PATERNOSTER BIBLICAL MONOGRAPHS

# Theodicy in Habakkuk

PATERNOSTER BIBLICAL MONOGRAPHS

# Theodicy in Habakkuk

## Grace Ko

Paternoster:

First published 2014 by Paternoster

Paternoster is an imprint of Authentic Media
52 Presley Way, Crownhill, Milton Keynes, Bucks, MK8 0ES, UK

www.authenticmedia.co.uk
Authentic Media is a division of Koorong UK, a company limited by guarantee

09 08 07 06 05 04 03   8 7 6 5 4 3 2 1

**British Library Cataloguing in Publication Data**
A catalogue record for this book is available from the British Library

ISBN 978–1–84227–850–5

Printed and bound in Great Britain
for Paternoster
by Lightning Source, Milton Keynes

*To Peter,*
*my beloved husband and partner in the Lord's ministry*

*and to the loving memory of my mother,*
*Mrs. Hing-Chun Chan Lu,*
*whose faith in the Lord emulated*
*"the righteous shall live by his/her faithfulness"*

# Series Preface

One of the major objectives of Paternoster is to serve biblical scholarship by providing a channel for the publication of theses and other monographs of high quality at affordable prices. Paternoster stands within the broad evangelical tradition of Christianity. Our authors would describe themselves as Christians who recognise the authority of the Bible, maintain the centrality of the gospel message and assent to the classical creedal statements of the Christian belief. There is diversity within this constituency; advances in scholarship are possible only if there is freedom for frank debate on controversial issues and for the publication of new and sometimes provocative proposals. What is offered in this series is the best of writing by committed Christians who are concerned to develop well-founded biblical scholarship in a spirit of loyalty to the historic faith.

# Series editors

# CONTENTS

# PREFACE

The idea of writing this dissertation was conceived in 2002 when I was teaching the book of Habakkuk in Sunday school. While preparing for the course, the issue of theodicy as well as the prophet's psalm of confidence captivated me. This led me to decide writing my dissertation, *Theodicy in Habakkuk*, and begin the journey of researching and unearthing this topic, a journey that took me seven years to complete. During which time, I experienced some personal heartaches and set-backs. First, my mom suffered a stroke, leaving her paralysed on her right side. Despite her failing health, her faith in the Lord remained strong. The Lord miraculously healed her, and she regained some mobility. Her unwavering faith and joy in the Lord was truly an inspiration and a comfort to many. Mom went to be with the Lord in 2010, shortly after I had successfully obtained my PhD degree, an accomplishment which brought her great joy.

Another set-back was the passing of my thesis advisor Dr. Brian Peckham of Regis College in 2008. He was an insightful and scintillating scholar admired by both colleagues and students alike. He had read through the first four chapters of my dissertation with great care, and provided me with pages of helpful, hand-written comments. I am forever indebted to him for his teaching and friendship.

I have incurred many debts while writing this dissertation, of which I will mention a few in particular. Dr. Glen Taylor of Wycliffe College graciously took over the role of thesis advisor and assisted me every step of the way. Without his encouragement and guidance, I would still be out in the woods. Dr. Michael Kolarchik of Regis College offered detailed comments that are always astute and invaluable. Dr. John Kessler of Tyndale Seminary, who provoked my initial thoughts on pursuing doctoral studies back in my Tyndale days, and has continued nurturing me since then, is a real godsend. I cannot express my gratitude to him enough.

Special thanks to Dr. Barbara Leung Lai of Tyndale Seminary, who demonstrates by example how to be a good shepherd-teacher; and to Dr. Marion Taylor of Wycliffe College, whose friendship and advices I will always treasure. These "women of noble character" are my role models in life

A word of appreciation must go to Dr. Dennis Ngien for suggesting me to submit my dissertation to Paternoster for publication consideration, and to the Paternoster Commissioning Editor, Dr. Mike Parsons, for the assistance I have received in the process of publishing this book. Last but not least, I would like to express my deepest gratitude for the loving support of my husband, Peter, whose contribution is immeasurable.

ברוך יהוה לעולם אמן ואמן

Grace Ko

# ABBREVIATIONS

| | |
|---|---|
| *AB* | *Anchor Bible* |
| *ABD* | *Anchor Bible Dictionary.* Edited by David Noel Freedman. New York: Doubleday, 1992. |
| *AOAT* | *Alter Orient und Altes Testament* |
| *AOTC* | *Abingdon Old Testament Commentaries* |
| *BA* | *Biblical Archaeologist* |
| *BDB* | Brown, F., S.R. Driver and C.A. Briggs. *A Hebrew and English Lexicon of the Old Testament.* Oxford: Clarendon, 1907. |
| *BHS* | *Biblia Hebraica Stuttgartensia.* Edited by K. Elliger and W. Rudolph. Stuttgart: Deutsche Bibelstiftung, 1997. |
| *BN* | *Biblische Notizen* |
| *BSC* | *Bible Study Commentary* |
| *BZAW* | *Beihefte zur ZAW* |
| *CBQ* | *Catholic Biblical Quarterly* |
| *CBR* | *Currents in Biblical Research* |
| *EBC* | *The Expositor's Bible Commentary* |
| *GKC* | *Gesenius' Hebrew Grammar.* Edited by E. Kautzsch and A. E. Cowley. Oxford: Clarendon, 1910. |
| *HSM* | *Harvard Semitic Monographs* |
| *HUCA* | *Hebrew Union College Annual* |
| *IDBSup* | Supplementary volume to *Interpreter's Dictionary of the Bible* |
| *Int* | *Interpretation* |
| *ITC* | *International Theological Commentary* |
| *IVP* | *InterVarsity Press* |
| *JBL* | *Journal of Biblical Literature* |
| *JETS* | *Journal of the Evangelical Theological Society* |
| *JNSL* | *Journal of Northwest Semitic Languages* |
| *JPS* | *Jewish Publication Society* |
| *JSOT* | *Journal for the Study of the Old Testament* |
| *JSOTSup* | *Journal for the Study of the Old Testament Supplement Series* |
| *JSS* | *Journal of Semitic Studies* |
| *KAT* | *Kommentar zum Alten Testament* |
| *LXX* | *Septuagent* |
| *MT* | *Masoretic Text* |
| *NAC* | *The New American Commentary* |
| *NASB* | *New American Standard Bible* |
| *NIB* | *The New Interpreter's Bible* |
| *NIBC* | *New International Biblical Commentary* |

| | |
|---|---|
| NICOT | New International Commentary on the Old Testament |
| NIV | New International Version |
| NJB | New Jerusalem Bible |
| NRV | New Revised Version |
| NSBT | New Studies in Biblical Theology |
| OTE | Old Testament Essays |
| OTL | Old Testament Library |
| RB | Revue Biblique |
| RSV | Revised Standard Version |
| SBL | Society of Biblical Literature |
| SJT | Scottish Journal of Theology |
| TDOT | Theological Dictionary of the Old Testament. Edited by G.J. Botterweck, H. Ringgren and H.J. Farbry. Translated by D.E. Green. 15 vols. Grand Rapids, 1974-2003. |
| TOTC | Tyndale Old Testament Commentaries |
| TynBul | Tyndale Bulletin |
| VT | Vetus Testamentum |
| VTSup | Vetus Testamentum Supplements |
| WBC | Word Biblical Commentary |
| WEC | The Wycliffe Exegetical Commentary |
| WTJ | Westminster Theological Journal |
| ZAH | Zeitschrift für Althebräistik |
| ZAW | Zeitschrift für die alttestamentliche Wissenschaft |

# CHAPTER 1

# Introduction

The book of Habakkuk is unique among the prophetic books in many ways. Not only does it differ from the other books in form and style,[1] but more importantly, it differs in content as well. It does not contain the usual prophetic disputation against the people of Israel in order to pronounce Yahweh's judgment as just and righteous. It does not call for repentance nor does it allow room for people to change their heart and return to the Lord. Rather, Habakkuk questions Yahweh's justice. It laments God's inactivity to punish in the face of injustice and looks for God's action to save and to put things right (1:2-4). But when Yahweh announces that he is raising up the Chaldeans against Israel (1:5-11), Habakkuk challenges Yahweh's decision, and is angered by God's apparent bad judgment in his choice of agent (1:12-17). Thus Habakkuk struggles with the issue of theodicy,[2] stands on the side of the Israelites,[3] and accuses Yahweh of his "complicity in allowing Chaldean depredations."[4]

---

[1] Form is defined here as the typical structure and shape of an individual passage or unit, while style is the choice of words, manner of expression and sentence construction. In the case of Habakkuk, the book lacks the usual prophetic formulae such as "Thus says the Lord," "declares the Lord," etc. Claus Westermann classified Habakkuk as cult prophecy, which contains elements of the service of worship, and is distinct from the other basic forms of prophecy. See C. Westermann, *Basic Forms of Prophetic Speech*, trans. H.C. White (Philadelphia: Westminster, 1967), 92-93.

[2] First coined by Gottfried von Leibniz (1646-1716) to refer to the work of defending the idea of a just God in the face of what seems contrary evidence, this word means "justice of God." See R.L. Sturch, "Theodicy," in *New Dictionary of Christian Ethics and Pastoral Theology* (Downers Grove: IVP, 1995), 843.

[3] Some argue that Habakkuk only stood up for himself since Israel is not mentioned in 1:2-4, but Yahweh's first response (2nd person masculine imperatives on 1:5) and Habakkuk's second complaint ("we shall not die" in 1:12) show that Habakkuk was speaking on behalf of the righteous within the Judean society. Julia M. O'Brien, who points out that Habakkuk consistently speaks for himself throughout the book, nevertheless, says that in Habakkuk the personal is also the communal. For a detailed discussion, see her book, *Nahum, Habakkuk, Zephaniah, Haggai, Zechariah, Malachi*. AOTC (Nashville: Abingdon, 2004), 59-60.

[4] D.S. Vanderhooft, *The Neo-Babylonian Empire and Babylon in the Latter Prophets*, HSM 59 (Atlanta: Scholars Press, 1999), 157.

The problem created by the issue of theodicy is acute for Habakkuk, as the apparent inactivity of God clashes with the traditional understanding of God's attributes.[5] First, Habakkuk does not accept the traditional prophetic resolution of the issue by laying blame on Israel's sin,[6] even though he is fully aware of the wickedness in Israel's society.[7] Secondly, he refuses to accept Yahweh's appointment of foreign invaders as righteous punishment. In fact, the divine response in 1:5-11 that he is raising up Chaldeans further infuriates Habakkuk to a point that he openly questions Yahweh's character: "Your eyes are too pure to behold evil, and you cannot look on wrongdoing; why do you look on the treacherous, and are silent when the wicked swallow those more righteous than they?" (1:13).[8] This bold accusation of divine injustice has a huge implication, especially when it is made by someone who is a prophet, a called messenger of God. David W. Baker comments that the prophet was supposed to urge the people to return to the covenant when they strayed from it, but instead Habakkuk was "calling God into account when his actions did not seem to correspond to those demanded by the covenant."[9] Crenshaw suggests that this illustrates

---

[5] An apt summary of the attributes of God is nowhere better expressed than that in the creedal statement of Exod 34:6-7, "The Lord, the Lord, a God merciful and gracious, slow to anger, and abounding in steadfast love and faithfulness; keeping steadfast love for the thousandth generation {or [for thousands]}, forgiving iniquity, transgression and sin, yet by no means clearing the guilty, but visiting the iniquity of the parents upon the children and the children's children, to the third and fourth generation." As Van Leeuwen observes, this base text, which expresses Yahweh's bipolar attributes of mercy and justice, is one of the themes that shape the scroll of the Twelve into a theological whole. See the discussion in R.C. Van Leeuwen, "Scribal Wisdom and Theodicy in the Book of the Twelve," in *In Search of Wisdom: Essays in Memory of John G. Gammie*, ed. L.G. Perdue, B.B. Scott, and W.J. Wiseman (Louisville: Westminster John Knox, 1993); see also J.D. Nogalski, "Recurring Themes in the Book of the Twelve: Creating Points of Contact for a Theological Reading," *Int* 61 (2007): 132-5. Habakkuk's complaint that God does not act according to his character shows that he understands this assumption on God's character.

[6] James L. Crenshaw notes that there is always conflict between the prophets and the Israelites over the issue of God's justice whenever historical crises occur. See his book, *Prophetic Conflict: Its Effect upon Israelite Religion* (New York: Walter de Gruyter, 1971), 30-31.

[7] This assumes that the wicked in 1:4 are the oppressors from within the Judean society, and that the prophet is describing his life situation. But even if we think that the wicked are the foreign invaders, the book of Habakkuk still lacks the usual prophetic accusation against Israel, which is prevalent in prophetic literature.

[8] All Bible quotations, unless otherwise stated, are taken from the RSV of the Bible, copyright 1946, 1952, 1971, 1973 by the Division of Christian Education of the National Council of the Churches of Christ in the U.S.A.

[9] D.W. Baker, *Nahum, Habakkuk, Zephaniah*, TOTC (Downers Grove: IVP, 1988), 43.

"the confusion resulting from continued belief in Yahweh's justice regardless of the evidence undercutting such conviction."[10]

## Survey of scholarship on the study of the Book of Habakkuk

For a book that contains only three short chapters, Habakkuk has certainly generated a disproportionate amount of scholarly works. Peter Jöcken surveyed the work of more than three hundred scholars on the book of Habakkuk between 1820 and 1977.[11] Indeed, Rex Mason describes questions raised by the book of Habakkuk as a "minefield for critical study."[12] Historical questions, in a large part, relate to the identities of the "wicked" and the "righteous" in 1:4, 13; and 2:4. Researchers ask questions such as:[13] Who are the "wicked" and the "righteous"? Do these terms refer to the same groups mentioned in all the passages above, or do they refer to different groups in different contexts? Are the "wicked" internal oppressors within Judean society or are they foreign oppressors?[14] What is the historical setting of the book and of the prophet?[15] Other questions concerning the composition of the book include: Are there any redactional layers discernible in the book?[16] Is the psalm in chapter 3 an integral part of the whole book or a later addition?[17] How are the different sections of the book related to each other? What is the genre of the book?

---

[10] J.L. Crenshaw, "Theodicy in the Book of the Twelve," in *Thematic Threads in the Book of the Twelve*, ed. P.L. Reditt, and A. Schart (New York: Walter de Gruyter, 2003), 187.

[11] P. Jöcken, *Das Buch Habakuk*, Bonner Biblische Beiträge 48 (Köhn-Bonn: Peter Hanstein, 1977).

[12] R. Mason, *Zephaniah, Habakkuk, Joel*, Old Testament Guides (Sheffield: JSOT Press, 1994), 60.

[13] Mason gives a list of questions that invoke disputes among scholars. See ibid., 63-64.

[14] R.D. Patterson, *Nahum, Habakkuk, Zephaniah*, WEC (Chicago: Moody, 1991), 127, points out that the identity of "the wicked" in 1:2-4 and 1:13-17 is an important factor that could affect the unity of the composition.

[15] Many attempts have been made to reconstruct the historical setting of Habakkuk; one of them, in four steps from 605 to 594, is suggested by William L. Holladay. See his article, "Plausible Circumstances for the Prophecy of Habakkuk," *JBL* 120 (2001): 123-30. For a brief survey on scholars' opinions on the prophet and his time before 1994, see Mason, *Zephaniah, Habakkuk, Joel*, 81-84.

[16] Many scholars such as Heflin, Robertson, Patterson, and Thompson argue that the book is written by the prophet himself. Others such as Nogalski, Peckham, Seybold, Lescow, see complex redactional activities in the book. This issue will be discussed later.

[17] The issue concerning the integrity of chapter 3 to the book of Habakkuk is another major threat to the unity of the book. Scholars are divided on this issue: some see Hab 3 as an integral part of the book while others, most notably Hiebert, think that it is a later addition. I will discuss this issue in greater detail later.

*Historical issues: identification of the historical players and the dating of the book*

To understand the issue at hand, a brief description of the content of the book of Habakkuk is in order. The book begins with a superscription (1:1). It is immediately followed by Habakkuk's initial complaint of violence (1:2-4). A response, presumably from Yahweh, states that he is the one who raises Chaldeans (1:5-11).[18] Then comes the prophet's second complaint about God's choice of agent (1:12-17).[19] The second chapter begins with a narration by the prophet describing how he waits for God's response to his second complaint (2:1). Yahweh answers him by commanding him to write down the vision (2:2-5). Then a list of five woe oracles is pronounced (2:6-20).[20] The third chapter starts with a separate superscription and musical notation (3:1). The hymn which describes the theophany (3:3-15) is framed by the lament (I-speeches) from the prophet (3:2, and 16-19).

Even after a century of research, the identification of the "wicked" and the "righteous" remains a contentious issue; no clear consensus seems to be in sight.[21] Some scholars argue that the "wicked" in the book refers to the same group of people throughout the book. Earlier scholars identified various foreign invaders with the wicked. The list includes: Assyria; Egypt; the Greeks and Macedonians under Alexander; and even Nicanor.[22] Since "Chaldeans" are mentioned in 1:6 and later identified as "the wicked" who swallow "the righteous" (1:13), most scholars think that "the wicked" most likely refers to the Babylonians. But by identifying "the wicked" with the same group in both 1:4 (Habakkuk's initial complaint) and 1:13 (Habakkuk's second complaint after God's response) raises difficulties, for Habakkuk would not have any objections to God punishing the foreign oppressors. Moreover, if "the wicked" in 1:4 were the same group of foreigners in 1:13, then Yahweh's answer in 1:5 be-

---

[18] The purpose of Yahweh's raising up the Chaldeans is not explicitly mentioned here, but Habakkuk understood this to be God's judgment according to 1:12b.

[19] The identity of the agent is again not explicitly mentioned, but if we take this section to be Habakkuk's reaction to Yahweh's response in 1:5-11, then it is only logical that the agent has to be the Chaldeans.

[20] The whole section is the woe oracles except 2:14, which is a doxology, and 2:20, which is a call for worship. The recipient of the oracles is not explicitly mentioned; however the content of the oracles reveals that it is likely to be the Babylonians, especially 2:8-9 where plundering of the nations and pillaging of the peoples are mentioned, which fit the descriptions of the Chaldeans in 1:5-11, 15-17. Also this section addresses the prophet's previous concern that the Chaldeans pillage the nations without ending.

[21] Oskar Dangl gives an overview on various positions current in the 1990s concerning the identification of the wicked and the righteous in Habakkuk. See his article, "Habakkuk in Recent Research," *Currents in Research: Biblical Studies* 9 (2001): 139-44.

[22] M.D. Johnson, "The Paralysis of Torah in Habakkuk I 4," *VT* 35 (1985): 258.

comes illogical or out of place, for this would not be a surprise to the prophet if he was complaining about them.

More recent scholars, such as Marshall D. Johnson, Michael H. Floyd, David Cleaver-Bartholomew, and Gert T.M. Prinsloo, try to solve the literary issues by proposing that the first chapter is not a dialogue between Yahweh and the prophet, but rather Habakkuk's complaint. Johnson proposes that 1:5-11 does not portray the Chaldeans as an answer to the issue raised in 1:2-4, but rather as a heightened complaint.[23] Floyd argues that the vision is in 1:5-11, which is the cause of the prophet's complaint in 1:2-4.[24] Cleaver-Bartholomew holds a similar view, with the following chronology: (1) Yahweh's initial revelation (1:5-11), (2) Habakkuk's complaint (1:2-4, 12-17), (3) Habakkuk seeks further clarification (2:1), and (4) Yahweh's response (2:2-20).[25] Prinsloo applies the principles of unit delimitation on the first chapter of Habakkuk and argues that this should be read as a single pericope, and thus it should be a continuous lament rather than a dialogue. He interprets 1:5-11 as Habakkuk's recalling Yahweh's inexplicable deed, rather than Yahweh's response to the prophet's complaint in 1:2-4.[26] The weakness of this view is that the chronological order of the text has to be rearranged to fit the interpreter's conjecture. One would question the validity of this practice, for the text makes sense as it stands, and it gives no literary clues that 1:5-11 is antecedent to 1:1-4.

While he thinks that it is best to interpret the "wicked" as referring to the Babylonians throughout the book, Marvin A. Sweeney does not agree with the view that 1:2-17 is a complaint rather than a dialogue between Yahweh and the prophet.[27] He argues that since 1:5-11 only identifies the establishment of the Chaldeans but says nothing about the purpose of their establishment, and since 1:9 indicates that they come for violence, therefore the Chaldeans are not to be viewed as the means for correcting the injustice; rather they may be viewed as its cause.[28] However, this argument is not strong, for if 1:5-11 is Yahweh's response to Habakkuk's previous complaint in 1:2-4, as Sweeney claims, it is only natural that Yahweh is indicating what he intends to do to deal with the injustice. Secondly, Habakkuk's further complaint in 1:12-13 plainly indicates

---

[23] Ibid., 261.

[24] M.H. Floyd, "Prophetic Complaints about the Fulfillment of Oracles in Habakkuk 1:2-17 and Jeremiah 15:10-18," *JBL* 110 (1991): 397-418.

[25] D. Cleaver-Bartholomew, "An Alternative Approach to Hab 1,2-2,20," *Scandinavian Journal of the Old Testament* 17 (2003): 206-25.

[26] G.T.M. Prinsloo, "Habakkuk 1—A Dialogue? Ancient Unit Delimiters in Dialogue with Modern Critical Interpretation," *OTE* 17 (2004): 621-45.

[27] M.A. Sweeney, "Habakkuk" in *Berit Olam: Studies in Hebrew Narrative and Poetry. The Twelve Prophets*, vol. 2 (Collegeville: The Liturgical Press, 2000), 455-57.

[28] M.A. Sweeney, "Structure, Genre, and Intent in Habakkuk," *VT* 41 (1991): 67.

that it is Yahweh who set the Chaldeans[29] as judgment (לְמִשְׁפָּט) and established them to requite (לְהוֹכִיחַ), both stating the purpose of the Chaldeans' establishment.

On the other hand, Robert D. Haak identifies the wicked to be from within Judean society in both 1:4 and 1:13. After an extensive historical-critical analysis, he argues that the wicked are to be identified with Jehoiakim and his pro-Egyptian team, while the righteous are to be identified with Jehoahaz, who was deposed by Pharaoh Necho II, and those who hope for the restoration of Jehoahaz.[30] Most scholars, however, do not identify the wicked and the righteous with the royal figures. Furthermore his insistence on portraying Habakkuk to be a staunchly pro-Babylonian prophet seems to contradict the tone of the text, which has a negative view of the Chaldeans. Also, while the woe oracles in 2:6-19 may have elements similar to Jeremiah's woe oracle against Jehoiakim in Jer 22:13-19, it is doubtful that these oracles are directed against Jehoiakim in their present context, especially in verses 2:5, 8, where "peoples" and "nations" are mentioned as the victims of oppression caused by the "wicked." Haak attempts to solve this problem by stating that "the references are not to Jehoiakim but rather to the Egyptians."[31] The problem with this view is that there is no mention of Egypt in the text. To address the issue that some oracles are similar to the ones pronounced against Jehoiakim by Jeremiah, William L. Holladay proposes that there are two recensions, one addressed to Jehoiakim, which included 2:5a, 6-7, 10abβ, 11, and 12; and the other addressed to Nebuchadrezzar, which added 2:5bβγδ, 8, 10bα, and 13-20.[32] Brevard S. Childs sees the woe oracles in 2:6-19 as a reshaping of earlier traditional material to apply it against the Babylonians.[33]

Georg Fohrer identifies two separate foreign powers as the wicked mentioned in different passages in the book: the Assyrians in 1:4 and the Babylonians in 1:13. He postulates that "Habakkuk is announcing that Assyrian rule, under which Judah suffered along with other nations, is about to be destroyed by the Babylonians, acting as Yahweh's instrument."[34] The obvious weakness of this argument is that it is inconceivable that Habakkuk would have any difficulty over the downfall of Assyria, and that he would have called the Assyrian more righteous than the Babylonian (1:13). The prophet's reaction makes sense

---

[29] Some may argue that the Chaldeans are not mentioned here, but the only logical antecedent to the pronominal suffixes of שַׂמְתּוֹ and יְסַדְתּוֹ in 1:12 is the Chaldeans in 1:5-11.

[30] R.D. Haak, *Habakkuk*, VTSup 44 (Leiden: Brill, 1991), 111-39.

[31] Ibid., 137.

[32] Holladay, "Plausible Circumstances," 125-30.

[33] B.S. Childs, *Introduction to the Old Testament as Scripture* (Philadelphia: Fortress, 1979), 452.

[34] G. Fohrer, *Introduction to the Old Testament*, trans. David Green (London: SPCK, 1970), 455.

only if the righteous in 1:13 is Israel considered as a whole and the wicked are the Babylonians sent by God.[35]

The majority of scholars hold the traditional view, which argues that the "wicked" in 1:4 and in 1:13 are two different groups: the former are those from within Judean society, while the latter are identified with the Chaldeans. This view has a long history. It is interesting to note that the earliest interpretation to identify the "wicked" as those within Judean society may have been the Qumran sectarians who identified the "wicked" as the Hasmonean priests. The Pesher of Habakkuk states, "Its prophetic meaning is that the 'wicked' is the Wicked Priest, the 'righteous' is the Righteous Teacher."[36] But this view is not without difficulties. As its critics hold, if Babylonians are being sent by God to punish Israel, why would the latter be described as "more righteous" than the former (1:13);[37] and why did the prophet complain about the judgment when it was him who asked for divine justice in the first place (1:1-4)?[38] As early as 1925, W.W. Cannon tried to answer these challenges by suggesting that the prophet's thought developed as events happened and that the oracles in the book of Habakkuk were not all written at the same time.[39] In other words, the prophet made his initial complaint to the Lord when he saw injustice in Judean society. But after he saw the rise of the Chaldean empire and its ruthlessness, he worried for Judah and made a second complaint. J.J.M. Roberts seems to follow the same argument: after analyzing the evidence from the text and the historical situation, he states that "the individual oracles that make up this compositional whole were originally given at widely separated times in the prophet's ministry."[40]

The greatest objection to taking the "wicked" as those from within Judean society in 1:2-4 is that there is no mention of Israel in the whole passage. However, while the text does not clearly identify who "the wicked" were in 1:2-4, the mention of "law (תּוֹרָה) is paralyzed," may indicate that the injustice is done from within Judean society. Some may argue that it was foreign occupation that caused the law to be numbed. But a survey of the use of "law" (תּוֹרָה) shows that it is never used as a complaint against foreign rule. Rather it is often used to accuse the Israelites, especially the leaders, of forsaking the law. Also, as Armerding states, normally when "justice" (מִשְׁפָּט) and "violence" (חָמָס) are juxtaposed, the "wicked" are Israelites unless otherwise stated (e.g. Exod 23:1-

---

[35] D.W. Baker, *Nahum, Habakkuk, Zephaniah*, 46.

[36] See the restored text in W.H. Brownlee, *The Midrash Pesher of Habakkuk* (Missoula: Scholars Press, 1979), 45.

[37] This question is not difficult to answer, for this is precisely Habakkuk's concern that God uses a "less righteous" nation to punish Israel.

[38] Mason, *Zephaniah, Habakkuk, Joel*, 67.

[39] W.W. Cannon, "The Integrity of Habakkuk cc. 1, 2," *ZAW* 43 (1925): 62-90.

[40] J.J.M. Roberts, *Nahum, Habakkuk, and Zephaniah: A Commentary*, OTL (Louisville: Westminster John Knox, 1991), 82.

9; Isa 5:7-15; and I would add Micah 3:9).[41] Indeed, as suggested by Richard D. Patterson, to identify two different groups of the wicked—that 1:2-4 refers to the Judean citizens and 1:13-17 refers to the Babylonians—is the simplest way of understanding the text and would pose the least literary difficulties.[42]

Closely associated with the issues of the identification of the wicked and the righteous is the issue with regard to the dating of the book. The proposed dates range from the ninth century BCE, according to an early Jewish rabbinic tradition that speculated that Habakkuk was the son of the Shunammite woman who lived in the reign of King Jehoram of Israel (2 Kgs 4:16), to the Maccabean period, according to Paul Haupt who identifies the wicked to be Nicanor.[43] Most scholars take the mention of Chaldeans in Hab 1:6 seriously as a clear historical clue for a date.

Earlier scholars such as Bernhard Duhm, followed by C.C. Torrey, tried to argue for a fourth century date by emending *Kasdim* to *Kittim*, a term used to designate Cypriots or Greeks in general.[44] This view was refuted when the Qumran text of the Habakkuk scroll actually reads *Kasdā'im* (הַכַּשְׂדְּאִים) while the *pesher* (1QpHab), which reflects a later situation contemporary with the Qumran community, interprets it as *Kittî'im* (הַכִּתִּיאִים).[45]

Fohrer, following his identification of Assyrians as the "wicked" mentioned in 1:4, dates the book after 626 BCE, when the Chaldeans arrived on the historical scene after the successful revolt of Nabopolassar, and before the fall of the Assyrian Empire in 612. He points out that Habakkuk must have appeared before 622, just a little later than Nahum.[46]

For those scholars who take the "wicked" in 1:4 as referring to people within Judean society, there are three proposals for the period. Patterson supports the Jewish tradition[47] that Habbakuk was active during the reign of Manasseh (698-642 BCE), when the Judean apostasy was at its worst, and the prophetic words of the rising of the Chaldeans would require the most prophetic foresight.[48] C.H. Bullock sees the early days of Josiah's reign between 641-627 BCE as the most appropriate date for the book, when the Judean sins enumerated in 1:2-4

---

[41] C.E. Armerding, "Habakkuk," in *EBC*, ed. F.E. Gaebelein (Grand Rapids, Zondervan, 1985), 499.

[42] Patterson, *Nahum, Habakkuk, Zephaniah*, 128.

[43] Ibid., 116.

[44] Ibid., 116.

[45] Brownlee, *Midrash Pesher of Habakkuk*, 59. In Qumran *pesher Kittî'im* probably refers to the Romans.

[46] Fohrer, *Introduction to the Old Testament*, 455.

[47] *Seder Olam* (or *Seder Olam Rabbah*), a Jewish historical work that summarizes the history of the world and of the Jews in particular from creation to the second century CE., associated Habakkuk with Manasseh's reign. See Patterson, *Nahum, Habakkuk, Zephaniah*, 115-16.

[48] Ibid., 139-40.

were in evidence and the prophecy of the Chaldean power would come as a surprise to the people.[49]

Although there is still a wide range of opinions as to the dating of the book, most scholars now regard the reign of King Jehoiakim (609-598 BCE) as the most likely period for the ministry of prophet Habakkuk.[50] Roberts argues that God's announcement (1:5-6) could only be a surprise to the Judean audience if the prophecy was made before the Chaldeans defeated the Egyptians at Carchemish in 605 BCE. However, Habakkuk's description of the Chaldeans in 1:11-17 and the nation's characterization as oppressor in 2:6-19 presuppose a much longer experience of Babylonian rule over Judah, probably after Nebuchadnezzar's first invasion of Jerusalem in 597 BCE. Hence he proposes some of Habakkuk's oracles date from before 605 and others from after 597 BCE.[51] Holladay, developing Robert's analysis, suggests plausible historical contexts for Habakkuk's prophecy in four steps from 605 to 594: The prophet is bewildered by Judean injustice (1:2-4); God responds that the Chaldeans will be a chosen instrument for punishment (1:5-11). The prophet further complains that the Chaldeans are themselves heartless (1:12-17); then God assures him of divine sovereignty and control so that the Chaldeans will ultimately fall (ch. 2), and offers a vision of God's march into the Promised Land (ch. 3).[52] Some scholars such as Mason are more cautious and are content with a date in the last part of the seventh century.[53] C.E. Armerding finds it best to see the dialogue in the book as "Habakkuk's spiritual struggles over a long period of time, possibly beginning as early as 626 and continuing as late as 590 or after."[54] Waylon Bailey agrees with the date under the reign of Jehoiakim, but suggests that a broader time span is possible.[55] James Bruckner thinks that each section of Habakkuk is best understood in its specific historical context, and that the subject matter of the book covers sixty-six years from 605 to 539 BCE.[56]

In my opinion, if one takes Yahweh's answer in 1:5 seriously that the raising up of the Babylonians would "utterly astound" the prophet, then the time of the initial complaint and the first divine response has to be dated prior to the Battle of Carchemish in 605 BCE, because the Babylonians only became a significant threat to Judah after 605 BCE. The most likely date for this section (1:2-11) is during the early period of Jehoiakim's reign before 605 BCE. Then Babylonian

---

[49] C.H. Bullock, *An Introduction to the Old Testament Prophetic Books* (Chicago: Moody, 1986), 182-83.

[50] Dangl, "Habakkuk in Recent Research," 141.

[51] Roberts, *Nahum, Habakkuk, and Zephaniah*, 82-84.

[52] Holladay, "Plausible Circumstances," 123-30.

[53] Mason, *Zephaniah, Habakkuk, Joel*, 83-84.

[54] Armerding, "Habakkuk," 493.

[55] W. Bailey, "Habakkuk" in *Micah, Nahum, Habakkuk, Zephaniah*, NAC, vol 20 (Nashville: Broadmen & Holman Publishers, 1998), 259.

[56] J. Bruckner, *The NIV Application Commentary: Jonah, Nahum, Habakkuk, Zephaniah* (Grand Rapids: Zondervan, 2004), 202.

aggression was increasingly felt by Judah after the defeat of the Egyptians at Carchemish, which then prompted the second complaint by the prophet (1:12ff). Therefore I concur with the view that Jehoiakim's reign (609-598 BCE) is the most likely setting for the book. The closing remark of Habakkuk in 3:16 which indicates that the day of calamity is yet to come also confirms this date.

*Literary critical issues: history of the composition of the book*

Some scholars employ literary criticism[57] to tackle questions concerning the history of the composition of the book. Mason gives a well-organized survey of various scholars' positions for and against the unity[58] of the book.[59] Although some scholars, such as R.H. Pfeiffer[60] and R.P. Carroll, read it as a "ragbag of traditional elements" put together in an "apparently slapdash fashion,"[61] most agree that the book is a coherent literary unit in its present form, even if it may not have been written by one author.[62] Prinsloo, among others, argues that a close reading of the book shows that Habakkuk is best read as a literary unit.[63]

Among those who argue for the literary unity of the text, their positions may be further distinguished by their view of the history of the composition of the book: some presume an original unity of the entire book; some presume only minor redactional activities on the book; while a few argue for a more complex literary composition process.[64]

*Unity of the entire book*
J.N. Boo Heflin asserts that the Book of Habakkuk is indeed a well-constructed literary unit written by Habakkuk, recording his ministry which extended over several years.[65] He also warns against extensive changes to the received text of

---

[57] Here literary criticism refers to the analysis of Scripture (often known as source criticism) that engages in finding the source of a text.

[58] Here "unity of the book" means that the book can be read as a literary unit which can be defended on the literary grounds of structural analysis and intratextual elements, rather than a collection of unrelated materials. This does not preclude the existence of redactional activities.

[59] Mason, *Zephaniah, Habakkuk, Joel*, 66-79. For studies in the 1990s, see Dangl, "Habakkuk in Recent Research," 135-39.

[60] Pfeiffer read it as a collection of "more or less disconnected prophetic utterances." See his book, *Introduction to the Old Testament* (London: Black, 1952), 597.

[61] R.P. Carroll, "Habakkuk," in *A Dictionary of Biblical Interpretation* (London: SCM, 1990), 269.

[62] M.A. Sweeney, "Habakkuk, Book of," in *The Anchor Bible Dictionary*, ed. D.N. Freedman (New York: Doubleday, 1992), 3:3.

[63] G.T.M. Prinsloo, "Reading Habakkuk as a literary unit: Exploring the possibilities," *OTE* 12 (1999): 515-35.

[64] Danyl, "Habakkuk in Recent Research," 135-39.

[65] J.N.B. Heflin, *Nahum, Habakkuk, Zephaniah, and Haggai*, BSC (Grand Rapids: Zondervan, 1985), 77.

the book, for despite its textual difficulties, the book of Habakkuk is open to meaningful interpretation without resorting to deletion, emendation, or transposition of major sections.[66]

O. Palmer Robertson thinks that the book of Habakkuk consists of authentic words of the seventh century prophet, and that there is no evidence that provides adequate ground for denying the integrity of the material.[67]

Patterson also favors the unity of the book; to him the "carefully crafted literary structure" strongly indicates that it was designed by the author himself.[68]

James W. Watts argues for the unity of the book by suggesting that "a single writer composed the work by incorporating older materials (most notably 3:3-15) into an exploration of Yahweh's power in the face of military disaster."[69] While some may argue that the incorporation of older material is a redactional activity, it can also be regarded as the creativity of the prophet by adapting existing material for the artistic expression of his view.

Michael E.W. Thompson admits the eclectic nature of the book but argues that the unique combination of the genres is Habakkuk's "maverick" way of tackling the theodicy theme.[70] Indeed, the mixing of genres could be another witness to the creativity of the author.

Bailey thinks that the essential unity of the book appears best as one looks at the literary devices the author used to create a book. He lists twenty-one rhetorical features that are employed by the prophet to give artistic form and meaning to his message.[71] He also criticizes House's over-emphasis of the unity on the Twelve and the existence of an "implied author" who "stands behind the scenes of the Twelve"[72] as "not describing Habakkuk from the viewpoint of the prophet and his audience," but from the postexilic work of the "implied author."[73]

Except for Otto Eissfeldt, the proponents of the unity of the entire book all see Habakkuk as the author of the book and regard the so-called evidence for the stratification of redactional layers as the literary devices used by the prophet to create a book.

Eissfeldt maintained that the content of the book of Habakkuk does form a unity and that all three chapters originated from the prophet himself; however

---

[66] Ibid., 77-78.

[67] O.P. Robertson, *The Books of Nahum, Habakkuk, and Zephaniah*, NICOT (Grand Rapids: Eerdmans, 1990), 38-40.

[68] Patterson, *Nahum, Habakkuk, Zephaniah*, 127-29.

[69] J.W. Watts, "Psalmody in Prophecy: Habakkuk 3 in Context," in *Forming Prophetic Literature: Essays on Isaiah and the Twelve in Honor of John D.W. Watts*. JSOTSup 235 (Sheffield: Sheffield Academic Press, 1996), 217-21.

[70] M.E.W. Thompson, "Prayer, Oracle and Theophany: The Book of Habakkuk," *TynBul* 44 (1993): 33-53.

[71] Bailey, "Habakkuk," 269.

[72] P. House, *The Unity of the Twelve*, JSOTSup 97 (Sheffield: Almond Press, 1990), 230.

[73] For a detailed discussion, see Bailey, "Habakkuk," 261-65.

*in form* these passages could not be regarded as a literary unity, but rather as "a loose collection" of a group of songs of lamentation and oracles (1:2-2:4), a series of six cries of woe (2:5-20), and the prayer of chapter 3.[74] This view was in direct contrast with some earlier form critics who argued for the unity of Habakkuk precisely based on the liturgical form of the book.[75] While it is debatable whether there were cultic prophets in ancient Israel,[76] this shows that it is precarious to judge a book's unity based purely on the form-critical approach. Also forms are theoretical abstractions of real literature, not vice versa.[77] Hence it is better to say that the book of Habakkuk as a literary unity based on its content and its rhetorical devices, and that these various literary forms are artistically and deliberately employed by the prophet in a logical structure to convey his message rather than a "loose collection." Bailey is certainly right when he says, "Most prophetic books require dissecting into brief oracles in order to understand the message. Habakkuk almost demands that the reader read the entire book before the message becomes clear, the component parts serving more to support the entire message than to provide an individual message of its own."[78]

*Unity with some redactional activities*
As Bailey notes, the eclectic nature of literary genres in the book of Habakkuk and the literary ties to the other books of the Twelve automatically raises the issue of unity.[79] Scholars readily attribute some parts of the book to the incorporation of earlier material (either by the author himself or as an addition by a later generation) and to the redactional work by a later generation. For example, Elizabeth Achtemeier, while admitting that the core of the work "comes out of a concrete historical situation," nonetheless points to the author's adaptation of earlier materials (2:5-20), a strong autobiographical (1:2-3, 12; 2:1-2; 3:1, 16, 18-19) and biographical emphasis (1:1; 3:1), and subsequent use of portions of the book within Israel's cult (3:1, 3, 9, 13, 19), and concludes that "both Habakkuk himself and later editors have given the work a universal and timeless validity which has made it a witness to every age."[80]

W. Rudolph, while arguing strongly for the basic unity of the book, dates several verses as late: 2:6a, 13a, 14, 17b, 19b; 3:6b (including the first two words of verse 7), and 3:17.[81] These late additions seem to be editorial com-

---

[74] O. Eissfeldt, *The Old Testament: An Introduction*, trans. P.R. Ackroyd (New York: Harper and Row, 1965; reprint, 1966), 420-1. Italics his.

[75] For a detailed discussion, see Mason, *Zephaniah, Habakkuk, Joel*, 68-72.

[76] R. de Vaux, *Ancient Israel: Its Life and Institutions*, trans. J. McHugh (Grand Rapids: Eerdmans, 1977), 384-86.

[77] Prinsloo, "Reading Habakkuk as a literary unit," 517.

[78] Bailey, "Habakkuk," 269.

[79] Ibid., 268.

[80] E. Achtemeier, *Nahum-Malachi*, Interpretation (Atlanta: John Knox, 1986), 32.

[81] W. Rudolph, *Micha-Nahum-Habakuk-Zephania*, KAT 13:3 (Gutersloh: Mohn, 1975), 195.

ments rather than redactions, for they do not significantly alter the meaning of the text.[82] While I do not deny the possibilities of later editorial additions, I wonder why these verses could not have come from the prophet himself.

Roberts sees different stages of Habakkuk's activities reflected in individual texts: sections 1:2-4 and 1:5-6 originated in the period 609-605 BCE, whereas 1:11-17 was written after 597 BCE by a creative redactor who rewrote and expanded Habakkuk's original oracles, turning the woe oracles in 2:6-20 against a Judean oppressor such as Jehoiakim into oracles against a foreign oppressor. Meanwhile the vision in 3:3-15 appears to be a reworking of an archaic poem by the prophet to express his visionary experience.[83]

In sum, these scholars attempt to describe and explain the apparently incongruous verses in the book and to propose a historical situation surrounding those verses by resorting to later editors. While it is quite plausible that editorial additions exist, it is nearly impossible to single out individual verses and attribute those to a particular epoch. Thus any proposal must remain provisional. Moreover, there is not sufficient evidence to indicate that those verses could not have come from the prophet himself. In an article discussing the problem of historical reconstruction in prophetic books, Roy F. Melugin cautions that persuasive evidence for historical reconstruction is very often unavailable, and so questions the ability of historical criticism to reconstruct its historical situation.[84]

*A complex redactional history*
Other scholars such as Eckart Otto, Peckham, Nogalski, Seybold, and Lescow, assume an even more complex history of composition.

Otto discerns five redactional layers in the book of Habakkuk.[85] The first layer is the proclamation of the prophet Habakkuk in 1:2-4, 12a, 13-14, in which he complained against injustice within Judean society, and the subsequent answer from Yahweh in 2:1-5abα. Then the woe oracles from the prophet are pronounced in 2:6b, 7, 9, 10abβ, 12, 11, 15-16. The second layer is the inclusion of the oracles in 1:5-11, 12b to give a new interpretation of an anti-Babylonian thrust. It is at this stage that a structure of double lament and oracle was shaped. The third layer is the anti-Babylonian tradition by a redactor in 1:15-17, 2:5bβ, 6a, 8, 10bα, 13, 14, 17. The fourth is the early post-exilic addi-

---

[82] It is understandable why he would regard these as editorial additions for it is apparent that both 2:6a and 13a begin with a rhetorical question (הֲלוֹא) to smooth out the transitions, and 2:14 and 17b appear to be editorial comments: the former is a doxology, and the latter is a refrain, and 2:19b is to clarify the previous statement. Meanwhile 3:6b and 17 are not as clear cut as the other ones.

[83] Roberts, *Nahum, Habakkuk, and Zephaniah*, 82-84.

[84] R.F. Melugin, "Prophetic Books and the Problem of Historical Reconstruction," in *Prophets and Paradigms: Essays in Honor of Gene M. Tucker*, ed. S.B. Reid, JSOTSup 229 (Sheffield: SAP, 1996), 70.

[85] E. Otto, "Die Theologie des Buches Habakuk," *VT* 35 (1985): 284-95.

tion of 1:1, 2:18-3:16 as well as 3:3-15 and 16 to the third layer. And finally, the ritual-cultic addition in 3:1, 3, 9, 13, 17-19 put the psalm in chapter 3 to cultic use. This redactional process took place, according to Otto, between 612 BCE and the early post-exilic period.

Peckham asserted that the book of Habakkuk is a composite unity.[86] He posited that the book is "a composition of text and commentary,"[87] which consists of Habakkuk's original vision in the form of a lament and a later commentary that changes the lament into a book by a complex process of "modifying some stanzas and adding others."[88] He then tried to uncover the sources that underlie both the lament and the commentary. He concluded that both the lament and the commentary "interpret the same literary and historical traditions, but belong to different stages in their development. The lament explained that the resurgence of Babylon fulfilled all of Isaiah's expectations, and the commentary explained that the destruction of Babylon fulfilled all the conditions of the law."[89]

According to Nogalski, the book of Habakkuk was substantially expanded when it was integrated into the corpus of the Twelve Prophets.[90] He postulates that the core of Habakkuk has a "wisdom-oriented discussion concerning the prosperity of the wicked in Judah."[91] Then the "Joel-related layer," which consisted of a Babylonian commentary (1:5-11, 12b, 15-17), and portions of the woe oracles in 2:5-19, and then a concluding hymn in chapter 3, were added to it.[92] He further speculates that "*both* the wisdom-oriented layer and its Babylonian expansion are post-exilic."[93] But as Bailey rightly comments, "Such a complex history of Habakkuk is not necessary. It represents a minimalist view in regard to the work of the original prophet and removes the 'Babylonian commentary' into a period when Babylon had long vanished as the foe in focus for Israel."[94]

---

[86] B. Peckham, "The Vision of Habakkuk," *CBQ* 48 (1986): 617. See also, idem, *History and Prophecy: The Development of Late Judean Literary Traditions* (New York: Doubleday, 1993), 406-20.

[87] Peckham, "The Vision of Habakkuk," 618.

[88] Ibid., 621. See the chart that shows the detailed breakdown of Habakkuk's vision and the book's composition on pp. 621-22.

[89] Ibid., 634. See the critique by Ernst Wendland, "'The Righteous Live by Their Faith' in a Holy God: Complementary Compositional Forces and Habakkuk's Dialogue with the Lord," *JETS* 42 (1999): 593 n. 6.

[90] J.D. Nogalski, *Redactional Processes in the Book of the Twelve*, BZAW 218 (Berlin/New York: W. de Gruyter, 1993), 276.

[91] See the chart of "wisdom-oriented layer" and the "Babylonian commentary" in ibid., 143.

[92] Ibid., 129-81, 274-80.

[93] Ibid., 154. Italics are his.

[94] Bailey, "Habakkuk," 268.

Seybold thinks that the book of Habakkuk consists of three major layers:[95] The oldest layer is Habakkuk's original prophecy which consists of his lamentation in 2:1-3, 5-19 directed against internal injustice; and his vision of foreign invasion in 1:1, 5-11, 14-17. This original prophecy was written down by the prophet himself on tablets according to 2:1-3. Then the tradents during the exilic period (around 550 BCE) added the hymnic texts of 3:1, 3-7, 15, 8-13a with framework at 3:2, 16. Finally the post-exilic editors added a lamentation that permeates the entire book: 1:2-4, 12-13; 2:4, 20; 3:13b, 14, 17-19a. In Seybold's opinion 2:4, which is central to the text's theological history, can only be explained as the prayer of an accused man, and belongs to the latest text layer.

Theodor Lescow, on the other hand, maintains that the book has a three-phase model, which is arranged in a concentric manner of A > B < C.[96] According to him, there are three continuations in addition to the basic text which consists of a lamentation (A: 1:2-4, 13), an oracle (B: 2:1-4), and woe oracles (C: 2:6b, 9, 12, 15, 19a), arranged concentrically focusing on the oracle.[97] The first, late exilic continuation expanded the framework sections of A (by adding a response in 1:5-11 and a second lamentation in 1:12-17) and C (by expanding the woe oracles into a funeral hymn).[98] The second continuation was added by a post-exilic author who inserted 1:15-16 to turn the main section A into a structure to be read concentrically; meanwhile the middle section of B (2:1-4) was left untouched.[99] The final continuation, which consists of the psalm in chapter 3, was done in the post-Persian period.[100] Thus, to him, the central portion of 2:1-4 belongs to the oldest core layer of Habakkuk.

Danyl notes the diverse conclusions made by Seybold and Lescow: the former thinks that 2:4 belongs to the latest text layer while the latter thinks that it belongs to the oldest layer. He then comments that their hypotheses raise the question of their methodologies.[101] He agrees with Mason's observation that these redactional-critical approaches tend to be subjective and run the risk of circular argument "if redactional layers are isolated only or primarily on the basis of a prior conviction as to what can and cannot be original to the prophet."[102]

In sum, when various redactional analyses are evaluated, it becomes clear that no consensus can be made on the redactional history of the book of Habakkuk. It is not surprising, though, that the search for the history of the book would yield such diverse results because various redactional theories depend on

---

[95] I was not able to obtain Seybold's book; the following description of his work is based on Dangl's article, "Habakkuk in Recent Research," 137-38.
[96] T. Lescow, "Die Komposition der Bücher Nahum and Habakuk," *BN* 77 (1995): 60.
[97] See his analysis of Habakkuk by using different font type in ibid., 77-79.
[98] Ibid., 80-81.
[99] Ibid., 82.
[100] Ibid., 84-85.
[101] Danyl, "Habakkuk in Recent Research," 139.
[102] Mason, *Zephaniah, Habakkuk, Joel*, 79.

the presuppositions of their practitioners. Furthermore, as Prinsloo suggests, once the book is finalized, the history of the book becomes vague,[103] so we may never be able to know definitively the redactional history of the book.

*Habakkuk 3*
The third chapter of the book is most problematic in terms of literary criticism. Not only is this chapter a distinct text within the book in terms of form and content, its absence from the Qumran *pesher* on Habakkuk prompts many scholars to conclude that it is not originally part of the book. It may be absent from the Qumran text because this chapter was not appropriate for the situation and purposes of the Qumran community.[104] Another reason, suggested by Peckham, is that the superscription and the subscription in 3:1 and 19 turned this chapter into a psalm, which is distinct from the prophecy, and so to the Qumran community it was no longer part of the prophetic book.[105] Yitzhak Avishur also sees that the Qumran sectarians were primarily interested in prophecy, and since Habakkuk 3 is basically a psalm and not a prophectic work, there was no need for a *pesher* on it.[106] Moreover, as Haak notes, among the *pesharim* from Qumran, no commentaries on complete books have been found.[107] Thus the absence of the third chapter of Habakkuk in 1QpHab cannot be taken conclusively as evidence that it was not originally part of the book.

Earlier generations of scholars tended to regard the psalm in chapter 3 as a late addition, probably around the post-exilic period.[108] These scholars include Julius Wellhausen, A.B. Davidson, Karl Marti, W. Nowack, S.R. Driver, and G.G.V. Stonehouse.[109] The reasons for doubting the authenticity of Habakkuk 3 are mainly literary and stylistic.[110] These critics argue that the genre and the

---

[103] Prinsloo, "Reading Habakkuk as a Literary Unit," 517.

[104] Patterson, *Nahum, Habakkuk, Zephaniah*, 128.

[105] Private comment by Professor Peckham.

[106] Y. Avishur, *Studies in Hebrew and Ugaritic Psalms* (Jerusalem: Magnes, 1994), 124.

[107] Haak, *Habakkuk*, 7-8.

[108] A.B. Davidson was somewhat uncertain whether Habakkuk 3 belongs to the prophecy of Habakkuk or is an independent poem. However, he mentioned that the musical directions in the poem may be assumed to be post-exilic. Also the "manner" of the third chapter "has affinities with lyrics of a pretty late age." See his book, *Nahum, Habakkuk, and Zephaniah*, Cambridge Bible (Cambridge: Cambridge University Press, 1896), 58-59.

[109] J. Wellhausen, *Die Kleinen Propheten* (Berlin: Georg Reimer, 1898); Davidson, *Nahum, Habakkuk and Zephaniah*; K. Marti, *Das Dodekapropheten* (Tübingen: J.C.B. Mohr, 1903); W. Nowack, *Die Kleine Propheten* (Göttingen: Vandenhoeck & Ruprecht, 1903); S.R. Driver, *The Minor Prophets, II. Nahum, Habakkuk, Zephaniah, Haggai, Zechariah, Malachi* (Edinburgh: T.C. & E.C. Jack, 1906); G.G.V. Stonehouse, *The Book of Habakkuk* (London: Rivingtons, 1911). Marti's comment, *Das Dodekapropheten*, 330, represented the most extreme position. He reduced the authentic words of Habakkuk to just a few verses in 1:5-10, 14-15 (16).

[110] For a detailed discussion, see Avishur, *Studies in Hebrew and Ugaritic Psalms*, 122-24.

content of Habakkuk 3 differ from the previous two chapters. While the previous two chapters are prophetic, the third is a hymn to God as a warrior. Also, unlike the previous two chapters, Habakkuk 3 is studded with difficulties.

Most recent scholars, however, regard chapter 3 as an authentic work of the prophet. Wendland asserts that "chapter three functioned as an integral and indispensable part of the 'rhetoric' of Habakkuk from the very beginning of the book's compositional history. His prophecy would simply not be the same—either without it, or with it being regarded as some sort of later, supplementary appendix."[111] Recently, Prinsloo, after careful analysis of Habakkuk 3 both as a literary unit and within its immediate literary context, concludes that chapter 3 in its present literary context is the climax of the book.[112]

One of the recent scholars who staunchly opposes the current consensus on the authenticity and the integrity of Habakkuk 3 in the book is Theodore Hiebert. He argues that problems with the current consensus on the unity of Habakkuk exist at "all levels of form and content."[113] According to him, the authenticity of the title in chapter 3 cannot be assumed without critical consideration because titles are "redactional elements in Israelite literature" and reflect a secondary setting.[114] Secondly, chapter 3 cannot be identified as a lament encompassing a vision because the poem is formally a hymn of victory celebrating the victories of the divine warrior, which is "atypical of classical prophecy."[115] Thirdly, he rejects a connection between the content of chapter 3 and the first two chapters.[116] For example, the plea for the salvation of Yahweh's "anointed" in chapter 3 comes into direct conflict with a common interpretation of 1:1-4, where wickedness, violence, and impotence of the Torah are understood to be the result of the corrupt leadership of Judah. Moreover there is no mention of Babylon being the enemy in the third chapter.[117] He also opines that the problems raised in chapter 1 are already resolved in chapter 2, that is, the righteous are admonished to be faithful regardless of the circumstances (2:4); and the Babylonians are expected to be destroyed by the natural retribution when the oppressed ones rise up against them (2:6-17).[118] Fourthly, to him, the archaic character of chapter 3 supports the thesis that this psalm originally existed independently of its present canonical context in the book of Habakkuk. And finally, he argues that apocalyptic fervor of the late sixth and early fifth centuries seems to be the most probable setting for the incorporation into the

---

[111] Wendland, "The righteous Live by Their Faith," 602.

[112] G.T.M. Prinsloo, "Reading Habakkuk 3 in its Literary Context: A Worthwhile Exercise or Futile Attempt?" *Journal for Semitics* 11 (2002): 83-111.

[113] T. Hiebert, *God of My Victory: The Ancient Hymn in Habakkuk 3*, HSM 38 (Atlanta: Scholars Press, 1986), 135.

[114] Ibid., 131.

[115] Ibid., 134.

[116] Ibid., 134.

[117] Ibid., 135.

[118] Ibid., 135.

writings of Habakkuk of such an archaic triumph hymn, which is to be understood "eschatologically rather than historically."[119]

In my opinion, authenticity and the integrity of Habakkuk 3 to the book, though related, are two different issues, and should be kept separate. We may never be able to find a definitive historical answer to the former question since we have no information on the life of Habakkuk. Meanwhile the book in its present form may still demonstrate a literary unity. Hiebert is right to remind us that the superscriptions are redactional materials which reflect secondary settings, and thus "are not *prima facie* evidence for the original setting of a poem."[120] However, even if the superscriptions in 1:1 and 3:1 are secondary, it does not follow that the content of the section is secondary. It is best to read the superscriptions as the editorial notes to clarify or inform later generations of the content of the section, rather than as grounds to deny the integrity of Habakkuk 3 to the prophecy. And at the very least it shows that tradition remembered Habakkuk as the author of this psalm very early on.

Hiebert argues that the musical notations, which are present only in chapter 3 and nowhere else outside the psalter,[121] signify that this psalm was a separate piece which was later incorporated into the book. He further raises the question "why Habakkuk employed liturgical notes here but not with other pieces in Chapters 1 and 2 which reflect cultic forms and vocabulary."[122] Contrary to Hiebert's opinion, Watt explains that the musical notations and the liturgical markings were intentionally mixed literary conventions employed by the writer so as to alert the reader to the liturgical nature of the poem.[123] This marking of Habakkuk 3 is necessary to mark it explicitly as an inset hymn within a poetic context so as to "[refocus] thematic attention on Yahweh as warrior and savior of Israel."[124] Thus these markings reflect "a self-conscious evocation of liturgical worship for literary effect within the book of Habakkuk."[125] Another reason, proposed by Davidson, is that though the poem was an integral part of the prophecy, it was used in the liturgical service, which explains the presence of the musical notations. However he admitted that such a use of any part of a prophetic book has no parallel.[126]

Hiebert opines that "understood as a hymn of triumph, Habakkuk 3 no longer fits its context" as a lament, and concludes that the form of Habakkuk 3 is best described as a song of victory,[127] originating in the era of Israel's earliest

---

[119] Ibid., 137.

[120] Ibid., 131.

[121] The liturgical rubrics of this chapter prompt some scholars to speculate that Habakkuk was a cultic prophet.

[122] Hiebert, *God of My Victory*, 134.

[123] Watts, "Psalmody in Prophecy," 212.

[124] Ibid., 213.

[125] Ibid., 218.

[126] Davidson, *Nahum, Habakkuk and Zephaniah*, 58.

[127] Hiebert, *God of My Victory*, 118.

literary conventions.[128] However, while few would dispute 3:3-15 is a victory hymn, many would argue that it is framed by a lament (vv. 2, 16-19). Most of the lament's traditional elements appear within those few verses: address and petition in v. 2, assurance, vow of praise, and expression of trust in vv. 16-19.[129] The complaint itself is missing, probably because it is voiced earlier.[130] Furthermore, a lot of lament psalms contain elements of the song of victory to refer to God's past deeds of salvation (for example, Pss 74:12-17; 77:14-20 [Eng 13-19]). Hence the author of this psalm follows the tradition of professing God's salvific deeds in a lament.

Moreover, Habakkuk 3 as a fitting end to the prophet's complaint finds support in Job and some psalms (notably Ps 77), where arguments over theodicy also conclude with a theophany.[131] The resolution of the prophet's complaint is due to the daunting religious experience[132] created by the theophany which changes the prophet's perspective—from asking the question "why" to a deep understanding of "who" God really is. Since God's being cannot be separated from his actions, meditation on God's deed in the past evokes hope and assurance of God's salvific action in the future. This hope then gave the prophet a quiet confidence for him to "wait" for the promised day of deliverance.[133]

Hiebert considers the mention of the salvation of the "anointed" to be in direct conflict with the view of 1:1-4 where the leaders were accused of paralyzing Torah.[134] However the "anointed" does not have to be the reigning king during Habakkuk's time but could be an ideal king much like the one expected in Micah 5:1-5. Moreover, if we take 3:8-15 as recalling the Exodus experience, then the "anointed" may refer to Moses.[135]

Hiebert observes that verbal syntax of Habakkuk 3 contains prefix/suffix alternation to describe events in the past and may indicate that this chapter is an archaic poem because it employed preterite forms.[136] But, as suggested by Peckham, Hiebert should have shown why the poem could not have come from

---

[128] Ibid., 121.

[129] For a detailed discussion on the structure and history of lament, see C. Westermann, *Praise and Lament in the Psalms*, trans. K.R. Crim, and R.N. Soulen (Atlanta: John Knox, 1981), 165-213.

[130] Watts, "Psalmody in Prophecy," 214.

[131] D.E. Gowan, "God's Answer to Job: How Is It an Answer?" *Horizons in Biblical Theology* 8 (1986): 93, suggests that the Lord's speeches in Job are introduced as a theophany, "Then the Lord answered Job out of the whirlwind" (38:1, 40:6).

[132] R. Otto describes three elements to that experience as "*mysterium*," "*tremendum*" and "*fascinansum*." For a detailed discussion, see his book, *The Idea of the Holy: An Inquiry into the Non-Rational Factor in the Idea of the Divine and Its Relation to the Rational*, trans. J.W. Harvey (London: Oxford University Press, 1925), 12-41.

[133] J.G. Janzen, "Eschatological Symbol and Existence in Habakkuk," *CBQ* 44 (1982): 411.

[134] Hiebert, *God of My Victory*, 134-35.

[135] Patterson, *Nahum, Habakkuk, Zephaniah*, 248.

[136] Hiebert, *God of My Victory*, 139.

other periods. For as it stands now, an eighth or seventh-century date is not excluded for Habakkuk 3.[137] Moreover, even if Hiebert successfully argues that the poem is archaic, there is no evidence to suggest that the prophet could not have incorporated or re-used an archaic psalm himself to express his religious experience.[138] As Andersen rightly concludes, Habakkuk could have produced the whole work and that he did indeed pray this prayer, though he thinks that the poem might have been an ancient one that Habakkuk appropriated.[139]

Hiebert rightly observes that Habakkuk 3 is not a new poem and identifies the differences between Habakkuk 3 and other new divine warrior psalms composed during the sixth and the fifth centuries in other prophetic books.[140] Also he mentions that the group who edited the book of Habakkuk was probably the same group who edited Isaiah and Zechariah. But this begs the question why the later editors of the sixth and fifth centuries did not compose a new poem as they did with other prophetic books but incorporated such an ancient poem. Would this not suggest that chapter 3 was already an integral part of the book when the book of Habakkuk was finally incorporated into the prophetic corpus?

### Textual critical issues

The text of the book of Habakkuk, particularly the third chapter, also poses many problems. W.F. Albright proposed some thirty-eight corrections of the Masoretic text in chapter three alone.[141] Textual difficulties, which include obscurities, *hapax legomena*, grammatical and scribal problems, abound in the book.[142] That may explain why the text of the LXX differs from that of the MT. The text from 1QpHab also has some significant variants from MT.[143] Brownlee lists more than fifty of the principal variants for the first two chapters. He also notes that on the whole the orthography (spelling) of the MT is more classical and not so full as that found in the Dead Sea Scrolls. The plene script is overwhelmingly more frequent in the Dead Sea Scrolls.[144] This phenomenon,

---

[137] B. Peckham, review of *God of My Victory*, by T. Hiebert, *Hebrew Studies* 30 (1989): 143-45.

[138] Wendland, commenting on Hiebert's suggestion that this hymn is a post-exilic composition to emphasize God's final victory over evil, states that, "As if the prophet himself could not have conceived of such a glorious outcome!" See his article, "The righteous Live by Their Faith," 600.

[139] F.I. Andersen, *Habakkuk: A New Translation with Introduction and Commentary*, AB 25 (New York: Doubleday, 2001), 260.

[140] For a discussion on the differences between the characteristics of the new poems and Habakkuk 3, see Hiebert, *God of My Victory*, 140.

[141] W.F. Albright, "The Psalm of Habakkuk," in *Studies in Old Testament Prophecy* (Edinburgh: T & T Clark, 1950), 10.

[142] Patterson, *Nahum, Habakkuk, Zephaniah*, 132.

[143] W.H. Brownlee, *The Text of Habakkuk in the Ancient Commentary from Qumran* (Philadelphia: Society of Biblical Literature and Exegesis, 1959), 109-13.

[144] Ibid., 100.

together with other orthographic features, indicate that the Qumran text represent a late or dialectic spelling.[145] Brownlee stresses that "in all cases of doubt, the safer criterion would be to follow the MT."[146] Despite these many deviations, Haak still concludes that "there is a basis for the textual study of Habakkuk within the consonantal tradition represented in the MT. Regardless of the general theory of textual transmission and development espoused, it appears that there existed only minor variations of a single consonantal text in the case of this prophecy."[147] According to him, divergences from the MT are due to peculiarities of the translators or the interpreters or that their vocalization of the Hebrew consonantal text differed drastically from that reflected in the MT.[148]

This confusion is also the subject of Paul E. Copeland's study. He analyzes ancient Greek (LXX; and Codex Barberini) and Aramaic Targum versions of Hab 3:2 and concludes that due to the uncertainty of the MT, these ancient versions came up with different interpretations. While the Targum is clearly based on a Masoretic-type text and translated the phrase בקרב שנים[149] as "In the midst of the years," LXX understood the phrase as "In the middle of the two living creatures (i.e. Cherubim)," which indicates the Lord's appearance between the two cherubim to reveal himself. These diverse interpretations on the phrase "בקרב שנים" may indicate that the MT version of Hab 3:2 "has served as 'pre-text' to widely divergent expositions, several of which have shaped the text form of ancient translation."[150]

Many scholars regarded the text presented by the MT as corrupt.[151] Earlier scholars tended to correct the MT by using other versions, but this practice has since been called into question. The opinion with regard to the accuracy of the MT is currently divided: some scholars, such as Ralph L. Smith, Haak, Robertson, and Patterson, show great confidence in the MT, while others, such as B. Margulis, Hiebert, and more recently, Aaron Pinker[152] continue to emend the text heavily.[153]

---

[145] Ibid., 106.

[146] Ibid., 113.

[147] Haak, *Habakkuk*, 7. Brownlee, on the other hand, mentions that many divergent texts were current from which the Qumran sectarians might well select the reading most advantageous to their purpose. See his book, *The Text of Habakkuk*, 118.

[148] For a detailed discussion, see Haak, *Habakkuk*, 1-11.

[149] For a detailed discussion see P.E. Copeland, "In the Midst of Years," in *Text as Pretext: Essays in Honour of Robert Davidson*, ed. R.P. Carroll, JSOTSup 138 (Sheffield: SAP, 1992), 99-105.

[150] Ibid., 105.

[151] For a brief survey of the textual-critical research on the book of Habakkuk up to 1992, see Sweeney, "Habakkuk, Book of," 3: 2-3.

[152] See the many articles by Pinker, "Better Bitter River," *ZAW* 114 (2002): 112-15; idem., "Casternets," *ZAW* 114 (2002): 618-21; idem., "God's C3 in Habakkuk 3," *ZAW* 115 (2003): 261-65; idem., " 'Captors' for 'Years' in Habakkuk 3:2," *RB* 112 (Jan 2005): 20-26; idem., "The Lord's Bow in Habakkuk 3,9a," *Biblica* 84 (2003):

Smith declares that the Hebrew text of Habakkuk is in fair shape despite some obscure passages.[154] Robertson, after evaluating the Qumran text and LXX, decides that the MT is well preserved and is to be preferred.[155] Patterson recognizes the textual difficulties in the MT version of Habakkuk, particularly in the third chapter. However he warns not to "overly dramatize" the difficulties and states in confidence that despite the presence of a few individual textual problems, the Hebrew text of Habakkuk is in fair shape.[156] F.F. Bruce recognizes the textual problems in the book of Habakkuk; however, he warns against "conjectural emendation," and states that "[t]he Masoretic Text, especially its consonantal framework, should not be abandoned without good reason."[157] Haak asserts that "the consonantal tradition reflected in the MT lies behind the other traditions and that the readings of the MT are usually equal or superior to the other Hebrew readings."[158] However, while he confirms the consonantal tradition reflected in MT as those found in other early versions, the same uniformity cannot be said with regard to the vocalization preserved by the MT.[159] According to him, "the vocalization tradition is primarily a tradition of interpretation of the consonantal text." Hence he seeks "to understand the consonantal text of Habakkuk as it was understood in the late 7th-early 6th century B.C.E."[160]

Margulis argues that in order to avoid the "overwhelmingly midrashic and isogetic interpretations" on some "unintelligible" Old Testament texts, it is better to do "honest and responsible attempts at improving on the Hebrew *textus receptus*."[161] Thus he engages in the reconstruction of the text, emending the text profusely.[162] However, the issue of subjectivity is precisely the problem with the approach that he is proposing. Hiebert, in an attempt to show how "inclusion functions to mark the discrete sections of Habakkuk 3 and to give shape

417-20; idem., "On the Meaning of מטיו in Habakkuk 3,14a," *Biblica* 86 (2005): 376-86.

[153] For the text-critical research in 1990s, see Dangl, "Habakkuk in Recent Research," 131-35.

[154] R.L. Smith, *Micah-Malachi*, WBC (Waco: Word, 1984), 96.

[155] Robertson, *The Books of Nahum, Habakkuk, and Zephaniah*, 40-42.

[156] Patterson, *Nahum, Habakkuk, Zephaniah*, 132-33.

[157] F.F. Bruce, "Habakkuk," in *The Minor Prophets: An Exegetical and Expository Commentary*, ed. T.E. McComiskey, vol. 2, *Obadiah, Jonah, Micah, Nahum, and Habakkuk* (Grand Rapids: Baker, 1993), 835.

[158] Haak, *Habakkuk*, 5.

[159] Ibid., 8. Ernst Würthwein also comments that vocalization of MT does not have the same significance as the consonantal text, and that alterations in the pointing do not qualify properly as emendations. For a detailed discussion on the methods of textual criticism, see his book, *The Text of the Old Testament: An Introduction to the Biblia Hebraica*, trans. Erroll F. Rhodes (Grand Rapids: Eerdmans, 1979), 111-19.

[160] Haak, *Habakkuk*, 9-10.

[161] B. Margulis, "The Psalm of Habakkuk: A Reconstruction and Interpretation," *ZAW* 82 (1970): 409.

[162] Ibid., 412-33.

to the poem as a whole,"[163] finds it necessary to emend the MT text thirty-eight times in just eighteen verses. But, as Wendland argues, "the credibility of a close discourse study of the original Hebrew stands in inverse proportions to the number of changes that are made to it in one's analysis and interpretation, especially those which affect the consonantal text (MT). Any critical alteration in this respect, no matter how seemingly valid in terms of theoretical principles, always weakens one's argument in relation to the textual organization as a whole."[164]

In sum, in spite of the textual difficulties and obscurities, the MT, especially the consonantal tradition reflected in it, is still regarded by most scholars as reliable and superior to other versions. Thus extreme caution should be exercised before one resort to alter the text, and the tentativeness of any emended text should be acknowledged.

### *Structure of the book*

Childs states that most scholars agree that the structure[165] of the book of Habakkuk includes three major literary sections: the dialogue between Habakkuk and God in 1:1-2:4[5], a series of woe oracles against the Chaldeans in 2:5[6]-20, and the concluding psalm in chapter 3.[166] Other scholars such as Maria Eszenyei Széles, Sweeney, Bruce, and others, propose another alternative structure by dividing the book into two sections: the oracle of Habakkuk in chapters 1 and 2, and the prayer of Habakkuk in chapter 3.[167] Sweeney argues that this division is to be preferred for the superscriptions in Hab 1:1 and 3:1 suggests a two-part instead of a three-part structure.[168]

As Bailey rightly observes, the argument on the structure of the book boils down to "whether one wants to follow traditional form critical markers or whether one decides to look for literary markers in the present canonical form of the book. Interestingly, whichever of these two choices one makes, the other subdivisions of the book remain virtually the same."[169]

By taking both superscriptions in 1:1 and 3:1, as well as the internal literary markers into consideration, I propose to divide the book into three interrelated

---

[163] T. Hiebert, "The Use of Inclusion in Habakkuk 3," in *Directions in Biblical Poetry*, ed. E. Follis, JSOTSup 40 (Sheffield: JSOT, 1987), 119-22.

[164] Wendland, "The Righteous," 600.

[165] Structure here refers to the internal organization of a text, its linguistic patterns, sequence, and development.

[166] Childs, *Introduction to the Old Testament as Scripture*, 448.

[167] See M.E. Széles, *Wrath and Mercy: A Commentary on the Books of Habakkuk & Zephaniah*, trans. G.A.F. Knight, ITC (Grand Rapids: Eerdmans, 1987), 7; and M.A. Sweeney, "Habakkuk" in *The Harper Collins Bible Commentary*, rev. ed., ed. J.L. Mays (San Francisco: Harper, 2000), 668; and Bruce, "Habakkuk," 831.

[168] Sweeney, "Structure, Genre, and Intent in Habakkuk," 64.

[169] Bailey, "Habakkuk," 256-57.

scenes.[170] Following the superscription of 1:1, scene 1 comprises Habakkuk's first complaint (1:2-4), Yahweh's first response (1:5-11), and Habakkuk's second complaint (1:12-17). Then the narration of 2:1 which depicts Habakkuk waiting at the rampart for the divine response begins scene 2. Yahweh's response comes in 2:2-5, which is followed by five woe oracles (2:6-20). The superscription of 3:1 precedes the third scene which records Habakkuk's petition (3:2), a theophany (3:3-15), and Habakkuk's reaction (3:16-19a). The musical notation in the subscription of 3:19b together with the superscription of 3:1 form an *inclusio* to this chapter.

### Debate on the genre of the book

This near consensus on structure, however, does not solve the problem of disagreement concerning the genre[171] of the book. Various genres proposed by scholars include prophetic liturgy, a report on the prophet's visionary experience, a wisdom text which deals with the issue of theodicy,[172] a lament, and a *maśśā'* (commonly translated as "oracle").[173]

The headings of the book and the presence of the musical notations indicate to some scholars that the book of Habakkuk is a cultic liturgy.[174] Hermann Gunkel identified this type of liturgy as the prophetic liturgy, which is a prophetic individual complaint song with a subsequent oracle of being heard, and is created by the prophet based on the model of the cult.[175] Albright saw the book of Habakkuk as composed by a single author who was a temple-musician in the last years of the First Temple.[176] E. Nielsen asserted the integral unity of Habakkuk and affirmed that it is a liturgical composition intended for the cult,

---

[170] Other scholars who outline the book into three main parts similar to mine include Bruckner, *The NIV Application Commentary*, 204; O'Brien, *Nahum, Habakkuk*, 59.

[171] Genre refers to the contribution of style and type of literary work. The term implies that a literary text can be classified within a type based upon literary conventions. For the importance of genre to our understanding of literary work, see K. Koch, *The Growth of the Biblical Tradition: The Form Critical Method*, trans. C.M. Cupitt (London: Adam and Charles Black, 1969), 4. For a more recent reassessment on the benefits of a generic approach to biblical texts, see T. Longman III, "Form Criticism, Recent Developments in Genre Theory, and the Evangelical," *WTJ* 47 (1985): 60-67.

[172] Sweeney, "Structure, Genre, and Intent in Habakkuk," 63.

[173] Richard D. Weis translates the term *maśśā'* as "prophetic exposition of divine revelation." For a detailed discussion and a survey of the use of this term, see R.D. Weis, "Oracle" in *ABD*, ed. D.N. Freedman (New York: Doubleday, 1992), 5:28-29.

[174] For the involvement and the role of prophet in Israel's worship, see A.R. Johnson, *The Cultic Prophet and Israel's Psalmody* (Cardiff: University of Wales Press, 1979).

[175] H. Gunkel, *Introduction to Psalms: The Genres of the Religious Lyric of Israel*, trans. J.D. Nogalski (German original, Göttingen: Vandenhoeck & Ruprecht, 1933. Macon: Mercer University Press, 1998), 314.

[176] Albright, "The Psalm of Habakkuk," 9.

or an imitation of such a form.[177] J.H. Eaton examines the features of the text and affirms that it is a liturgical text. He postulates that the setting is in the Autumn Festival.[178] Ivan Engnell stated that prophetic literature may be divided into two main types: the liturgy type and the *dīwān* type. The prophetic liturgy literature, in which Habakkuk belongs, has a more consistent poetic form, while the *dīwān* type has come to mean the collected work of a poet.[179] Széles speculates that Habakkuk was called, trained, and received his message "through the instrumentality of the liturgy in public worship," and thus she concludes that Habakkuk was a "cultic prophet."[180] J.D.W. Watts follows the story of "Daniel, Bel, and the Snake" in the Apocrypha, and thinks that the liturgical elements in the book of Habakkuk support the view that "he was one of the Levites who conducted temple worship in Jerusalem."[181] G. Fohrer sees the book as prophetic imitation of a cultic liturgy.[182] More precisely, he sees chapters 1 and 2 as a prophetic imitation of a cultic liturgy, in which Habakkuk is the sole speaker.[183] But as for the third chapter, he regards it as a vision report which describes the vision in 2:2-4, but not the vision itself, for "it is far too extensive to be such an oracle."[184] Jörg Jeremias also believed that Habakkuk was a pre-exilic cult prophet, and that the book of Habakkuk is basically a "lament liturgy." He also saw Habakkuk as influenced by the canonical prophets for he proclaimed divine judgment against Israel though he also predicted salvation for the righteous.[185] Jöcken, on the other hand, maintained that there is nothing to suggest either the pre-exilic Habakkuk was a cultic prophet, or that a post-exilic redaction tried to establish him as one.[186]

W. Rudolf also doubts whether Habakkuk can be classified as the "cultic prophet." He argues that the dialogues between God and the prophet in the first

---

[177] E. Nielson, "The Righteous and the Wicked in Habaqquq," *Studia Theologica* 6 (1953): 59.

[178] J.H. Eaton, "The Origin and Meaning of Habakkuk 3," *ZAW* 76 (1964): 144-71. Johnson thinks the psalms that are defined as "prophetic liturgy," were originally associated with one of Israel's regular religious festivals. See Johnson, *The Cultic Prophet*, 5.

[179] I. Engnell, *Critical Essays on the Old Testament*, trans. J.T. Willis (London: SPCK, 1970), 166-67.

[180] Széles, *Wrath and Mercy*, 5.

[181] J.D.W. Watts, *The Books of Joel, Obadiah, Jonah, Nahum, Habakkuk and Zephaniah* (Cambridge: Cambridge University Press, 1975), 121-22.

[182] G. Fohrer, "Das 'Gebet des Propheten Habakuk' (Hab 3,1-16)," in *Mélanges bibliques et orientaux en l'honneur de M. Mathias Delcor*, ed. A. Caquot, S. Légasse, and M. Tardieu, AOAT 215 (Neukirchen: Neukirchener Verlag, 1985), 159-67.

[183] Fohrer, *Introduction to the Old Testament*, 453.

[184] Ibid., 454.

[185] J. Jeremias, *Kultprophetie und Gerichtsverkundigung in der späten Königszeit Israels* (Neukirchen-Vluyn: Neukirchener Verlag, 1970), 90-104.

[186] P. Jöcken, "War Habakuk ein Kultprophet?" In *Bausteine Biblischer Theologie*, ed. H.J. Fabry (Bonn: Bonner Biblische Beiträge, 1977), 332.

two chapters cannot be regarded as liturgy, for other prophets such as Amos also had similar experience and no one would classify Amos a cult prophet.[187] He prefers to view the book of Habakkuk as a report on his visionary experience.[188] Gerald Janzen takes the verb "saw" (חָזָה) on the superscription in 1:1 seriously, for it identifies 2:2-4 with its repeated noun "vision" (חָזוֹן) as "the rhetorical and hermeneutical center of the book."[189] Peckham saw the book as a composition of text, which records Habakkuk's vision in a lament, and a commentary by a later redactor.[190] And recently, Andersen asserts that the book of Habakkuk "reports and records the prophet's vision of God," which was granted "only after strenuous and dangerous prayers."[191]

A third view regards this book as a wisdom text which deals with the issue of theodicy. Donald E. Gowan, analyzing Habakkuk in terms of six types of literary evidence, demonstrates that Habakkuk has close affinities with "skeptical wisdom."[192] However, Gary Tuttle opines that Gowan's evidence on the relation between Habakkuk and skeptical wisdom is not convincing. Instead, Habakkuk can be shown to have affinities with traditional wisdom.[193] Dennis R. Bratcher thinks that the central issue is that God is not acting according to the traditional principles which Habakkuk expects.[194] Otto argues that the theology of the book of Habakkuk is the theology of its tradition-historical development.[195] Each new, painful and unfortunate event in the historical situation raises the question of theodicy and demands actualization of its theological tradition. A.H.J. Gunneweg thinks that the centre of Habakkuk lies in 2:4, which has a wisdom theme that deals with the fate of the righteous sufferer.[196] Bullock comments that "Habakkuk was bold enough to broach the subject of divine justice," and that he probed the issue on an "international plane."[197] Thompson recognizes the eclectic nature of the text, and argues that the author

---

[187] For a detailed discussion on his view, see W. Rudolf, *Mica-Nahum-Habakuk-Zephanja* (Gütersloh: Mohn, 1975), 193-94. It is noteworthy that Childs also argues against the liturgical view, stating that the autobiographical shaping of the present text contradicts it. See his book, *Introduction to the Old Testament as Scripture*, 452.

[188] Rudolf, *Mica-Nahum-Habakuk-Zephanja*, 193.

[189] J.G. Janzen, "Eschatological Symbol and Existence in Habakkuk," *CBQ* 44 (1982): 396.

[190] Peckham, "The Vision of Habakkuk," 617-36. See also, idem., *History and Prophecy*, 408-409.

[191] Andersen, *Habakkuk*, 12.

[192] D.E. Gowan, "Habakkuk and Wisdom," *Perspective* 9 (1968): 157-66.

[193] G.A. Tuttle, "Wisdom and Habakkuk," *Studia Biblica et Theologica* 3 (1973): 14.

[194] D. Bratcher, *The Theological Message of Habakkuk* (Ann Arbor: University Microfilm International, 1984), 66-67.

[195] Otto, "Die Theologie des Buches Habakuk," 284.

[196] A.H.J. Gunneweg, "Habakuk und das Problem des leidenden sdyq," *ZAW* 98 (1986): 400-15.

[197] Bullock, *Prophetic Books*, 183.

had borrowed from wisdom and Isaianic traditions to resolve a difficult theological problem—the issue of theodicy.[198]

A fourth view, held by scholars such as Haak and Prinsloo, sees the book of Habakkuk as a lament. Haak sees the entire book of Habakkuk in the form of a complaint.[199] Prinsloo sees the first part of Habakkuk, which composed of the first two chapters, as lament against wickedness and Yahweh's perverted sense of justice, and the third chapter as a lament poem.[200] But Andersen argues that it is too general to classify Habakkuk 3 as a lament by only an opening invocation (3:2a) followed by a prayer for divine intervention (3:2b).[201] He further stresses the importance of distinguishing "complaint" from "lament."[202] He refers the term "lament" to the prayer of misery appealing to God's mercy while a "complaint" can take the form of protest and an appeal to God's justice.[203] Andersen also criticizes Haak as making some forced argument to fit the whole book of Habakkuk into the template of a cultic complaint, and that Haak's explanation that the "second complaint is an elaboration of the situation already described in the first complaint"[204] is an overstatement, for his argument undermines the distinctiveness of the "woe oracles."[205] Indeed, he may be right when he states, "We are prepared to argue for the *thematic* unity of the book in an overarching literary structure. But none of the familiar genres supplies the model for the whole book."[206] Wendland thinks that the framework of the book assumes the literary form of the traditional lament, which provides the "formal, semantic and emotive backbone of the entire discourse," and as an *inclusio* framing other poetic types to dramatize the discourse. This type of arrangement, he terms it "poetic-prophetic" genre.[207]

Floyd, and Cleaver-Bartholomew follow Richard Weis' research and argue that *maśśā'* is a genre of prophetic literature.[208] Floyd thinks that the first chapter of Habakkuk should not be understood as a dialogue between the prophet and Yahweh, but rather as a prophetic complaint concerning the fulfillment of

---

[198] Thompson, "Prayer, Oracle and Theophany," 33-53.

[199] Haak, *Habakkuk*, 19.

[200] Prinsloo, "Reading Habakkuk as a Literary Unit," 520-22.

[201] Andersen, *Habakkuk*, 20.

[202] G.M. Tucker makes a distinction between "lament" and "complaint." He reserves the term lament for the dirge, or the funeral song; but when there is still hope that disaster may be averted, complaints are made to God to save. See G.M. Tucker, *Form Criticism of the Old Testament*. Guides to Biblical Scholarship (Philadelphia: Fortress, 1971), 81.

[203] Andersen, *Habakkuk*, 21.

[204] Haak, *Habakkuk*, 138.

[205] Andersen, *Habakkuk*, 21.

[206] Ibid., 21 (Italics his).

[207] Wendland, "The Righteous Live by Their Faith," 607.

[208] For Floyd's argument, see his article, "The מַשָּׂא (*maśśā'*) as a Type of Prophetic Book," *JBL* 121 (2002): 401-22.

an oracle.[209] He argues that 1:5-11 should not be read as a response from Yahweh to the prophet's complaint, for one would expect to find a salvation oracle typical of a response to a complaint.[210] But as Herbert Marks remarks, "it is precisely the disjunctions—the fact that prophetic complaint and divine response appear to be at cross-purposes—that account for its resonance."[211] My opinion is that the surprising twist on the conventions of a salvation prophecy adds to the effect of Yahweh's surprising announcement that the hearers are going to be astounded. Cleaver-Bartholomew also argues against a sequential reading of Hab 1:2-2:20,[212] but sees Habakkuk as a *maśśā'* (מַשָּׂא). However, *maśśā'* as a prophetic genre has not been widely followed by most commentators. Also even if one accepts *maśśā'* as a prophetic explanation of the previous divine revelation, it does not necessarily follow, as what Cleaver-Bartholomew claims, that Hab 1:5-11 should be read as a "previously delivered divine oracle which is elucidated at a later time."[213] A more natural reading would be that 2:2-5 is a revelation (or *maśśā'*) in response to the previous divine oracle of 1:5-11.

In sum, although there is no clear consensus on the genre of the book, most would agree that the book consists of various genres subsumed under a framework of a prophetic complaint. This prophetic complaint is couched in a traditional lament form. The eclectic nature of the book, however, should not be viewed as a loose collection of unrelated material. Rather, it is best to see that the prophet employed various literary devices and conventions available to him to create a book that could deliver his message in the most effective and dramatic way.

## *Synchronic reading of the book*

In light of the paucity of concrete historical data that the book of Habakkuk contains,[214] and the failure of historical-critical research to provide definitive answers to its questions,[215] some scholars, such as Bratcher and B.Y. Leigh,

---

[209] Floyd, "Prophetic Complaint," 406-407.

[210] Ibid., 402.

[211] H. Marks, "The Twelve Prophets," in *The Literary Guide to the Bible*, ed. R. Alter and F. Kermode (Cambridge: Belknap Press, 1987), 219.

[212] Cleaver-Bartholomew, "An Alternate Approach," 207-11.

[213] Ibid., 212.

[214] The only clear historical datum that the book provides is the mentioning of the Chaldeans in Hab 1:5-10. Other possible clues include: the name of Habakkuk which has an Assyrian cognate, as well as his title as a prophet.

[215] Prinsloo states that in spite of a magnitude of publications, "no satisfactory answer can be given to even one of the problem areas." See his article, "Reading Habakkuk as a Literary Unit," 515. Indeed Childs may be right when he laments that historical criticism fails to work in finding the message in the book of Habakkuk. He writes, "The frequent assumption of the historical critical method that the correct interpretation of a biblical text depends upon the critic's ability to establish a time-frame for its

seek to approach the text by employing a synchronic study of the book.[216] By doing a rhetorical and structural analysis of the book, one can "find access into the heart of the book"[217] and "uncover the dynamics of personal and social identification and transformation."[218] This emphasis on the literary approach to the study of the book of Habakkuk is a welcomed supplement to the traditional research, and may indeed "burst the boundaries of traditional form criticism,"[219] and lead to constructive results that traditional historical criticisms could not attain.

## Purpose

The book of Habakkuk begins with the prophet's complaint to God about his contemporary social conditions, and ends with a theophany as well as a resolution of the prophet's problem. The theme of the book finds parallels with wisdom literature,[220] especially Job,[221] and with lament psalms, most notably, Psalm 77[222] and 73,[223] and to some extent, Jeremiah's confession (Jer 12:1-6; 15:10-21; 17:14-18; 18:18-23; 20:7-13, 14-18).[224]

---

historical background breaks down in the case of Habakkuk. The danger is acute that a doctrinaire application of historical criticism not only fails to find an access into the heart of the book, but by raising a series of wrong questions it effectively blocks true insight." See his book, *Introduction to the Old Testament as Scripture*, 454-55. For a response to various critiques of historical criticism, see A.L. Nations, "Historical Criticism and the Current Methodological Crisis," *SJT* 36 (1983): 59-71.

[216] See Bratcher, *Theological Message of Habakkuk*; B.Y. Leigh, "A Rhetorical and Structural Study of the Book of Habakkuk" (Ph.D. diss., Golden Gate Baptist Theological Seminary, 1994).

[217] Bratcher, *Theological Message of Habakkuk*, 19.

[218] Dangl, "Habakkuk in Recent Research," 153-54.

[219] Ibid., 154.

[220] Wisdom literature here refers to the biblical corpus made up of Job, Proverbs and Ecclesiastes. Donald Gowan thinks that Habakkuk has close affinities with the "skeptical wisdom" of Job, Koheleth, Proverb 30, and some of the Psalms. See his article, "Habakkuk and Wisdom," 158.

[221] Habakkuk finds similarity in Job in that they both dare to challenge God's justice. In chapter 9 Job ponders the possibility of entering into litigation with God, and in 23:4-5 he demands to see God to plead his case before God. The language used in Job 23:4-5 is strikingly similar to Hab 2:1. Moreover, both books resolve their issues after the theophany. As for the style, both books employ dialogues as a mean to present their concerns.

[222] Ps 77 is strikingly similar to Habakkuk in its structure, form, and content. It begins with a lament (vv 1-10 [Eng 9]), then comes the remembrance of God's mighty deeds in the past (vv 11 [Eng 10]-16 [Eng 15]), and ends with a theophany (vv 17 [Eng 16]-20 [Eng 19]). The description of theophany in vv. 17-20 parallels that in Hab 3:8-10.

[223] The similarity between Ps 73 and Habakkuk lies in the psalmist's struggle to resolve his issue. The psalmist has a problem with the prosperity of the wicked but finds solace after he enters into the sanctuary. Many interpreters regard Ps 73 as a wisdom psalm because of its concern of the retribution motif (cf. Pss 37 & 49). However,

The purpose of this book is to explain the resolution of the issue of theodicy in the book of Habakkuk. While earlier researchers usually concentrate on the historical questions about Habakkuk, the present study intends to focus on the presentation and the resolution of the issue of theodicy in a prophetic book.

This involves showing how the writer of Habakkuk presents his case to his audience, and how he comes to the final resolution of his problem. It is hoped that by engaging in a close reading of the text, paying attention to its rhetorical devices, surprise elements, twists and turns of the event, I can uncover literary clues in the text that demonstrate the dynamic transformation of the prophet's faith—from doubt to triumph in faith, and that we can glean insight on how to resolve this universal human experience.

Since the subject matter in this book is theodicy, an issue that some pious Israelites constantly struggled with, it is pertinent to study biblical passages that deal with theodicy, particularly how theophany would help to settle the issue. I shall limit my investigation to the theophany in Job 38-41, and to a lesser extent, Psalm 77, and to the personal resolutions seen in Psalm 73 and Jeremiah's confessions.

Many scholars would agree that Habakkuk is unique among the prophetic literature in its presentation of the message. It is helpful to see how Habakkuk fits into the prophetic tradition, particularly how it differs from other prophetic literature in handling the issue of theodicy, as well as its presentation of the issue.

While this book deals with the subject of theodicy, it is not a philosophical discussion of this topic. The scope of my investigation is anchored strictly within the framework of the Old Testament studies so as to see how the ancient Israelites deal with the matter.

## Methodology

In this thesis I will study the MT, with reference to the other versions when needed. I will employ a literary approach to the text. The literary approach used here is not the biblical literary criticism practiced by German scholars in search

---

scholars including Bentzen, Mowinckel, Murphy, and Kuntz all believe that Ps 73 should belong to a thanksgiving psalm due to its form and literary style. See A. Bentzen, *Introduction to the Old Testament* (Copenhagen: Gad, 1958), 1:161; S. Mowinckel, "Psalms and Wisdom," in *Wisdom in Israel and in the Ancient Near East*, ed. M. Noth, and D. Winton Thomas (Leiden: Brill, 1960), 208; R.E. Murphy, "A Consideration of the Classification, 'Wisdom Psalms,'" in *Congress Volume: Bonn, 1962*, VTSup 9 (Leiden: Brill, 1963), 164; K. Kuntz, "The Canonical Wisdom Psalms of Ancient Israel—Their Rhetorical, Thematic, and Dimensions," in *Rhetorical Criticism: Essays in Honor of James Muilenburg*, ed. J.J. Jackson and M. Kessler, Pittsburg Theological Monograph Series 1 (Pittsburgh: Pickwick Press, 1974), 207.

[224] Although Jeremiah's complaints are mostly personal in nature, he also questions God's justice in 12:1-2, and laments that God has abandoned Judah in 14:19.

of the source of the text.[225] Rather, it is a new literary analysis of the Bible, stimulated by James Muilenburg's 1968 presidential address to the Society of Biblical Literature, to move beyond form criticism to what he called "rhetorical criticism."[226] Muilenburg describes his method as tracing the movement of the writer's thought by "exhibiting the structural patterns that are employed for the fashioning of a literary unit, whether in poetry or prose, and in discerning the many and various devices by which the predictions are formulated and ordered into a unified whole."[227] This method focuses on the final form of the text and studies the way the language of texts is deployed to convey meaning.[228]

Rhetorical critics begin by defining the boundaries of the passage, and then analyzing its linguistic elements—verbal structures, grammar, meter, word play, and strophes—paragraph by paragraph, sentence by sentence, and word by word. Using this method, as it has developed since Muilenburg, I will study the final form of Habakkuk to discover the relation between all the parts of the text and their contribution to the understanding of the prophet's message. I concur with Martin Kessler who suggests that "rhetorical criticism may serve as a suitable rubric for the kind of biblical criticism which deals with the literary analysis of the Massoretic text."[229] However, the weakness of this method is that it normally does not deal with larger concerns such as genre, themes, plot, or characters.[230]

Since the purpose of this book is to explore not just the message of Habakkuk (*what it says*) but also its presentation of the message (*how it says*), it is necessary to supplement the rhetorical analysis with other literary analytical methods that deal with such literary issues as the plot, the genre, the theme of

---

[225] Klaus Koch's definition of German biblical literary criticism is "the analysis of biblical books from the standpoint of lack of continuity, duplications, inconsistencies and different linguistic usage, with the object of discovering what the individual writers and redactors contributed to a text, and also its time and place of origin." See Koch, *The Growth of the Biblical Tradition*, 69-70.

[226] Later, it is called "literary criticism." See L. Ryken, "The Bible as Literature: A Brief History," in *A Complete Literary Guide to the Bible*, ed. L. Ryken, and T. Longman III (Grand Rapids: Zondervan, 1993), 60; but some refer to it as one of the older streams of literary criticisms, together with new criticism and structuralism, as opposed to the newer literary criticisms which include feminist criticism, materialistic or political criticism, psychoanalytic criticism, and deconstruction. See D.J.A Clines, and J.C. Exum, "The New Criticism," in *The New Literary Criticism and the Hebrew Bible*, ed. J.C Exum, and D.J.A. Clines (Sheffield: SAP, 1993; reprint, Valley Forge: Trinity Press, 1994), 16.

[227] J. Muilenburg, "Form Criticism and Beyond," *JBL* 88 (1969): 8.

[228] Clines, and Exum, "The New Criticism," 16.

[229] M. Kessler, "A Methodological Setting for Rhetorical Criticism," *Art and Meaning: Rhetoric in Biblical Literature*, ed. D.J.A. Clines, D.M. Gunn, and A.J. Hauser, JSOTSup 19 (Sheffield: JSOT, 1982), 10.

[230] P.R. House, *Zephaniah: A Prophetic Drama*, JSOTSup 69 (Sheffield: Almond Press, 1988), 15.

the book, and the characters involved. The plot is the events of the story line, usually motivated by conflict, which generates suspense and leads to a conclusion. Plot analysis is not just to recount the events of the story line, but to explain the reasons and the relationships of those events. [231] Although Hebrew poetry is not usually used to tell a tale, in Habakkuk the use of narrative insert, dialogue, and narrative impulse within the poem, helps to unfold the events. [232] Wendland mentions that "the book [of Habakkuk] as a whole clearly reveals the characteristic sequence of a simple 'plot,' at least in rudimentary form" with its different stages of problem/conflict, complication, climax, then resolution/outcome. [233]

In the broadest level of classification, genre consists of poetry and prose. The insertion of prose interjection in Habakkuk is often used by the critics as evidence of later redaction(s). While I do not deny the existence of redaction, it is not the main concern of this thesis. Rather, the interjection of prose in the poetry is viewed as an authorial intentional device to guide the reader as to how to read the passage.

I will begin by determining the compositional units of the book, using the procedure outlined by Muilenburg in his seminal paper "Form Criticism and Beyond." The isolation of the pericopes is important in grasping the writer's intent and meaning, since it is usually at the beginning of the passage where the major motif is presented. [234] The literary units will be defined by rhetorical devices employed by the writer, such as *inclusio*, change of style, insertion of a prose interjection in the midst of poetry, presence of superscription and subscription. In order to avoid the objection that "too much subjectivity is involved in determining where the accents of the composition really lie," [235] objective guidelines are set to observe the climactic or ballast lines which are present within the pericope. Plot analysis and genre investigation will also be done to see how the writer presents his case through intricate plot and eclectic use of various forms.

The structure of each pericope will also be examined to determine the movement and the development of the writer's thought. The component parts of the pericope are termed strophes. The term strophe here is defined as a series of parallel figures (bicola or tricola) with a discernible beginning and ending, possessing identifiable unity in thought, structure, and style. Strophe may not have a consistent rhythmic or metrical regularity, [236] and may mean "a verse

---

[231] See ibid., 61; T. Longman III, "Biblical Narrative," in *A Complete Literary Guide to the Bible*, ed. L. Ryken, and T. Longman III (Grand Rapids: Zondervan, 1993), 71.

[232] For the dynamic movement in the poetry to move from line to story, see R. Alter, *The Art of Biblical Poetry* (New York: Basic Books, 1985), 27-61.

[233] Wendland, "The Righteous Live by Their Faith," 607.

[234] Muilenburg, "Form Criticism," 9.

[235] Ibid., 9.

[236] Muilenburg, "Form Criticism," 12, warned of the danger of emendation in order to produce regularity.

paragraph of indeterminate length uncontrolled by any formal artistic scheme."[237] Strophes will be identified by literary features such as anaphora, repetition of key words, parallel structures, refrains, emphatic particles, and rhetorical questions.[238] The study of strophes is important for they demonstrate the turning points or the shifts and breaks within a composition, and allow us to trace the movement and the development of the writer's thought.

Then I will explore characterization in the book to see how the writer presents the main characters of the book. Characterization can be done by examining the character traits—by what the character says about himself, by what other characters says about him, and by his actions.[239] Another way of exploring characterization is to trace the development of a character as the plot progresses. In the book of Habakkuk, the dialogues and the monologues not only help to propel the plot, they also provide a window for us to see what is in the speaker's mind. This is important especially when we seek to understand how the prophet comes to his final resolution on the issue of theodicy. The theme of the book will then be drawn by exploring the images, symbols, actions, and personalities. These elements interact with one another to create a larger thematic unit.[240]

In addition to literary and rhetorical criticism, I will also examine the inner biblical exegesis[241] to see how the writer of Habakkuk uses and reinterprets the traditions to forward his message. This is particularly important in the woe oracles, when the prophet applies earlier woe sayings against Jehoiakim to his anti-Babylonian sentiment, and in the third chapter, when the writer employs an ancient victory hymn to describe the theophany, which leads to the final resolution of his concern. Five types of intertextuality will be examined: quotations, allusions, catchwords, themes and motifs, and framing devices.

## Presuppositions

In view of the methodologies employed in this study, two presuppositions must be made. The first one is that the final form of the text is valuable aside from its historical background. The text, with its artistic expressions and specific liter-

---

[237] R.N. Soulen and R.K. Soulen, *Handbook of Biblical Criticism*, 3d ed. (Louisville: Westminster John Knox, 2001), 180.

[238] Bratcher, *Theological Message*, 28. I follow Peckham's method for some of the divisions of strophes. I will discuss this further in the following chapter.

[239] House, *Zephaniah*, 68.

[240] Ibid., 74.

[241] Michael Fishbane, who is interested in exegesis found within the Hebrew Bible, believes that the content of the tradition (the *traditum*) in the Hebrew Bible was the complex result of a long and varied process of transmission, or *traditio*. And the Hebrew Bible itself demonstrates the inner biblical exegesis by reworking and reinterpreting the *traditum*, e.g., the Chronicler's reworking of the Book of Kings. For a detailed discussion, see *Biblical Interpretation in Ancient Israel* (Oxford: Clarendon, 1985), 5-6.

ary features, is a valid medium to convey a message. This statement does not preclude the possibility of redactions. The study on the redactional layers is valuable in that it reflects the history of interpretation and appropriation of the passage by later generations to address their specific historical realities. However due to the speculative nature of this method, and the paucity of historical data within the book,[242] a study on the final text may yield a more profitable result. Hence the goal of this study is to understand the meaning of the final text as it stands rather than a reconstruction of what the original intention of the author might have been.

The second presupposition is that the book is a unity rather than an unrelated collection of eclectic sayings. While the book of Habakkuk contains diverse literary elements,[243] it is a well-constructed masterpiece that holds all these integral parts together to form a literary unit. With these presuppositions, the present study proceeds to concentrate on the features that give coherence to the book as a literary unit.

---

[242] Childs thinks that the final editor has purposefully arranged his material so as to disregard the complexities of the original historical setting of these oracles in order to convey a theological perspective which views human history from the divine perspective. See Childs, *Introduction*, 452-53.

[243] Heflin, *Nahum*, 74, identifies elements such as poetry, prophecy, wisdom, liturgy, and autobiography.

# CHAPTER 2

# Close reading of the Book of Habakkuk

In this chapter, I intend to do a detailed analysis on the literary elements of the Book of Habakkuk. By studying the book closely, it is hoped that the progression and development of the inner thought of the author can be seen, and that his goal of communication can be uncovered. In order to do that, literary boundaries of the book will first be demarcated.[1] Then a fresh translation from the Masoretic text will be done, along with a section on comments where I will discuss the meaning of the text stanza by stanza, and how those stanzas relate to each other to bring out the message of the book. Following that, an analysis on the literary genres of the book will be done to find out the reason why those particular genres are used.

### Demarcation of large literary units

To demarcate the literary units, the following literary elements are considered: the presence of headings in the text, the change of genre, change of scene, speaker (including personal forms of verbs, pronouns and pronominal suffixes), subject matter, and the repetition of words and phrases, as well as the presence of *inclusio*.[2]

The macrostructure of the book of Habakkuk is quite clearly defined, for the two superscriptions (1:1 and 3:1) provide a major division in the book. The headings "oracle" (מַשָּׂא) and prayer (תְּפִלָּה) inform the reader concerning the various forms of the texts, which in turn alert the reader to use the appropriate reading strategy. Although superscriptions are usually regarded as late additions, they nevertheless reflect the understanding of later generations on the nature and concept of the book, and thus have theological value.[3] Within the first major section, it can be further divided into two scenes. Scene 1 records

---

[1] Muilenburg indicated that the first concern of a rhetorical critic is to delimit the scope of the literary unit. See his discussion, "Form Criticism and Beyond," 9.

[2] Wendland mentions that there are five common signals of a beginning (*aperture*) in biblical poetry: a formulaic opening, an imperative, a vocative, explicit mention of the divine name, and a rhetorical question. See his discussion, "The Righteous Live by Their Faith," 592.

[3] Childs, *Introduction to the Old Testament as Scripture*, 520.

the dialogues between the prophet and Yahweh, while the interlude in 2:1 indicates a change of scene (at the rampart), and an interjection of monologue. The opening verse in chapter 2 signals a break from the previous section as well as serves as an introduction to what follows.[4] Moreover, this short verse also provides vital information about the prophet's attitude and posture. He is described as standing firm, looking out for the invading army, and waiting for Yahweh's response. The second major section contains the third scene, which is enclosed by a superscription and a subscription.[5] Subunits within each scene can easily be defined by the changes in speakers (1:2-4, 5-11, 12-17; 2:2-5), and subject matters (2:6-20; 3:2, 3-15, 16-19a). In light of these literary clues, I divide the book into three inter-related scenes and propose the following overall outline of the book.

**Superscription**                                             1:1

<u>Scene 1</u>

| | |
|---|---|
| Habakkuk's First Complaint | 1:2-4 |
| Yahweh's First Response | 1:5-11 |
| Habakkuk's Second Complaint | 1:12-17 |

<u>Scene 2</u>

| | |
|---|---|
| Interlude: Habakkuk's Action | 2:1 |
| Yahweh's Second Response | 2:2-5 |
| Five Woes against Chaldeans | 2:6-20 |

**Superscription**                                          3:1

<u>Scene 3</u>

| | |
|---|---|
| Habakkuk's Petition | 3:2 |
| Theophany | 3:3-15 |
| Habakkuk's Reaction | 3:16-19a |

**Subscription**                                         3:19b

The lay-out of the macrostructure of the book shows that each scene contains a somewhat concentric pattern that centers on Yahweh's response or his theophany. And if we treat scene 2 as the center of the entire book, then the climax of the book seems to fall on Yahweh's answer in 2:2-5.

---

[4] Prinsloo also notices its introductory character, see "Reading Habakkuk as a Literary Unit," 520.

[5] The presence of the superscription and subscription strongly indicates that the poem may have achieved the status of an independent literary composition. See B. Childs, "Psalm Titles and Midrashic Exegesis," *JSS* 16 (1971): 141.

Grammatically, 1:2-4 features first and second person masculine singular verbs and suffixes, with the prophet as the addresser and Yahweh as the addressee (1:2a). The form in this section is similar to the community lament usually found in the Psalter.[6] In fact, Westermann identifies Habakkuk 1 as one of the "complete examples of the community lament genre."[7] But Wendland thinks that it takes the whole book of Habakkuk, rather than just chapter one, to fit the pattern of community lament proposed by Westermann.[8]

While the divine response is rarely preserved in the Psalter,[9] the book of Habakkuk has clearly marked sections that record Yahweh's response (1:5-11 and 2:2-5). The beginning of Yahweh's first response at 1:5 is marked by a change in subject, and a series of second person masculine plural imperatives.[10] The change from singular to plural number in 1:5 confirms that this is a communal complaint rather than a personal one. Although it is not clearly indicated here that it is an answer from Yahweh, the change in speaker can be deduced from the content of the speech, for no one else other than Yahweh could have raised up the Chaldeans (v.6).[11] Moreover, this pattern of divine response is repeated again in 2:2, where it is clearly marked as Yahweh's answer, and it begins with imperatives as well. The sudden change of speaker at 1:5 could be a deliberate literary device to amplify the surprise element that is present in the speech (1:5a), and to prepare the audience for the totally unexpected divine response (1:6-11). It is observed by many scholars that usually the divine response to a complaint would be expected to be a comforting one, and that it would contain some elements of salvation; yet in 1:5-11, no such elements were found. This prompts some scholars, such as Floyd and Cleaver-Bartholomew, to reject this section as Yahweh's response.[12] However, Yahweh's statement in

---

[6] Westermann identifies five elements which are basic to the structure of a community lament: (1) address (or introductory petition), (2) lament, (3) confession of trust, (4) petition (double wishes for us and foes), and (5) a vow of praise. See his book, *Praise and Lament in the Psalms*, 52. W.H. Bellinger Jr. notes that in Habakkuk, although the form of the lament is singular, "the reference is clearly communal since the person is put into the context of a corrupt society which provides the occasion for the lament." See his book, *Psalmody and Prophecy*, JSOTSup 27 (Sheffield: JSOT Press, 1984), 83.

[7] C. Westermann, *The Psalms: Structure, Content, and Message*, trans. Ralph D. Gehrke (Minneapolis: Augsburg, 1980), 29.

[8] Wendland, "The Righteous Live by Their Faith," 601.

[9] Westermann, *Psalms*, 43.

[10] Wendland notes that the use of imperatives is an indicator of the beginning of a section in biblical poetry. See "The Righteous Live by Their Faith," 592.

[11] Pinker is certainly off base when he attributes 1:6 to be the speech made by Habakkuk and accuses the prophet of being presumptuous. See his article, "Was Habakkuk Presumptuous?" *JBL* 32 (2004): 31.

[12] *Contra* Childs' view that 1:5-11 is an ironic reply to 1:2-4, Floyd, "Prophetic Complaint," 402, sees no evidence to show that 1:5-11 is a play on the convention of a

1:5 that the audience would be totally astounded by the oracle seems to anticipate the reaction. The surprise element would make sense only when it is Yahweh's unexpected response to a complaint by a righteous person. The conventional divine response to a righteous complaint would be a salvation oracle, but
instead a judgment oracle is pronounced. This is the surprise effect that the author tries to achieve. Habakkuk's second response in 1:12-17 begins with a
rhetorical question addressing to Yahweh. The rhetorical question is again repeated at 1:17a to form an *inclusio* to this section.

The second scene begins with an interlude (2:1-2aα). The change of scenery
and the speech format (from dialogue to monologue) serve as a break to delay
and to heighten the expectation of the divine response which turns out to be the
climax of the book. Unlike Yahweh's first response in 1:5-11, this section (2:2-
5) is explicitly marked as Yahweh's response (2:2aα).

The section on the five woe oracles (2:6-20) begins with a rhetorical question (2:6a) and is not difficult to delimit the subunits within it (6b-8, 9-11, 12-
14, 15-17, and 18-20). Each subunit is led by the word הוֹי "woe," except the
last one which appears in verse 19 instead of verse 18.[13] There is also a debate
on the identity of the speaker in this section. Some scholars, such as
Armerding, Robertson, and Wendland, see the five woes as Yahweh's judgment on the Babylonians.[14] But according to Tucker, woe speeches, almost
without exception, "are not given as the words of Yahweh and therefore are not
oracles."[15] Hiebert sees a new speaker in this section: the oppressed nations
"who now break their silence to address their oppressor."[16] Other scholars, such
as Bruce and Smith, either ignore the issue or conclude that the speaker in this

---

prophecy of salvation. Cleaver-Bartholomew, "An Alternative Approach," 208-209,
holds a similar position to Floyd.

[13] Cannon, together with some scholars, thought that "woe" oracles must begin with הוֹי,
and he changed the sequence of the two verses. See Cannon, "Integrity of Habakkuk," 88. Andersen, on the other hand, thinks that "the fifth 'woe oracle' moves logically from stage to stage," and that the impact of the literary contrast is lost if the two
verses are reversed. See Anderson, *Habakkuk*, 257.

[14] Armerding, "Habakkuk," 510, treats the entire passage of 2:2-20 as Yahweh's judicial procedure against the Babylonians. Robertson, *Nahum, Habakkuk, and Zephaniah*, 185, sees Yahweh as the God of history who must ensure "public vindication of
the righteous and the shaming of the arrogant." Wendland, "The Righteous Live by
Their Faith," 598, thinks that since there is no shift in speaker in the section, it is
most logical to assume that Yahweh is the speaker.

[15] G.M. Tucker, "Prophetic Speech," in *Interpreting the Prophets*, ed. James Luther
Mays and Paul J. Achtemeier (Philadelphia: Fortress, 1987), 33. However, his statement that "the woe cry does not convey a revelation concerning the future" may be
overstated, for even in the three passages that he cites (Amos 5:18-20; 6:4-7; Isa 5:8-
12), they contain revelations regarding the future of Israel and Judah.

[16] T. Hiebert, "The Book of Habakkuk: An Introduction, Commentary, and Reflections," in *NIB* (Nashville: Abingdon, 1996), 7:646.

section cannot be clearly identified.[17] My opinion is that these woe oracles, as they now stand, are pronouncements being put into the mouth of the nations to create an irony. The first word on 2:6b before the pronouncement of woe (הוֹי) is "and it may say" (וְיֹאמַר). The antecedent of this verb is a "satire, mocking riddles" (2:6a) which the nations say about the Chaldeans. Hence the woe oracles are the content of the mocking riddles pronounced by the oppressed nations. The irony is created when the oppressor becomes the object of mockery and the oppressed ones are the ones who pronounce judgment on him. This irony is further illustrated by the woe oracles that follow: the creditor becomes the debtor (2:6b-7), the plunderer becomes the one being plundered (2:8), the one who acquires gains by evil means acquires shame (2:9), and the one who intoxicates others will end up drinking the cup of wrath from the Lord (2:13-16). The interjection of doxology by Habakkuk in 2:14 and 2:20 also heightens the irony.[18] Habakkuk interrupts the nations at strategic points to show the truthfulness of Yahweh: at the end of the third woe which may be a quotation from other prophets,[19] and after the fifth woe to contrast with the idols.

The third scene is clearly delimited by the superscription at 3:1 and the subscription at 3:19b. The presence of musical terms (שִׁגְיֹנוֹת at 3:1 and לַמְנַצֵּחַ בִּנְגִינוֹתָי at 3:19b) indicates the liturgical function of this hymn. Though there is an on-going debate as to whether this chapter was originally part of the book, the purpose of this paper is to find out the function and the relationship of this chapter to the entire book, rather than engaging in the debate. The designation, "a prayer (תְּפִלָּה) of Habakkuk the prophet," clearly informs us of the nature of the passage.[20]

Since the book of Habakkuk is a poetic composition, the structure of the book can also be demarcated by means of stanzas and strophes. Analyzing the strophes and stanzas on a micro-level may help us to see the narrative impulse of the poem,[21] and to trace the movement and development of the writer's

---

[17] Bruce simply calls this section "The Oppressor Denounced," and ignores the issue. See his commentary, "Habakkuk," 862-65. Smith gives a detailed discussion on this issue but concludes that "we cannot be certain about the speaker in this section." See his commentary, *Micah-Malachi*, 110-111.

[18] *Contra* Roberts who thinks that 2:13a and 14 are later glosses and that these glosses "miss the point of the original *hôy*-saying in Hab. 2:12 + 13b." See his commentary, *Nahum, Habakkuk*, 123.

[19] Scholars have long noticed that the third woe is reminiscent of other prophetic sayings such as Micah 3:10; Jer 51:58; and Isa 11:9. See Fred Kelly, "The Strophic Structure of Habakkuk." *American Journal of Semitic Languages and Literatures* 18 (1901/1902): 99. See also, Peckham, "The Vision of Habakkuk," 632.

[20] For a discussion on prayer in the Old Testament and its relationship to the issue of theodicy, see S.E. Balentine, "Prayers for Justice in the Old Testament: Theodicy and Theology," *CBQ* 51 (1989): 597-616.

[21] Alter, *The Art of Biblical Poetry*, 28-29, indicates that the semantic parallelism in Hebrew poems usually works towards "a focusing, a heightening, a concretization, a development of meaning," as well as "a consequentiality of images and ideas that is

thought. Wilfred G.E. Watson defines stanza as a subunit within a poem, and a strophe as a subunit within a stanza.[22] Stanza division usually depends on the content, though there are certain stanza-markers such as refrain, acrostic, key-words, particles, gender patterns, chiasm, change of speaker, and tricolon that can help to demarcate a stanza.[23] A strophe is a verse-unit of one or more cola, with a discernible beginning and ending, possessing identifiable unity in thought, structure, and style.[24] I will incorporate the division of stanzas and strophes in the following section.

## Translation and division of the book

The following translation is based on the Masoretic Text (MT) of the *Biblia Hebraica Stuttgartensia*.[25] Habakkuk's Hebrew is difficult at times: he some-times omits suffixes, definite articles, and conjunctions; also it is not always clear what the antecedent is. Hence it is not possible to be too literal; I will use more idiomatic English in my translation in order to make sense. Moreover, the tenses in the book oscillate from perfect to imperfect. Since both perfect and imperfect aspects may indicate a present time frame,[26] my translation will re-flect English present tense whenever possible. In the case where modal value is warranted, the verb in question will be translated with the appropriate modal form, such as "can," "should," "may," "must," and etc. For example, to reflect a first person singular cohortative of resolve, it will be translated "I *will*." The italics are used to distinguish it from the simple future tense. In order to show the structure of the whole passage, explanation on each strophe will be deferred to the next section entitled "Comments."

---

incipiently narrative and may include brief sequences of explicit narrative develop-ment."

[22] For a detailed discussion on stanza and strophe, see W.G.E. Watson, *Classical He-brew Poetry: A Guide to its Techniques*, JSOTSup 26 (Sheffield: JSOT Press, 1984), 160-200.

[23] Ibid., 163-64.

[24] Soulen, *Handbook of Biblical Criticism*, 180.

[25] *Biblia Hebraica Stuttgartensia*, 5th ed, ed. Hans Peter Rüger (Stuttgart: Deutsche Biblegesellschaft, 1997).

[26] For discussions and examples on the use of perfective and imperfective in present time frame, see R.J. Williams, *Hebrew Syntax: An Outline*, 2d ed. (Toronto: Univer-sity of Toronto Press, 1976), 29-32 §161-75; also see B.K. Waltke and M. O'Connor, *An Introduction to Biblical Hebrew Syntax* (Winona Lake: Eisenbrauns, 1990), 487-89, 492-93, 504-509; as well as B. Peckham, "Tense and Mood in Biblical Hebrew," *ZAH* 10 (1997): 139-68.

### Superscription[27] (1:1)

1:1   The oracle that Habakkuk[28] the prophet saw.

הַמַּשָּׂא אֲשֶׁר חָזָה חֲבַקּוּק הַנָּבִיא:

## Scene One

**I**   *Habakkuk's First Complaint (1:2-4)*

Stanza 1

    *Strophe 1*

1:2   How long? O Yahweh

עַד־אָנָה יְהוָה

        I cry for help[29] and you do not listen;

שִׁוַּעְתִּי וְלֹא תִשְׁמָע

        I cry out to you "Violence!"

אֶזְעַק אֵלֶיךָ חָמָס

                and you do not save.

וְלֹא תוֹשִׁיעַ

    *Strophe 2*

1:3   Why do you make me see iniquity,

לָמָּה תַרְאֵנִי אָוֶן

        and you make me look at trouble?

וְעָמָל תַּבִּיט

        and destruction and violence are before me;

וְשֹׁד וְחָמָס לְנֶגְדִּי

and there is strife, and contention arises.

וַיְהִי רִיב וּמָדוֹן יִשָּׂא:

    *Strophe 3*

1:4   Therefore law grows numb

עַל־כֵּן תָּפוּג תּוֹרָה

        and judgment never goes forth.

וְלֹא־יֵצֵא לָנֶצַח מִשְׁפָּט

---

[27] For a detailed discussion on the importance of superscriptions in composition and redaction, see J. Watts, "Superscriptions and Incipits in the Book of the Twelve," in *Reading and Hearing the Book of the Twelve*, SBL Symposium Series 15, eds. J.D. Nogalski and M.A. Sweeney (Atlanta: SBL, 2000). Gene M. Tucker mentions that the superscription in "Habakkuk is noteworthy as the only superscription which identifies the prophet as such (*hannābî'*); and that the superscription is followed immediately, not by a prophetic address, but by an address to God." See his article, "Prophetic Superscriptions and the Growth of a Canon," in *Canon and Authority*, eds. G.W. Coats and B.O. Long (Philadelphia: Fortress, 1971), 61.

[28] For a detailed discussion on the name of Habakkuk, see Andersen, *Habakkuk*, 88-90.

[29] The tense here is a perfect tense, but it can be regarded as a persistent (future) perfective. See Waltke and O'Connor, *Biblical Hebrew Syntax*, 489-90. Also, according to Peckham, "Tense and Mood in Biblical Hebrew," 147, a verb first *qātal* clause marks simultaneous time which, following on a present, future, modal or nominal clause, is present tense. Since the first clause "How Long Yahweh?" is the mark of complaint, the following clauses are verb first and thus present tense.

For [the] wicked surround the righteous;

כִּי רָשָׁע מַכְתִּיר אֶת־הַצַּדִּיק

therefore judgment goes forth perverted

עַל־כֵּן יֵצֵא מִשְׁפָּט מְעֻקָּל:

## II     *Yahweh's First Response (1:5-11)*

### Stanza 2

*Strophe 1*

1:5     See among the nations and look!

רְאוּ בַגּוֹיִם וְהַבִּיטוּ

Be astonished! Be astounded!

וְהִתַּמְּהוּ תְּמָהוּ

For I am working a work in your days;

כִּי־פֹעַל פֹּעֵל בִּימֵיכֶם

you would not believe if it were told.

לֹא תַאֲמִינוּ כִּי יְסֻפָּר:

*Strophe 2*

1:6     For behold, I am about to raise the Chaldeans,

כִּי־הִנְנִי מֵקִים אֶת־הַכַּשְׂדִּים

the nation, the fierce and the impetuous one;

הַגּוֹי הַמַּר וְהַנִּמְהָר

the one who goes to the breadth of the earth,

הַהוֹלֵךְ לְמֶרְחֲבֵי־אֶרֶץ

to possess dwelling places not his own.

לָרֶשֶׁת מִשְׁכָּנוֹת לֹא־לוֹ:

### Stanza 3

*Strophe 1*

1:7     Terrible and dreadful is he;

אָיֹם וְנוֹרָא הוּא

from him his judgment and his dignity go forth.

מִמֶּנּוּ מִשְׁפָּטוֹ וּשְׂאֵתוֹ יֵצֵא:

*Strophe 2*

1:8     And his horses are swifter than leopards,

וְקַלּוּ מִנְּמֵרִים סוּסָיו

and are keener than wolves of evening;

וְחַדּוּ מִזְּאֵבֵי עֶרֶב

and his horsemen spring about,

וּפָשׁוּ פָּרָשָׁיו

and his horsemen come from afar;

וּפָרָשָׁיו מֵרָחוֹק יָבֹאוּ

they fly like an eagle hastening to devour.

יָעֻפוּ כְּנֶשֶׁר חָשׁ לֶאֱכוֹל:

### Stanza 4

*Strophe 1*

1:9     All of it come for violence,

כֻּלֹּה לְחָמָס יָבוֹא

everyone of them marches forward;

מְגַמַּת פְּנֵיהֶם קָדִימָה

and he gathers captives like sand.

וַיֶּאֱסֹף כַּחוֹל שֶׁבִי:

*Strophe 2*

1:10  And he mocks at the kings,

וְהוּא בַּמְּלָכִים יִתְקַלָּס

and rulers are a laughing matter to him;

וְרֹזְנִים מִשְׂחָק לוֹ

he laughs at every fortification,

הוּא לְכָל־מִבְצָר יִשְׂחָק

and he heaps up soil and captures it.

וַיִּצְבֹּר עָפָר וַיִּלְכְּדָהּ:

*Strophe 3*

1:11  Then he sweeps through like the wind and is gone;

אָז חָלַף רוּחַ וַיַּעֲבֹר

and he becomes guilty.

וְאָשֵׁם

[He] whose strength is his god!

זוּ כֹחוֹ לֵאלֹהוֹ

**III**     *Habakkuk's Second Complaint (1:12-17)*

<u>Stanza 5</u>

*Strophe 1*

1:12  Are you not from ancient time? O Yahweh

הֲלֹא אַתָּה מִקֶּדֶם יְהוָה

my God, my Holy One, let us not die!

אֱלֹהַי קְדֹשִׁי לֹא נָמוּת

O Yahweh, for judgment you have set him;

יְהוָה לְמִשְׁפָּט שַׂמְתּוֹ

O Rock, for reproof you have established him.

וְצוּר לְהוֹכִיחַ יְסַדְתּוֹ:

*Strophe 2*

1:13  Too pure are [your] eyes to see evil,

טְהוֹר עֵינַיִם מֵרְאוֹת רָע

and to look at trouble you are not able.

וְהַבִּיט אֶל־עָמָל לֹא תוּכָל

Why do you look on the treacherous ones,

לָמָּה תַבִּיט בּוֹגְדִים

[and] you remain silent

תַּחֲרִישׁ

when the wicked swallows

בְּבַלַּע רָשָׁע

the one more righteous than him?

צַדִּיק מִמֶּנּוּ:

*Strophe 3*

1:14    And you have made human being like fishes of the sea,

וַתַּעֲשֶׂה אָדָם כִּדְגֵי הַיָּם

like a critter [with] no ruler over him.

כְּרֶמֶשׂ לֹא־מֹשֵׁל בּוֹ:

## Stanza 6

*Strophe 1*

1:15    All of it with a hook he brings up;

כֻּלֹּה בְּחַכָּה הֶעֱלָה

he drags it with his net,

יְגֹרֵהוּ בְחֶרְמוֹ

and he gathers it with his fishing net.

וְיַאַסְפֵהוּ בְּמִכְמַרְתּוֹ

Therefore he rejoices and he exults.

עַל־כֵּן יִשְׂמַח וְיָגִיל:

*Strophe 2*

1:16    Therefore he sacrifices to his net,

עַל־כֵּן יְזַבֵּחַ לְחֶרְמוֹ

and he burns incense to his fishing net.

וִיקַטֵּר לְמִכְמַרְתּוֹ

For in them his portion is rich,

כִּי בָהֵמָּה שָׁמֵן חֶלְקוֹ

and his food is sleek.

וּמַאֲכָלוֹ בְּרִאָה:

*Strophe 3*

1:17    Will he therefore empty his net;

הַעַל כֵּן יָרִיק חֶרְמוֹ

and continually kill nations

וְתָמִיד לַהֲרֹג גּוֹיִם

and not spare?

לֹא יַחְמוֹל:

## Scene Two

**I**    *Interlude: Habakkuk's Action (2:1)*

## Stanza 1

*Strophe 1*

2:1    On my guard post I *will* stand

עַל־מִשְׁמַרְתִּי אֶעֱמֹדָה

and I *will* station myself on the rampart;

וְאֶתְיַצְּבָה עַל־מָצוֹר

and I *will* keep watch to see

וַאֲצַפֶּה לִרְאוֹת

what he might speak to me,

מַה־יְדַבֶּר־בִּי

and what I might reply concerning my reproof.

וּמָה אָשִׁיב עַל־תּוֹכַחְתִּי:

**II**     *Yahweh's Second Response (2:2-5)*

*Strophe 2*

2:2     And Yahweh answered me and he said:

וַיַּעֲנֵנִי יְהוָה וַיֹּאמֶר

Write down the vision,

כְּתוֹב חָזוֹן

and make it plain on the tablets;

וּבָאֵר עַל־הַלֻּחוֹת

in order that the one reading it may run.

לְמַעַן יָרוּץ קוֹרֵא בוֹ:

2:3     For yet the vision is for the appointed time;

כִּי עוֹד חָזוֹן לַמּוֹעֵד

and it will run breathlessly to the end

וְיָפֵחַ לַקֵּץ

and it will not lie.

וְלֹא יְכַזֵּב

If it were to tarry, wait for it;

אִם־יִתְמַהְמָהּ חַכֵּה־לוֹ

for it will certainly come, it will not delay.

כִּי־בֹא יָבֹא לֹא יְאַחֵר

Stanza 2

*Strophe 1*

2:4     Behold [his soul] is inflated,

הִנֵּה עֻפְּלָה

his soul is not upright in him.

לֹא־יָשְׁרָה נַפְשׁוֹ בּוֹ

But [the] righteous in his faithfulness will live.

וְצַדִּיק בֶּאֱמוּנָתוֹ יִחְיֶה:

*Strophe 2*

2:5     And furthermore, wine [is] treacherous;

וְאַף כִּי־הַיַּיִן בּוֹגֵד

a man is haughty and he will not abide,

גֶּבֶר יָהִיר וְלֹא יִנְוֶה

who enlarges his throat like Sheol;

אֲשֶׁר הִרְחִיב כִּשְׁאוֹל נַפְשׁוֹ

*Strophe 3*

and he is like death and he is not sated,

וְהוּא כַמָּוֶת וְלֹא יִשְׂבָּע

and he gathers to himself all the nations,

וַיֶּאֱסֹף אֵלָיו כָּל־הַגּוֹיִם

and he collects to himself all the peoples.

וַיִּקְבֹּץ אֵלָיו כָּל־הָעַמִּים:

*Strophe 4*

2:6     Will not these, all of them

הֲלוֹא־אֵלֶּה כֻלָּם

raise a proverb against him,

עָלָיו מָשָׁל יִשָּׂאוּ

and a satire, mocking riddles about him?

וּמְלִיצָה חִידוֹת לוֹ

and it will say,

וְיֹאמַר

## III    *Five Woe Oracles (2:6-20)*

### *The First Woe Oracle*

Stanza 3

*Strophe 1*

Woe to the one who increases [what is] not his!

הוֹי הַמַּרְבֶּה לֹּא־לוֹ

Until when?

עַד־מָתַי

And making heavy on himself pledges?

וּמַכְבִּיד עָלָיו עַבְטִיט:

*Strophe 2*

2:7    Will not your creditors suddenly arise,

הֲלוֹא פֶתַע יָקוּמוּ נֹשְׁכֶיךָ

and those who make you tremble will wake up?

וְיִקְצוּ מְזַעְזְעֶיךָ

And you will become booties for them.

וְהָיִיתָ לִמְשִׁסּוֹת לָמוֹ:

*Strophe 3*

2:8    Because you have plundered many nations,

כִּי אַתָּה שַׁלּוֹתָ גּוֹיִם רַבִּים

all the remnant of the peoples will plunder you;

יְשָׁלּוּךָ כָּל־יֶתֶר עַמִּים

because of human bloodshed and violence to the land,

מִדְּמֵי אָדָם וַחֲמַס־אֶרֶץ

to the city and all of its inhabitants.

קִרְיָה וְכָל־יֹשְׁבֵי בָהּ: פ

### *The Second Woe Oracle*

Stanza 4

*Strophe 1*

2:9    Woe to the one who gains evil profit for his house!

הוֹי בֹּצֵעַ בֶּצַע רָע לְבֵיתוֹ

to put his nest in the high place,

לָשׂוּם בַּמָּרוֹם קִנּוֹ

in order to be delivered from the hand of evil.

לְהִנָּצֵל מִכַּף־רָע:

*Strophe 2*

2:10    You have devised shame for your house,

יָעַצְתָּ בֹּשֶׁת לְבֵיתֶךָ

cutting off many peoples

46

קְצוֹת־עַמִּים רַבִּים

and bringing sin to your soul.

וְחוֹטֵא נַפְשֶׁךָ

2:11    For a stone cries out from the wall,

כִּי־אֶבֶן מִקִּיר תִּזְעָק

and a rafter answers it from the woodwork.

וְכָפִיס מֵעֵץ יַעֲנֶנָּה: פ

## The Third Woe Oracle

### Stanza 5

*Strophe 1*

2:12    Woe to the one who builds a city with bloodshed,

הוֹי בֹּנֶה עִיר בְּדָמִים

and the one who founds a town with injustice!

וְכוֹנֵן קִרְיָה בְּעַוְלָה:

*Strophe 2*

2:13    Is it not indeed from Yahweh of hosts

הֲלוֹא הִנֵּה מֵאֵת יְהוָה צְבָאוֹת

that the peoples must toil only for fire,

וְיִיגְעוּ עַמִּים בְּדֵי־אֵשׁ

and nations grow weary only for nothing?

וּלְאֻמִּים בְּדֵי־רִיק יִעָפוּ:

*Strophe 3*

2:14    For the earth will be filled with

כִּי תִּמָּלֵא הָאָרֶץ

the knowledge of the glory of Yahweh,

לָדַעַת אֶת־כְּבוֹד יְהוָה

as the waters cover over the sea.

כַּמַּיִם יְכַסּוּ עַל־יָם: ס

## The Fourth Woe Oracle

### Stanza 6

*Strophe 1*

2:15    Woe to the one who makes his neighbor drink,

הוֹי מַשְׁקֶה רֵעֵהוּ

pouring out your wrath,

מְסַפֵּחַ חֲמָתְךָ

and even make [them] drunk;

וְאַף שַׁכֵּר

so as to gaze upon their nakedness!

לְמַעַן הַבִּיט עַל־מְעוֹרֵיהֶם:

*Strophe 2*

2:16    You are sated with dishonor rather than glory.

שָׂבַעְתָּ קָלוֹן מִכָּבוֹד

Drink! even you, and be counted uncircumcised.

שְׁתֵה גַם־אַתָּה וְהֵעָרֵל

> The cup of the right hand of the Lord will turn upon you,
>
> תִּסּוֹב עָלֶיךָ כּוֹס יְמִין יְהוָה
>
> and emetic shame will be upon your glory.
>
> וְקִיקָלוֹן עַל־כְּבוֹדֶךָ:

### Strophe 3

2:17    For the violence of Lebanon will overwhelm you,

> כִּי חֲמַס לְבָנוֹן יְכַסֶּךָ
>
> and the devastation of beasts will terrify you;
>
> וְשֹׁד בְּהֵמוֹת יְחִיתַן
>
> because of human bloodshed and violence to the land,
>
> מִדְּמֵי אָדָם וַחֲמַס־אֶרֶץ
>
> to the city and all of its inhabitants.
>
> קִרְיָה וְכָל־יֹשְׁבֵי בָהּ: פ

### *The Fifth Woe Oracle*

**Stanza 7**

### Strophe 1

2:18    What profit is an idol?

> מָה־הוֹעִיל פֶּסֶל
>
> For the one who forms it has carved it,
>
> כִּי פְסָלוֹ יֹצְרוֹ
>
> a molten image and a teacher of falsehood.
>
> מַסֵּכָה וּמוֹרֶה שָּׁקֶר
>
> For he who forms his graven image trusts in it,
>
> כִּי בָטַח יֹצֵר יִצְרוֹ עָלָיו
>
> to make dumb worthless gods.
>
> לַעֲשׂוֹת אֱלִילִים אִלְּמִים: ס

### Strophe 2

2:19    Woe to the one who says to the wood, "Awake!"

> הוֹי אֹמֵר לָעֵץ הָקִיצָה
>
> "Arouse!" to a silent stone.
>
> עוּרִי לְאֶבֶן דּוּמָם
>
> He will teach?
>
> הוּא יוֹרֶה
>
> Behold, he is encased in gold and silver;
>
> הִנֵּה־הוּא תָּפוּשׂ זָהָב וָכֶסֶף
>
> and there is not any breath inside him.
>
> וְכָל־רוּחַ אֵין בְּקִרְבּוֹ

### Strophe 3

2:20    But Yahweh is in his holy temple;

> וַיהוָה בְּהֵיכַל קָדְשׁוֹ
>
> be silent in his presence all the earth.
>
> הַס מִפָּנָיו כָּל־הָאָרֶץ: פ

## Scene Three

### *Superscription*

3:1    A prayer of Habakkuk the prophet,

# Close reading on the Book of Habakkuk

תְּפִלָּה לַחֲבַקּוּק הַנָּבִיא

on *Shigyonoth*.

עַל שִׁגְיֹנוֹת:

## I     *Habakkuk's Petition (3:2)*

### Stanza 1

*Strophe 1*

3:2     O Yahweh, I have heard of your report;

יְהוָה שָׁמַעְתִּי שִׁמְעֲךָ

I fear, O Yahweh, your work.

יָרֵאתִי יְהוָה פָּעָלְךָ

*Strophe 2*

In [the] midst of years revive it,

בְּקֶרֶב שָׁנִים חַיֵּיהוּ

in [the] midst of years make it known.

בְּקֶרֶב שָׁנִים תּוֹדִיעַ

In turmoil, remember compassion.

בְּרֹגֶז רַחֵם תִּזְכּוֹר:

## II     *Praise: Theophany*

### Stanza 2

*Strophe 1*

3:3     God came from Teman,

אֱלוֹהַ מִתֵּימָן יָבוֹא

and the Holy One from Mount Paran. Selah.

וְקָדוֹשׁ מֵהַר־פָּארָן סֶלָה

His splendor covered heavens,

כִּסָּה שָׁמַיִם הוֹדוֹ

and his praise filled the earth.

וּתְהִלָּתוֹ מָלְאָה הָאָרֶץ:

*Strophe 2*

3:4     And the brightness was like the sunlight,

וְנֹגַהּ כָּאוֹר תִּהְיֶה

he had rays [coming] from his hand;

קַרְנַיִם מִיָּדוֹ לוֹ

and there [was] the hiding place of his strength.

וְשָׁם חֶבְיוֹן עֻזֹּה:

*Strophe 3*

3:5     Before him went pestilence,

לְפָנָיו יֵלֶךְ דָּבֶר

and plague came forth at his feet.

וְיֵצֵא רֶשֶׁף לְרַגְלָיו:

### Stanza 3

*Strophe 1*

3:6     He stood and he measured the earth;

עָמַד וַיְמֹדֶד אֶרֶץ

he looked and he startled nations,

רָאָה וַיַּתֵּר גּוֹיִם

and ancient mountains were shattered,

וַיִּתְפֹּצְצוּ הַרְרֵי־עַד

eternal hills were prostrate;

שַׁחוּ גִּבְעוֹת עוֹלָם

the ancient pathways before him.

הֲלִיכוֹת עוֹלָם לוֹ׃

*Strophe 2*

3:7   I saw the tents of Cushan under distress;

תַּחַת אָוֶן רָאִיתִי אָהֳלֵי כוּשָׁן

the curtains of the land of Midian quivered.

יִרְגְּזוּן יְרִיעוֹת אֶרֶץ מִדְיָן׃

## Stanza 4

*Strophe 1*

3:8   Did Yahweh rage against the rivers?

הֲבִנְהָרִים חָרָה יְהוָה

or was your anger against the rivers

אִם בַּנְּהָרִים אַפֶּךָ

or your fury against the sea;

אִם־בַּיָּם עֶבְרָתֶךָ

when you mounted your horses,

כִּי תִרְכַּב עַל־סוּסֶיךָ

your chariots of salvation?

מַרְכְּבֹתֶיךָ יְשׁוּעָה׃

*Strophe 2*

3:9   You exposed the nakedness of your bow;

עֶרְיָה תֵעוֹר קַשְׁתֶּךָ

arrows fulfilling [your] word. Selah.

שְׁבֻעוֹת מַטּוֹת אֹמֶר סֶלָה

You cleaved the rivers of the earth.

נְהָרוֹת תְּבַקַּע־אָרֶץ׃

## Stanza 5

*Strophe 1*

3:10   The mountains saw you [and] writhed;

רָאוּךָ יָחִילוּ הָרִים

a downpour of waters passed by.

זֶרֶם מַיִם עָבָר

The deep gave its voice,

נָתַן תְּהוֹם קוֹלוֹ

it raised its hands on high.

רוֹם יָדֵיהוּ נָשָׂא׃

*Strophe 2*

3:11   Sun, moon stopped in their high abode;

שֶׁמֶשׁ יָרֵחַ עָמַד זְבֻלָה

at the light of your arrows as they flew,

לְאוֹר חִצֶּיךָ יְהַלֵּכוּ

at the brightness of the lightning of your spear.

לְנֹגַהּ בְּרַק חֲנִיתֶךָ:

## Stanza 6

*Strophe 1*

3:12 In indignation you strode the earth;

בְּזַעַם תִּצְעַד־אָרֶץ

in anger you trampled nations.

בְּאַף תָּדוּשׁ גּוֹיִם:

*Strophe 2*

3:13 You came forth for the salvation of your people,

יָצָאתָ לְיֵשַׁע עַמֶּךָ

for the salvation of your anointed.

לְיֵשַׁע אֶת־מְשִׁיחֶךָ

You shattered the head from the house of the wicked,

מָחַצְתָּ רֹּאשׁ מִבֵּית רָשָׁע

laying bare from foundation to neck. Selah.

עָרוֹת יְסוֹד עַד־צַוָּאר סֶלָה: פ

## Stanza 7

*Strophe 1*

3:14 You pierced with his own arrows

the head of his warriors.

נָקַבְתָּ בְמַטָּיו רֹאשׁ פְּרָזוֹ {פְּרָזָיו}

They had stormed to scatter me.

יִסְעֲרוּ לַהֲפִיצֵנִי

Their exultation

עֲלִיצֻתָם

resembled devouring the helpless in secret.

כְּמוֹ־לֶאֱכֹל עָנִי בַּמִּסְתָּר:

*Strophe 2*

3:15 You trod on the sea [with] your horses;

דָּרַכְתָּ בַיָּם סוּסֶיךָ

the foaming of many waters,

חֹמֶר מַיִם רַבִּים:

## III    *Habakkuk's Reaction*
## Stanza 8

*Strophe 1*

3:16 I heard and my belly churned;

שָׁמַעְתִּי וַתִּרְגַּז בִּטְנִי

at the sound my lips quivered.

לְקוֹל צָלְלוּ שְׂפָתַי

Rottenness entered into my bones,

יָבוֹא רָקָב בַּעֲצָמַי

and underneath me I trembled.

וְתַחְתַּי אֶרְגָּז

Yet I must wait for the day of distress,

אֲשֶׁר אָנוּחַ לְיוֹם צָרָה

when he who will attack us to come up against the people.

לַעֲלוֹת לְעַם יְגוּדֶנּוּ:

*Strophe 2*

3:17    Though the fig tree does not blossom,

כִּי־תְאֵנָה לֹא־תִפְרָח

and there is no produce on the vines;

וְאֵין יְבוּל בַּגְּפָנִים

the yield of olive fails,

כִּחֵשׁ מַעֲשֵׂה־זַיִת

and fields do not yield food;

וּשְׁדֵמוֹת לֹא־עָשָׂה אֹכֶל

Cut off from the fold are the sheep,

גָּזַר מִמִּכְלָה צֹאן

and there are no cattle in the stables.

וְאֵין בָּקָר בָּרְפָתִים:

Stanza 9

*Strophe 1*

3:18    Yet I, in Yahweh, I *will* exult,

וַאֲנִי בַּיהוָה אֶעְלוֹזָה

I *will* rejoice in the God of my salvation.

אָגִילָה בֵּאלֹהֵי יִשְׁעִי:

*Strophe 2*

3:19a    Yahweh, the Lord is my strength,

יְהוִה אֲדֹנָי חֵילִי

and he will make my feet like the hinds,

וַיָּשֶׂם רַגְלַי כָּאַיָּלוֹת

and upon my high places he will make me tread.

וְעַל בָּמוֹתַי יַדְרִכֵנִי

**Subscription**

3:19b    To the director. With my string music.

לַמְנַצֵּחַ בִּנְגִינוֹתָי:

## Comments

*Superscription (1:1)*

The superscription in 1:1 "the oracles that Habakkuk the prophet saw" sets the tone for the whole book and gives an overview of the book. The Hebrew term used for "oracle" here is מַשָּׂא which is derived from the verb נָשָׂא meaning "to lift up, to carry."[30] Weis, in a 1986 study, defines מַשָּׂא as a genre and prefers to

---

[30] For a discussion on how מַשָּׂא is extended to mean "prophetic pronouncement," see H.P. Miller, "מַשָּׂא," *TDOT*, 9:20-24.

call it a "prophetic exposition of divine revelation."[31] He explains that מַשָּׂא is a response to a question asked regarding the divine intention or forthcoming action. On the basis of the prophetic exposition, מַשָּׂא also directs human action in the present or near future.[32] If his definition is accepted, then the superscription tells us that this is a prophetic exposition of the divine revelation which is revealed to him in a vision,[33] and that this vision also directs proper human behavior in the present situation. Though Weis's definition of מַשָּׂא as a genre is not widely followed, his study helps to illustrate how the superscription describes the content of the book. מַשָּׂא can sometimes be translated as "burden," deriving its meaning from the heavy load carried by the animals. Understanding it as "burden" would indicate some kinds of "troubles" that the prophet saw. Thus this explains how the complaints Habakkuk directs towards God would become part of the מַשָּׂא.

Habakkuk is designated as "prophet" (נָבִיא) in the superscription.[34] The word "prophet" (נָבִיא) is derived from the Akkadian verb *nabû* "to call, proclaim," but there is a debate on whether the term should be understood actively as "speaker, proclaimer," or passively as "called one."[35] I believe that both meanings are applicable here: a prophet is a person "called" by God to "proclaim" his message to the people. The designation of Habakkuk as a "prophet" (נָבִיא) in the superscription is important for it legitimizes his authority as well as gives him the right to stand before Yahweh as a representative of the people. And if we understand the word נָבִיא as "the called one," then it makes the ensuing complaint even more poignant, for the complaint and accusation come from one of Yahweh's own "called" prophets.

*Scene one*

*Stanza 1 Habakkuk's first complaint (1:2-4)*

---

[31] R.D. Weis, "A Definition of the Genre *Maśśā'* in the Hebrew Bible" (Ph.D. diss., Claremont Graduate School, 1986); idem, "Oracle," 28-29.

[32] According to Weis, a *maśśā'* is the prophet's response to a question raised by the community with regard to the lack of clarity between divine intention and human reality. See ibid., 28.

[33] The verb חָזָה is derived from the noun חָזוֹן which means something that is envisioned in the mind of the prophet or in a vision seen by the prophet. John Skinner reminded us that "the claim to have had a vision was taken seriously in ancient times as a proof of inspiration." See his discussion in J. Skinner, *Prophecy and Religion: Studies in the Life of Jeremiah* (Cambridge: Cambridge University Press, 1955), 10-14.

[34] The other two prophets who have the same designation in the Minor Prophets are Haggai (Hag 1:1; 3:1) and Zechariah (Zech 1:1, 7). The prophetic books of Haggai, Zechariah, along with Ezekiel, are the only ones which are not prefixed with superscriptions. Cf. Tucker, "Prophetic Superscriptions," 59, n.6.

[35] K. Möller, "Prophets and Prophecy," in *Dictionary of the Old Testament: Historical Books*, ed. B.T. Arnold and H.G.M. Williamson (Downers Grove: IVP, 2005), 825.

The first stanza introduces a complaint. The term "how long" (עַד־אָנָה) is a typical question introducing a complaint about others' behavior.[36] It is used in divine complaint about Israel's wayward behavior in Exod 16:28 and 14:11. It is also used when one person complains about another person or party as in Josh 18:3, and in Job's disputations with his friends in Job 18:2 and 19:2, as well as in Ps 62:3 when the psalmist turns to his enemies and complains against them. Sometimes, as in Hab 1:1, it is used by a person to complain against God (cf. Ps 13:2-3 [Eng 1-2]). It may even be used to address an inanimate object as in Jer 47:6. Thus Habakkuk uses a stereotypical expression to begin his complaint against Yahweh.

Habakkuk accuses Yahweh of ignoring his desperate cry for help: "I cry for help[37] and you do not listen. I cry out to you 'Violence,'[38] and you do not save." Usually when a faithful one cries to God for help, he/she expects God to hear and to act on his/her behalf. But here Habakkuk chides Yahweh for ignoring him, especially when his cry is caused by "violence" (חָמָס).

While the first strophe describes the prophet's urgent plea for help, he gives the detail of his complaint in the second strophe: he accuses God of making him see chaotic, unlawful commotion around him, "Why do you make me see iniquity and make me look at trouble;[39] and destruction and violence are before me; and there is strife, and contention arises." There is a partial chiastic parallelism within 3aα, i.e. "why (a) do you make me see (b) iniquity (c), and trouble (c') you make me look at (b')?"[40] This chiastic pattern is repeated again in

---

[36] Roberts, *Nahum*, 88.

[37] "I cry for help" (שִׁוַּעְתִּי), which occurs here and also in Pss 30:2; 40:2; 88:14; and Jonah 2:3, refers to a cry, specifically to God, for help.

[38] "Violence" usually refers to bloodshed (e.g., Gen 6:11, 13; 49:5; Judg 9:24; Ps 74:20; Isa 59:6; 60:18; Jer 6:7; 20:8; Ezek 7:23; 8:17; 28:16 etc.). "Violence" can also refer to injustice and wrong done to others such as harsh treatment, injurious treatment, wickedness, ruthlessness, denial of others' rights (e.g., Gen 16:5; 1 Chr 12:18; Job 16:17; Ezek 45:9; Amos 3:10; 6:13; Mic 6:12; Zeph 1:9; Mal 2:16). When it is used with the word "witness" (עֵד), it refers to the malicious or false witness (e.g., Ezek 23:1; Deut 19:16; Pss 27:12; 35:11).

[39] Roberts disagrees with the traditional division of the verse because he thinks that "iniquity and trouble" (אָוֶן וְעָמָל), and "destruction and violence" (וְשֹׁד וְחָמָס) are parallel pairs, each dependent on a single verb. Moreover, if one follows the traditional division of taking "trouble" (עָמָל) as the object of the verb "you see" (תַּבִּיט), then "the resulting parallelism between a causative and a simple transitive verb appears awkward." See Roberts, *Nahum*, 87-8.

[40] Grammatically, the Hiphil root of the verb נבט does not necessarily have a causative sense, which may have caused some ancient version to emend it to אביט (I see). LXX uses an infinitive (ἐπιβλέπειν "to look upon") to translate it and appends it to the previous question "Why do you show me troubles and grief to look upon?" The *textual apparatus* of the BHS, 1049, indicates that the Syriac version has אביט. However, C.F. Keil, *The Twelve Minor Prophets*, vol. 2, trans. J. Martin (Grand Rapids: Eerdmans, 1949), 56, noted the affinity of vocabulary in Hab 1:3aα and that of Balaam's

the last colon, "and there is (a) strife (b),[41] and contention (b') arises (a')."[42] The unusual arrangement of the two chiastic patterns at the beginning and the end of the verse is to emphasize the "destruction and violence" that are before the prophet. And the form of נבט may have double meanings due to the ambiguity of the Hiphil, which would make the complaint even more poignant: God looks at and remains inactive in the face of trouble and yet makes him look at iniquity (and trouble) helplessly. It is noteworthy that "violence and destruction" (חָמָס וָשֹׁד) is used by other prophets, such as Ezekiel (45:9) and Amos (3:10; 6:3),[43] to describe the behavior of Israelite leaders, or Jerusalem in general (Jer 6:7). So it is not unreasonable to see that Habakkuk uses the term "violence" in the first two opening strophes to describe the situation within Judean society. Though the agent of "violence" in 1:9 is clearly the Chaldeans, it does not follow that the agent of violence has to be the same in both 1:2-3 and 1:9. Moreover, by having different agents in these verses, it further emphasizes the universality of violence and the prophet's denouncement of it.

Habakkuk's initial complaint comes to a climax when he mentions, in the third strophe, that the law becomes ineffective,[44] which leads to the abortion of justice and the oppression of the righteous. When the word תּוֹרָה[45] is translated as "law;" it may refer to the Deuteronomic code.[46] The mention of תּוֹרָה being

---

words in Num 23:21, and argued that תַּבִּיט is to see, not cause to see. My proposal of the chiastic pattern within 3aα still stands even if we take the non causative meaning, "Why do you make me see iniquity, and trouble you look at?"

[41] *BHS*, 1049, notes that וַיְהִי רִיב "and there is strife" is a variant reading or a gloss based on what follows. However Michael O'Neal, *Interpreting Habakkuk as Scripture: An Application of the Canonical Approach of Brevard S. Childs*, Studies in Biblical Literature 9 (New York: Peter Lang, 2007), 37, points out that רִיב and מָדוֹן form a pair, and that it is better to retain both words.

[42] יִשָּׂא is Qal imperfect 3ms of נָשָׂא "to lift up," which may have an unusual intransitive or reflexive meaning "lift oneself up;" this also occurs in the texts of Hos 13:1; Nah 1:5; Ps 89:10[9]. *BHS* suggests to emend יִשָּׂא to אֶשָּׂא "I bear contention," or that some words may have dropped out of the text. My opinion is that it is best to leave the MT the way it is.

[43] According to Seidel's law, the reversal of the word order marks it as a quotation, so Amos is probably the source. Seidel's law is first proposed by M. Seidel in his article, "Parallels between the Book of Isaiah and the Book of Psalms" [Hebrew] *Sinai* 38 (5616 [1956]): 150. For a discussion on Seidel's law and its application, see B.M. Levinson, *Deuteronomy and the Hermeneutics of Legal Innovation* (New York: Oxford University Press, 1997), 18-20.

[44] The verb פוג means "to grow numb, be cold, be helpless." When it is used with "law," it has the meaning of "be ineffective." See BDB, 806.

[45] תּוֹרָה may refer to a body of prophetic teaching or sometimes priestly teaching. For a thorough study on the word תּוֹרָה and its usage in the Old Testament, see García López, "תּוֹרָה", *TDOT*, 15:609-44.

[46] Roberts, *Nahum*, 90, thinks that תּוֹרָה here refers to the scroll of the deuteronomic law that was found in the temple during Josiah's reign.

rendered ineffective may be Habakkuk's attempt to arouse Yahweh to action. The Israelites are frequently accused of not keeping or ignoring the divine law (e.g., Isa 24:5; 30:9; Hos 4:6; Amos 2:4). However, there is no evidence that the foreign nations are ever accused of not keeping תּוֹרָה.[47] It is interesting to note that Zephaniah also complains against Jerusalem's prophets and priests, and accuses them of doing "violence to the law" (חָמְסוּ תוֹרָה Zeph 3:4bβ). Andersen states that the slacking of Torah is due to Yahweh's inactivity, hence implicates Yahweh of not performing his duty as judge.[48] As a consequence of Torah being ineffective, "justice/judgment" (מִשְׁפָּט) either never goes forth or goes forth "perverted" (מְעֻקָּל).[49] Thus the juxtaposition of the numbness of Torah and the perversion of judgment seems to confirm that Habakkuk is complaining about an internal social injustice,[50] which leads to the flourishing of the wicked and the suppression of the righteous, and implicates God for allowing such things to happen.

In sum, in the first stanza, Habakkuk begins his complaint with a typical negative prayer[51] accusing God of not listening to his cry for help and ignoring his plea for deliverance from violence. He gives a description of the destruction and violence around him and complains that Yahweh just stands idly by and allows the lawlessness and the injustice to go on. While the text does not specify the perpetrators of violence, the mention of law and judgment in v. 4 makes it highly probable that the prophet is complaining against violence within Judean society.

---

[47] It is suggested by some that the destruction and violence in v. 3 is done by the foreign nations and the problem in 1:3-4 is to indicate that the law is powerless to resolve the dispute, for one cannot take the foreign offenders to court. The problem with this understanding is that of all the sins that the prophets accuse the foreign nations of committing (e.g. Amos, Isaiah, Jeremiah, etc.), Torah is never mentioned. On the contrary the Israelite leaders are always accused of violating God's Torah.

[48] Andersen, *Habakkuk*, 119.

[49] The Pual participle of the verb עקל "be bent out of shape, crooked" only appears here. Elsewhere, Micah uses a similar verb and accuses the Israelite leaders of perverting justice and making crooked (יְעַקֵּשׁוּ) all that is straight (Mic 3:9). Patterson, *Nahum*, 143, comments, "The application of the root to the perverted justice of Judahite society is obvious."

[50] López comments that the parallel listing of Torah being ineffective and judgment (מִשְׁפָּט) not going forth reflects the situation following the death of Josiah, when Jehoiakim refused to follow up his father's reform. López, *TDOT*, 15:625-26.

[51] Fredrik Lindström, "Theodicy in the Psalms," *Theodicy in the World of the Bible*, ed. A. Laato and J.C. De Moor (Leiden: Brill, 2003), 263, points out that there are positive and negative prayers in the individual complaint psalms; the former appeal to God for help while the latter turn into accusation. Habakkuk is unique in the prophetic literature by using a negative prayer to begin his dialogue with God.

*Stanza 2 Yahweh's response: the rise of Chaldeans (1:5-6)*

The shift of the verbs to masculine plural imperatives (רְאוּ "see," הַבִּיטוּ "look," הִתַּמְּהוּ "be astonished," תְּמָהוּ "be astounded") at the beginning of this new stanza indicates that there is a change in speaker. The addresser is Yahweh and the addressees are likely to be Habakkuk and his circle of people. In the first strophe of stanza 2, God breaks the silence and addresses the prophet's question of divine inactivity by telling him that he is in fact doing a work that is so astonishing that they will not believe it. The use of literary device is brilliant: The repeating rhyme of "û" sound gives some force to the imperatives.[52] Also, the author uses different stems of the same root verb תָּמַה to emphasize the surprise element and to create a sense of bewilderment, as well as the same root פעל to emphasize the work which God is working in their days would be a total surprise to them.[53]

The raising up of the Chaldeans is the surprise work that Yahweh is working in the prophet's time. This strophe is peculiar for it does not have a finite verb, "For behold I am about to raise (מֵקִים)[54] the Chaldeans. The nation, the fierce and the impetuous one,[55] the one who goes (הַהוֹלֵךְ) to the breadth of the earth to possess (לָרֶשֶׁת) dwelling places not his own." Perhaps the peculiarity is to high-light the revelation of God's plan and the introduction of the Chaldeans. Also the alliteration of *ha* (הַ) to describe the Chaldeans unites the rest of the verse. The imminent coming of the Chaldeans is emphasized and their invasion is inevitable. Elsewhere in the Old Testament, the Israelites are told to possess the land that is given to them by God. But here the Chaldeans are sweeping across the land out of their own might to possess places that do not belong to them. This paves the way to the description of the Chaldeans in the next two stanzas.

---

[52] Notice that the rhyme "û" sound goes all the way to the last colon of v. 5, תַאֲמִינוּ.

[53] Although the Hebrew text does not supply a subject for the participle of the verb פעל, the context clearly shows that God is the subject. LXX understands it this way, and explicitly uses the first person pronoun (ἐγώ) to indicate that God is the subject of the verb. Also the next verse has the first person pronominal suffix attached to הִנְנִי "be-hold I," followed by a participial form of the verb, thus confirming my translation "I am working a work."

[54] The Hiphil participle masculine singular of the verb קוּם (מֵקִים) is used to indicate imminent action. See Williams, *Hebrew Syntax*, 39 §214. Patterson, *Nahum*, 150, al-so mentions that the construction הִנְנִי מֵקִים is often used to refer to future events. Of the eight occurrences of this verb form (מֵקִים) in the Old Testament, God is the sub-ject in seven of them. Amos 6:14 warns the Israelites that God is raising a nation against them with the same three opening words "For behold I am about to raise..." (כִּי הִנְנִי מֵקִים).

[55] In order to keep the alliterative effect, Patterson, *Nahum*, 150, follows the NJB and translates הַמַּר וְהַנִּמְהָר "fierce and fiery."

*Stanza 3 Description of the Chaldeans (1:7-8)*

In stanza 3 Yahweh continues to describe the Chaldeans.[56] Babylon is further described as "dreadful and fearsome" (אָיֹם וְנוֹרָא), and respecting no other authority or law except his own. Not only do the words "judgment" (מִשְׁפָּט) and "go forth" (יֵצֵא) in v. 7b act as literary links with v. 4 where Habakkuk complains about the judgment within Judean society not going forth, they also give an ironic twist: since the Judean leaders refuse to bring out the upright judgment of Torah, they must suffer the barbaric judgment of the Babylonian king.

The swiftness and the fierceness of Babylon are described by using the imagery of various wild beasts, "And his horses are swifter than the leopards and are keener[57] than wolves of evening;[58] and his horsemen[59] spring about, and his horsemen[60] come from afar; they fly like an eagle hastening to devour." The assonance of the *û* (ו) sound punctuates throughout this verse creating a poetic rhythm that is fitting to describe the fast movement of the army. The use of onomatopoeia[61] in "and his horsemen spring about" ( וּפָשׁוּ פָּרָשָׁיו) is brilliant; not only do the two words sound alike and together give the rushing sound of horses, the two verbs פָּרַשׁ and פּוּשׁ[62] also give the image of the fast moving cavalry galloping across the land like eagles from afar to devour. It is interesting to note that in Jer 4:13, the enemy from the north is also described as "his horses are swifter than eagles" (סוּסָיו קַלּוּ מִנְּשָׁרִים). This confirms that the Chaldeans are well-known for their speed in the ancient world.

*Stanza 4 Brutality of the Chaldeans (1:9-11)*

Stanza 4 describes the purpose and the attitude of the Chaldeans. The purpose for their coming is clear: "for violence" (לְחָמָס). The word "violence" is the same word that the prophet uses when he describes the situation in vv. 2 and 3. This prompts some scholars to think that Habakkuk is complaining about the Babylonian invasion all along. But that is not necessarily the case. The violence caused by the Chaldeans would be a fitting warning or punishment to the Jude-

---

[56] The masculine singular pronoun of "he" (הוא) is used to describe the Chaldeans as a mighty warrior, or alternatively, as suggested by Patterson, *Nahum*, 150, הוא can be taken to mean Nebuchadnezzar, the Babylonian king.

[57] Patterson thinks that the verb חָדַד would be better translated as "fierce," which refers to the "keen sensibilities of the wolf, alert to the prey and to every situation. As applied to horses it must refer to their skill and spiritedness in battle situations." Patterson, *Nahum*, 151.

[58] Apparently in Palestine, wolves hunt in the evening, which means that they would be more fierce and eager to attack. See Bailey, *Micah*, 305-306.

[59] The noun פָּרָשׁ means both "horse" and "horseman," which seems to pose a problem for translating the verse. For a detailed discussion, see Bailey, *Micah*, 306.

[60] The anadiplosis (the repetition of the last part of a line at the beginning of the next line) of the word פָּרָשָׁיו is used here.

[61] Rhetorical term that means the use of a word whose sound is used for its own effect.

[62] פָּרַשׁ in Qal form has the meaning of "spreading out," and פּוּשׁ has the meaning of "pawing the ground."

ans if they are bent on violence. Moreover, this may explain the prophet's bewilderment of the divine response, for he is expecting divine intervention to stop the violence, not to create more violence.

The phrase מְגַמַּת פְּנֵיהֶם קָדִימָה is notoriously difficult to translate. Translation of this clause depends on the first and the third words.[63] The word מְגַמַּת only occurs here and its meaning is uncertain. Its root is generally considered to have derived from גמם, which has an Arabic cognate meaning "abundance, become abundant, company (of people)."[64] A less likely root is from גמא, meaning "swallow," with the derived meaning of "eagerness."[65] The root of the word קָדִימָה is קדם which has the meaning of "march forth or advance."[66] קָדִימָה also has the meaning of "East, or east wind."[67] The east wind is the violent, scorching wind from the desert, which is an image that looks attractive to a lot of the commentators, especially when it fits well with the next clause "and he collects captives like sand."[68] NIV tries to retain both the meaning of advancing army and east wind by translating the clause, "Their hordes advance like a desert wind." However, Armerding thinks that this translation "rests more on the parallel passage in Jeremiah 4:11-13 than on the Hebrew text."[69] In this verse, קָדִימָה may mean "eastward" or "forward." In order to make the meaning clear, I translate this clause, "everyone of them (lit. the horde of their faces) marches forward."

The imagery of "sand" (חוֹל)[70] is used to describe the incalculable quantity of captives gathered by the Chaldeans so as to emphasize their mighty, ruthless military power which sweep across the land. Hence this strophe describes the conquest of the Chaldeans: they come for violence, and march forward as a unit, and gather numerous captives.

Then the second strophe gives the details of the arrogance and the military might of the Chaldeans. Not only does the use of personal pronoun "he" (הוּא)

---

[63] For a detailed discussion, see Patterson, *Nahum*, 151-52.

[64] BDB, 168.

[65] This translation was suggested by Ewald, Keil, and Delitzsch. See BDB, 170.

[66] BDB, 869.

[67] Ibid., 870.

[68] Brownlee, *Midrash*, 68, translates the Qumran text (1QpHab) to read, "the mutterings of/their face are the east wind" (מְגַמַּת פְּנֵי הֶם קָדִים), meaning that the fierceness of the invading army is like the scorching desert wind. In this study, the Qumran text is taken from 1QpHab, since the Hebrew text of Habakkuk from Wadi Murabba'at is virtually identical to the MT. For a concise discussion on the ancient manuscripts of the Twelve Minor Prophets found in the Judean desert, see Russell Fuller, "The Form and Formation of the Book of the Twelve: The Evidence from the Judean Desert," in *Forming Prophetic Literature: Essays on Isaiah and the Twelve in Honor of John D.W. Watts*, ed. J.W. Watts & P.R. House, JSOTSup 235 (Sheffield: Sheffield Academic Press, 1996), 86-101.

[69] Armerding, "Habakkuk,"503.

[70] This imagery is reminiscent of God's promise to Abraham that his descendants will be as numerous as sand (Gen 22:17; 32:13; Isa 48:19; Hos 2:1 [Eng 1:10]).

at the beginning of the two clauses in this verse serve as an anaphora,[71] it also acts as a *Stichwort* to link to verse 7, which reminds the reader how terrible and dreadful the Babylonians are. Grammatically speaking, the use of an independent pronoun with a finite verb is for emphasis on the subject.[72] The use of paronomasia[73] abounds in this verse: the sound of $\bar{a}$ at the end of a word occurs six times. Patterson also notes the sound of *s* in five occasions, with three of them in successive words.[74] The most obvious example involves the words מִשְׂחָק and יִשְׂחָק which both have the same root שׂחק (laugh). All these literary devices are used to emphasize the fearlessness of the Babylonians: kings and rulers are merely their laughing-stock, and all fortifications are nothing in their sight, certainly no match for their military might. There is a transposition of the consonant ב and צ in the word מִבְצָר "fortification" and the verb וַיִּצְבֹּר "heap up." The heaping up of soil to build a siege mound is a popular military tactic widely used in the ancient Near East.[75] This play on words seems to explain why the Babylonians laugh at the fortifications, for they know how to build the siege mound to overtake them. Thus this strophe describes the arrogance and the fearlessness of the Chaldeans and their military superiority over other nations.

The last strophe of this stanza gives a summary and a comment on the Chaldeans by Yahweh; "Then[76] he sweeps[77] through like the wind[78] and is gone;[79] and he becomes guilty.[80] He[81] whose strength is his god!" The swiftness of the

---

[71] A rhetorical term that means repetition of the initial word at the beginning of successive clauses.

[72] Williams, *Hebrew Syntax*, 22 §106.

[73] A rhetorical term which means play on words; or a pun.

[74] Patterson, *Nahum*, 153.

[75] Ibid., 153. For a brief description of this kind of warfare, see Bailey, *Micah*, 308.

[76] The article אָז "then" can be used in poetry to throw emphasis on a particular feature of the description. BDB, 23.

[77] Some argue that רוּחַ is a feminine noun and cannot be the subject of the verb חָלַף, but רוּחַ as a masculine noun is also attested, though less often. See Brownlee, *Midrash*, 81. Cf. Patterson, *Nahum*, 153.

[78] BHS, 1050, suggests that the word רוּחַ is probably כָּרוּחַ "like wind."

[79] The word וַיַּעֲבֹר has the meaning of "pass over, through, by, or pass on." It also has the meaning of "overstep or transgress," thus both NRV and JPS translate as "they transgress." However, in order to keep the simile with the wind, the clause אָז חָלַף רוּחַ וַיַּעֲבֹר is better translated as "Then he sweeps through like the wind and is gone."

[80] The verb וְאָשֵׁם has the meaning of "offend, be guilty, or be held guilty." According to the MT, this word has an *atnach* underneath it; thus it belongs to the first half of the verse. NIV and RSV take אָשֵׁם as the substantive use of the adjective and translate it as "guilty men," and put it with the second half of the verse. Patterson, *Nahum*, 153-4, takes it as an adjective in predicate relation to the following subject clause, and translates as "but he whose strength is his god will be held guilty." For a discussion on the placement of this word, see D.J. Clark, and H.A. Hatton. *A Translator's Handbook on the Book of Nahum, Habakkuk, and Zephaniah*, Helps for Translators (New York: United Bible Societies, 1989), 80. *BHS* textual apparatus notes that

Chaldeans is described as a powerful and destructive wind, which sounds like a tornado that leaves nothing standing on its path. Yahweh further comments that Babylon incurs guilt by regarding his strength as his God.

In sum, stanza 3 and 4 give a vivid and detailed portrayal of Babylon: his swiftness, fierceness, and military might have no comparison, which make him proud and arrogant. He has no regard for anyone except himself and he worships his own might as his God. This is the agent raised up by Yahweh as Judah's judgment.

*Stanza 5 Habakkuk's second complaint against Yahweh (1:12-14)*
Habakkuk is enraged by Yahweh's reply that he is bringing in the Chaldeans to solve Judean social injustice. He expresses his disapproval by asking the Lord a rhetorical question, "Are you not from ancient time?[82] O Yahweh." Patterson suggests that there are three nuances of the word קֶדֶם: (1) from of old; (2) from most ancient time; and (3) from everlasting.[83] He opts for the third meaning since the question is focused on God's existence, not his deeds. However, Armerding indicates that when this word is used with the preposition "from" (מִן) it usually refers to God's former deliverance of Israel in history.[84] It is quite possible that both God's existence and his deeds are in the prophet's mind. Then the prophet continues his lament and says, "My God, my Holy One, let us not die." The double invocation of "my God, my Holy One"[85] makes it sounds urgent and intimate.

The clause "let us not die/we will not die" (לֹא נָמוּת) is one of the eighteen *tiqqune sopherim* (תקוני ספרים) "scribal corrections."[86] The original is suppos-

---

Qumran scroll reads וישם and suggests וְיָשֶׂם to be connected with the second half of the verse, i.e., "and he set his strength to be his god." But some understand it as from the root שׁמם "to be desolate." Brownlee, *Midrash*, 80-1, attempts to retain all possible meanings by using a conflated translation for this verse, "Then, in accordance with the will, they transgressed, and passed on and were guilty, (and each one laid waste); And this one (appointed) his strength / to be their god."

[81] זֹה is a pronoun which can either be a demonstrative or a relative pronoun. BDB suggests that in Hab 1:11 it is used as a demonstrative pronoun. Gesenius, GKC, §138h, mentioned that זֹה can be used to introduce an independent relative clause. Reading it this way, it seems to emphasize that *this* is the one who incurs guilt because he only worships his own might.

[82] When used in a temporal sense קֶדֶם means "ancient, aforetime." God is usually described to be the one who did wonder from of old (Pss 74:12; 77:12; Isa 45:21; Mic 5:1).

[83] Patterson, *Nahum*, 163.

[84] Armerding, "Habakkuk," 505-506.

[85] The word קָדֹשׁ "my Holy One" is a *hapax legomenon*. While *BHS*, 1050, suggests to read קְדֹשִׁי אֱלֹהֵי "my holy God," the reading of MT is to be preferred. Also, as Patterson, *Nahum*, 163, points out, "the title 'Holy One' here anticipates its use in the epic psalm of the third chapter (3:3)."

[86] Würthwein, *Text of the Old Testament*, 18-19.

edly תמות לא "you will not die." Reading it as second person, it fits the context quite well for it parallels the former line that God is from ancient time and confirms God's existence.[87] However, as Ellis R. Brotzman mentions, there are uncertainties regarding the so-called *tiqqune sopherim*.[88] And as C. McCarthy says, "[i]n most cases (apart from 1 Sam 3:13; Zech 2:8 [H 12]; and Job 7:20) the MT and its context present no serious difficulty. Furthermore, the proposed alternative 'original reading' does not have significant textual support from the versions."[89] In this case "you will not die" does not find support in any manuscript;[90] meanwhile the MT is supported by the LXX and Symmachus and implicitly by 1QpHab.[91] Andersen thinks that נָמוּת can be a genuine alternative reading, though not with the first person meaning. He explains that the word could be a Niphal with a middle meaning, and proposes to translate לֹא נָמוּת as "the one who is not dead."[92] The only problem with this explanation is that, and even Andersen admits it, no Niphal form of the verb מוּת is recognized. Thus MT remains the best choice here: Habakkuk reminds Yahweh that he is God of Israel from ancient time and that he is the Holy One of Israel, thus he should not let Israel die.[93] Israel's survival does not depend on her own merit but on the faithfulness of her covenantal God, Yahweh.[94] Reading it this way, Habakkuk is pleading with God that despite God's harsh judgment, Israel, as God's own people, will not die.[95]

Then by using two synonymous parallel cola Habakkuk expresses his astonishment that Yahweh sets Babylon[96] for the purpose of judgment and reproof,[97] "O Yahweh, for[98] judgment you have set him. O Rock,[99] for reproof you have

---

[87] Smith, *Micah-Malachi*, 103.

[88] E.R. Brotzman, *Old Testament Textual Criticism: A Practical Introduction* (Grand Rapids: Baker Books, 1994), 116-18, states that reasons such as, variation in the lists of changes, the lack of consensus on the time when these changes supposedly took place, cast doubt on their existence.

[89] McCarthy, "Emendations of the Scribes [תקוני סופרים *Tiqqune Sopherim*]," *IDBSup* (Nashville: Abingdon, 1976), 264.

[90] Patterson, *Nahum*, 157.

[91] Armerding, "Habakkuk," 510.

[92] For details of his argument, see Andersen, *Habakkuk*, 176-78.

[93] J.J.O. van der Wal, "*Lō' Nāmūt* in Habakkuk I 12: A Suggestion," *VT* 38 (1988): 480-2, also sees this as the prophet's desperate cry to the Lord and suggests to translate this as "We should not die!"

[94] Keil, *Twelve Minor Prophets*, 63-64.

[95] For a discussion on other explanations for this clause, see Patterson, *Nahum*, 156-8.

[96] This may refer to Nebuchadnezzar for it is singular in Hebrew, "O Yahweh you have set him for judgment."

[97] Sweeney, "Structure," 67, argues that there is no clear indication of the purpose of the Chaldeans' establishment by Yahweh in 1:5-11. Yet here the prophet understands clearly that Yahweh's purpose of raising the Chaldeans is for judgment.

[98] The preposition לְ attached to it can be used to designate a cause. See BDB, 514-15.

established him." The key word "judgment" (מִשְׁפָּט), which is present in vv. 4 and 7, reappears. The invocation of the divine title "Rock" makes the complaint sound even more piercing: The Rock of Israel, who is supposed to be a source of salvation, turns out to be the One who is establishing the Chaldeans to do the destruction. The word "reproof" (הוֹכִיחַ)[100] means to "correct," with the purpose of bringing someone back onto the right track. So the purpose of God's establishment of the Chaldeans is clear: to chasten the Israelites in order to bring them back to the right path. But this further puzzles Habakkuk, for how can Yahweh use a morally debased nation to judge and reprove a more righteous nation? This is peculiar to Habakkuk, for while it is characteristic of the prophets to indict and warn Israel, Habakkuk rejects and complains God's appointment of Nebuchadnezzar as a judge and a reproof to his own people.

Habakkuk continues his complaint against God by appealing to God's nature, "Too pure[101] are your eyes[102] to see evil, and to look[103] at trouble[104] you are not able." Not only does the adjective "pure" (טָהוֹר) have a ritual meaning but here it also has the meaning of ethically pure and clean.[105] Since Yahweh is a holy and pure God, he should not be able to tolerate any mischief or morally wrong deeds. So Habakkuk challenges God and questions him why he remains silent when the righteous are oppressed by the wicked, "Why do you look on the treacherous ones, [and] you remain silent (תַחֲרִישׁ) when the wicked swallows the one more righteous than him?"[106] The positioning of the word (תַחֲרִישׁ) between the question "why do you look at the treacherous ones?" and the clause "when the wicked swallow the one more righteous than him," prompts

---

99 "Rock" (צוּר) is one of the titles of God (Deut 32:4; 1 Sam 2:2; 2 Sam 22:32; Isa 26:4 & etc.). In fact, the Lord is sometimes called the "Rock of Israel" (2 Sam 23:3; Isa 30:29). Other than having the meaning of permanence and stability, the word "rock" is usually associated with salvation, refuge, or strength (Deut 32:15; 2 Sam 22:47; Pss 62:8; 73:26).

100 This word also anticipates the term "my reproof" (תּוֹכַחְתִּי) in 2:1.

101 The adjective "pure" followed by the prefix preposition מִן to the verb (מֵרְאוֹת), denotes a comparative meaning of "too pure." See GKC, §133c.

102 Although the word for "eyes" (עֵינַיִם) does not have a pronominal suffix attached to it, the context shows that the prophet must have meant the eyes of the Lord, thus "your eyes are too pure to see evil."

103 Armerding, "Habakkuk," 506, explains that to "look" at a matter can imply that it is viewed with acceptance (cf. Pss 66:18; 138:6).

104 The noun "mischief, trouble" (עָמָל) recalls Habakkuk's initial complaints about God's inactivity in the face of trouble in verse 3.

105 BDB, 373.

106 Patterson, *Nahum*, 164, argues that the asyndetic (omission of conjunction between words, phrases, or clauses) structure of "[Why…] you are silent" (תַחֲרִישׁ) makes the question more dramatic. Bailey, *Micah*, 314 n.128, mentions that the "NIV takes this as resumptive use of the opening interrogative, 'Why?' thus, 'Why are you silent while the wicked swallow up those more righteous than themselves?'"

some commentators to read this word with the latter clause.[107] I think the word תַּחֲרִישׁ is in a pivotal position so that it can be read with both clauses, "Why do you look at the treacherous ones and remain silent? [You remain silent] when the wicked swallows up the one more righteous than him."[108] Reading it this way, it serves to highlight the fact that the Lord remains silent as he watches the havoc caused by the wicked.

Habakkuk's accusation comes to a climax when he accuses God of making humans vulnerable like fish, "And you have made human being like fishes of the sea, like a critter (or a creeping thing)[109] with no ruler over him." In Gen 1:26 and 28, human beings (אָדָם)[110] are commissioned to rule over the fish of the sea and the creeping things. This contradicts our text that says that there is no ruler over them. Furthermore, here human being is compared to these creatures which are vulnerable because they have no ruler to protect them.[111] The prophet uses this imagery of the reversal of the order of creation to implicitly accuse God as the one who brings such calamity on humanity for he makes (תַּעֲשֶׂה) them to be like that. The imagery of the sea creatures anticipates the following stanza which describes the invader as a fisherman.

*Stanza 6 Habakkuk's complaint against the Chaldeans (1:15-17)*
Habakkuk then turns his complaint against the Chaldeans by portraying Babylon as a fisherman, who drags and catches other nations like fish. The first word כֻּלֹה "all of it" that begins this stanza is the same word at the beginning of stanza 4 which tells us of the brutal nature of Babylon. Two words, "net" (חֵרֶם) and "fishing net" (מִכְמֶרֶת),[112] are used to describe the sweeping success of the Babylonian aggression against the nations. Their military success is the reason for their joy and happiness, "Therefore[113] he rejoices and he exults." The hendiadys

---

[107] Cf. Smith's translation, "Why do you look upon the faithless ones, and remain silent while the wicked swallows one more righteous than he?" See Smith, *Micah*, 102.

[108] For a description of the pivot pattern, see Watson, *Classical Hebrew Poetry*, 214-21.

[109] The word for "critter" or "creeping thing" (רֶמֶשׂ) is a collective noun that refers to the crawling things that move on the land, as well as the sea animals or the gliding things (cf. Ps 104:25). See BDB, 943.

[110] In Gen 1:26-28, the word אָדָם is a collective term for humankind, for all the verb forms are plural and the pronominal suffix oscillates between singular and plural.

[111] Armerding, "Habakkuk," 507, calls the comparison to fish "subhuman and vulnerable," and the sea creature "lacking the organization or leadership normally expected in human society."

[112] Both words also have the meaning of snare; in fact חֵרֶם is used for a hunter's net in Mic 7:2, while מִכְמֶרֶת has its cognates מִכְמָר and מַכְמֹר which mean "net, snare." For a discussion of the different types of net associated with these two words, see Patterson, *Nahum*, 165.

[113] The complex preposition that functions as adverbial "therefore" (עַל־כֵּן) usually introduces the statement of a *fact*, rather than a *declaration*. BDB, 487, italics theirs. Here it is used to state the reason for the Babylonians' happiness.

"rejoice and exult" (יִשְׂמַח וְיָגֵיל) are used to express total gladness.[114] Armerding mentions that these two words are used frequently in religious context of worship and praise (cf. 1 Chr 16:9; Isa 25:9; Joel 2:21, 23; Pss 16:9; 31:8; 118:24; Zech 10:7).[115] If that is the case, then this clause anticipates the following strophe.

In the second strophe, the repetition of the words, such as, "therefore" (עַל־כֵּן), "net" (חֵרֶם), and "fishing net" (מִכְמֶרֶת) from the previous verse suggests to the reader that these two verses should be read together. The imagery of religious worship continues with the use of the words "sacrifice" (יְזַבֵּחַ) and "burn incense" (וִיקַטֵּר).[116] The prophet is describing the Babylonians as honoring their own might and power rather than God. This echoes what Yahweh says in 1:11 that they incur guilt because they regard their strength as their God. The Babylonians attribute their success to their own power, "For[117] in them his portion is rich (שָׁמֵן) and his food is sleek (בְּרִיא)." Both שָׁמֵן and בְּרִיא have been used to describe the wicked ones who gain their wealth through unjust means and are boastful of their success (cf. Ezek 34:16; Jer 5:26-28; Ps 73:4; Deut 32:15).[118] Elsewhere, for example, in Isa 5:1 שָׁמֵן is also used to describe a fertile slope where God plants his vineyard. Thus this could mean that the military might of the Chaldeans enables them to occupy fertile lands and gain riches.

Just as the prophet begins stanza 5 with a rhetorical question, he ends stanza 6 with another rhetorical question, thus forming an *inclusio* for this section: "Will he therefore[119] empty his net and continually[120] kill nations and not spare?" Qumran text (1QpHab) reads "his net" (חֶרְמוֹ) as "his sword" (חַרְבּוֹ), due to the confusion of only one consonant.[121] To "empty, or draw" (רִיק) the "sword" (חֶרֶב) is quite a common expression as attested in Exod 15:9; Lev

---

[114] Patterson, *Nahum*, 166.

[115] Armerding, "Habakkuk," 507.

[116] Armerding, "Habakkuk," 508, points out that the Piel form of these two verbs is sometimes used of sacrifices of animals and incense made to other deities or in illegal worship.

[117] The conjunction כִּי "for" is used in a causal sense. See Williams, *Hebrew Syntax*, 72 §444.

[118] Patterson, *Nahum*, 166. See also, Armerding, "Habakkuk," 508.

[119] The interrogative ה is not present in Qumran, Greek, or Syriac versions, and verse 17 begins with "therefore" (עַל כֵּן) in those versions. Patterson, *Nahum*, 167, opines that there is no sufficient reason for the omission and prefers to maintain the MT reading. He also rejects Dahood's translation, "O Most High, Just One."

[120] According to the textual critical apparatus of *BHS*, 1050, the word "and continue" (וְתָמִיד) is not supposed to have ו (a dittograph); hence it suggests reading this word in connection with the previous clause, "Will he therefore continue to empty his net?" This reading is supported by Qumran and Syriac versions. However, the accentuation of the MT puts the word וְתָמִיד with the second half of the verse, "and continually kill nations."

[121] Peckham suggested that it is due to a pronunciation error when the scribe was reading aloud, for both ב (b) and מ (m) are bilabials. Private communication with Peckham.

26:33; Ezek 5:2, 12; 12:14; 28:7; 30:11. Also it makes very good sense with the context. However, MT is still preferred because not only does it fit the context well, it also maintains the imagery of the fisherman who keeps emptying his net, a metaphor developed in vv. 14-16. The word "sparing" (חָמַל) has the meaning of "compassion," as in Exod 2:6, "she had compassion on him." But it also means to "spare/save something," as in Jer 50:14, "do not spare any arrow."[122] Hence this word may have a double entendre here; the Chaldeans are accused of not having "compassion" on nations, and they "spare" no one.[123]

It is noteworthy that stanza 6 parallels stanza 4. Not only do they both describe the brutality of the Chaldeans, there are words and images that parallel each other. Both of the stanzas begin with the word "all of it" (כֻּלֹּה), followed by the description of the captivity of many people (vv. 9 and 15) by the Chaldeans. The happiness of the Chaldeans is portrayed with words such as "laugh" (יִשְׂחָק) in v. 10 and "rejoice and exults" (יִשְׂמַח וְיָגִיל) in v. 15, and their worshipping of their own might in vv. 11 and 16. Thus these two stanzas tell the reader that both Yahweh and Habakkuk agree on the assessment of the Chaldeans: they are brutal, arrogant, successful, and they worship their own might.

*Scene two*

*Stanza 1 Habakkuk's action and Yahweh's response (2:1-3)*
2:1 begins a new scene whereby the prophet depicts himself as a watchman. The verb forms in the first part of this verse are cohortative (אֶעֱמֹדָה וְאֶתְיַצְּבָה) to indicate a strong desire or resolve[124] on the part of the speaker, "On my post guard I *will* stand and I *will* station myself on the rampart." This type of chiastic couplet is usually used to open a stanza or poem.[125] The parallel pair of "post guard" (מִשְׁמֶרֶת) and "rampart or siege" (מָצוֹר) indicates that the scene is at the city walls where the watchmen keep watch for the advancing enemies so as to warn the citizens of the danger.[126] Elsewhere in the Old Testament, prophets are set by the Lord to be the watchmen for the house of Israel (Ezek 3:17-21; 33:2-6; cf. Isa 21:6-8; Hos 9:8). Habakkuk states his purpose of going up to the rampart, "and I *will* keep watch[127] to see[128] what he might speak to me,[129]

---

[122] Gesenius mentioned that the expression לֹא יַחְמֹל "may be regarded simply as equivalent to negative adverbial ideas," thus "unsparingly." GKC, §156g.

[123] Armerding, "Habakkuk,"508.

[124] Waltke and O'Connor, *Hebrew Syntax*, 573.

[125] Watson, *Classical Hebrew Poetry*, 205.

[126] For a description of the fortification of the city walls, see P.J. King, and L.E. Stager, *Life in Biblical Israel* (Louisville: Westminster John Knox, 2001), 231-36. See also Armerding, "Habakkuk," 509.

[127] The verb "I will keep watch" (וַאֲצַפֶּה) has the meaning of "to look out, spy, or keep watch;" in fact, a watchman is called צֹפֶה (substantive use of Qal active participle).

[128] The infinitive construct of a verb with the preposition לְ is used to express a purpose, thus לִרְאוֹת has the meaning of "so as to see."

and what I might reply[130] concerning my reproof."[131] As a watchman, Habakkuk goes to the rampart to see if the invading army is coming. He also expects a reply from God and gets ready to answer to his anticipated reproof.

The Lord then answers Habakkuk by commanding him to write down the vision in the second strophe, "Write down the vision and make it plain[132] on the tablets[133] in order that the one reading it may run." In Deut 27:8, Moses is instructed to write the law clearly on the stones.[134] Since the word "tablets" (הַלֻּחוֹת) chiefly refers to the stone tablets that the Ten Commandments were written on,[135] it is conceivable that plastered stone tablets are used later for writing prophecy.[136] Isaiah is ordered to write down the prophecy on a tablet in Isa 30:8.[137] The reason for writing on the stone tablets appears to be for its permanency, "that it may be with them, to be a witness forever" (Isa 30:8b).[138] This is further supported by the metaphoric saying "to write on the tablet of one's heart" in Jer 17:1; Prov 3:3; 7:3.

---

[129] The preposition בְּ with the first person pronominal suffix, along with the verb דבר means "speak to/with/in me" (cf. Zech 1:13).

[130] The verb אָשִׁיב in the last colon of this verse has a variant reading. *BHS* indicates that the Syriac version has the verb יָשִׁיב "he will reply" instead of MT אָשִׁיב. The verb אָשִׁיב is a Hiphil imperfect 1cs of שׁוּב, which has the meaning of "cause to return, bring back, restore." O'Neal, *Interpreting Habakkuk*, 41 n. 1b, takes it to mean "withdraw," and renders the clause, "and if I should withdraw my complaint." However, most of the scholars translate אָשִׁיב "I reply, answer."

[131] The word תּוֹכַחְתִּי also has the meaning of "argument, rebuke, or correction." The word can be taken to mean "the argument that I have made," or "the reproof that I receive." Armerding, "Habakkuk," 509, explains that it depends on whether one takes the possessive suffix "my" to be the agent of the noun, or its object. In both cases, the prophet is expecting a reply from God.

[132] The Piel imperative of the verb בָּאֵר means "to make distinct, plain" of letters on the tablets (הַלֻּחוֹת).

[133] Clark and Hatton, *Translator's Handbook*, 90, states that the material for the "tablets" can be clay, stone, wood or metal.

[134] However, David T. Tsumura, "Hab 2 2 in the Light of Akkadian Legal Practice," *ZAW* 94 (1982): 294-5, appeals to Akkadian legal practice and suggests that the term באר may have an Akkadian cognate *burru* which means "to confirm" by legal means. This suggestion, though attractive, lacks biblical support.

[135] BDB, 531.

[136] For a description of some of the archaeological findings on plaster text, see King and Stager, *Life in Biblical Israel*, 304-305.

[137] According to Peckham, לוּחַ was also a wooden tablet, usually a diptych or triptych with wax-covered surfaces so that the letters can be impressed on with a stylus. It was not permanent but meant to be carried by a messenger or a merchant. However, Isaiah's tablet might have been permanent. Private communication with Professor Peckham.

[138] The similarity of the command and the affinity of the vocabulary in Isa 30:8 and Hab 2:2, make one wonder whether Yahweh is quoting Isa 30:8 here.

The clause, "in order that the one reading it may run," has different translations, depending on the understanding of the syntax between the two verbs "run" (רוּץ) and "call out or read" (קָרָא). The NRV translates this as "so that a runner may read it," probably meaning that the message is clear and plain enough for someone to run and read it at the same time. Bailey tries to defend this reading by saying, "make the message plain enough so the person running (Hb. participle) may read the message."[139] The problem with this translation is that the word for "reading" (קוֹרֵא) is participial meanwhile the word for "run" is a finite verb (יָרוּץ).[140] Grammatically, the participle of a verb can be used substantively, thus קוֹרֵא can be translated "the one who reads."[141] NIV translates it "so that a herald may run with it," taking it to mean that a herald may run to spread the message. This translation has the advantage of keeping the imagery of the watcher issuing the warning and the herald relating the message to the general public.[142] Furthermore, professional messengers, who run to spread the message of their lords, are common in ancient royal courts such as those in ancient Mari and Babylon.[143] Thus Yahweh commands Habakkuk to write the vision plainly on the tablets so that whoever reads it may run either to spread the message or to run for refuge.

Yahweh continues admonishing Habakkuk to wait for the vision to come, "For yet[144] the vision is for the appointed time;[145] and it will run breathlessly[146]

---

[139] Bailey, *Micah*, 323.

[140] J.M. Holt points out that the main verb is יָרוּץ and the emphasis is not on "reading" but on "running." Thus the more accurate translation is that "the revelation is given so that a reader may run." For a detailed discussion, see his article, "So He May Run Who Reads it," *JBL* 83 (1964):298-300.

[141] The Qumran text has the definite article הקורא, "that he who reads it may run." Brownlee, *Midrash*, 107.

[142] Holt, however, sees "running" as a "figure of speech," and prefers to translate it as "so he who reads it may live obediently." See his article, "So He May Run Who Reads It," 301-302. Roberts, *Nahum*, 109, quotes the construction of Prov 18:10 and suggests the reason for running is "so that the one who reads might run into it (for refuge)."

[143] J.H. Walton, V.H. Matthews, and M.W. Chavalas, *The IVP Bible Background Commentary: Old Testament* (Downers Grove: IVP, 2000), 792.

[144] Some scholars, such as J. Gerald Janzen and Samuel E. Loewenstamm, argue that עוֹד "yet" should be emended to עֵד "witness" so as to parallel יָפֵחַ which, according to them, means "testifier." See Janzen, "Habakkuk 2:2-4 in the Light of Recent Philological Advances," *Harvard Theological Review* 73 (1980): 55-57.

[145] מוֹעֵד "appointed time" is usually prefixed with a preposition לְ meaning "at the appointed time" (לַמּוֹעֵד). See BDB, 417.

[146] The verb וְיָפֵחַ is a Hiphil imperfect 3ms of פּוּחַ, which has the meaning of "breathe, blow, puff, pant, and utter." BDB, 806, understands that the vision pants (or hastens) towards the end. *BHS*, 1051, suggests that the verb probably reads וְיָפִיחַ. The Greek text translates it as "ἀνατέλει", which probably understands the Hebrew verb to be יִפְרַח(וְ) "break forth, spring forth." Loewenstamm, Dahood and others see that the

to the end and it will not lie. If it were to tarry,[147] wait for it; for it will certainly come,[148] it will not delay." Habakkuk is told that the "vision"[149] (חָזוֹן), which he is commanded to write down, is to be fulfilled in the future. The futuristic aspect of the vision is emphasized by such words as "yet" (עוֹד),[150] "tarry" (יִתְמַהְמָהּ), "wait" (חַכֵּה). However, the imminence of the vision is also stressed by such phrases as "it will run breathlessly to the end," "it will not lie," "it will surely come," "it will not delay." Hence the prophet is admonished to wait patiently for its "appointed time" which lies solely on God's discretion. Incidentally, Isa 30:18 states that Yahweh "waits" to be gracious to those who would "wait" for him. To wait for God requires commitment and trust in the faithfulness of God. The affinity of Yahweh's reply here and Isaiah's passage (Isa 30:8) may mean to remind the reader of Isaiah's vision. Thus Yahweh states right at the beginning that the vision has an appointed time in the near future, which is likely to be in the prophet's days (1:5), and warns him to wait patiently for it.

*Stanza 2 Contrast of the arrogant and the righteous (2:4-6a)*
Stanza 2 consists of four strophes and each strophe has three lines. This stanza focuses on the message that Yahweh commands Habakkuk to write down. The first strophe (2:4) characterizes the wicked and the righteous, "Behold [his soul] is inflated (עֻפְּלָה),[151] his soul (נַפְשׁוֹ) is not upright (לֹא־יָשְׁרָה)[152] in him. But

---

Hebrew יָפֵחַ/יָפִיחַ is cognate with Ugarit *yph*, which means "witness, testifier." See Janzen, "Habakkuk 2:2-4," 55. Dennis Pardee, "*YPH* "Witness" in Hebrew and Ugaritic," *VT* 28 (1978): 213, opines that "Hebrew *yp(y)h* is a verbal adjective (active participle) which, like its synonym '*ēd*, functions as a noun." This understanding finds support from biblical texts, particularly Prov 6:19; 12:17; 14:5, 25; 19:5, 9. In all of these texts יָפִיחַ is parallel with עֵד, that prompts some scholars to emend עוֹד in this verse to עֵד, and translate it as "For the vision is a witness to the appointed time, a testifier to the end—it does not lie." Moreover, the word כְּזָבִים is present in all passages except Prov 12:17. In fact, Prov 14:5 also has the verb יְכַזֵּב which is present in Hab 2:3 as well. While it is attractive to translate יָפִיחַ/יָפֵחַ "witness, testifier," it still makes sense to translate it "breathe out or utter" in all the above texts. In order to keep the imagery of "running" as in the previous verse, 2:3 may be translated, "For yet the vision is for the appointed time. It will run breathlessly to the end and it will not lie."

[147] יִתְמַהְמָהּ is the Hithpalpel imperfect 3ms of the verb מָהַהּ which means "tarry, linger, delay."

[148] The infinitive absolute and the imperfect of the verb בּוֹא "to come" are used to emphasize that the vision will certainly come and that it will not delay any further ( לֹא יְאַחֵר). *BHS*, 1051, indicates that many manuscripts have וְלֹא instead of לֹא.

[149] It is suggested by some that the vision is Yahweh's speech in 1:5-11.

[150] The word עוֹד "yet" may allude to Isa 30:8 where the vision is for "another day."

[151] The verb עֻפְּלָה is a Pual perfect 3fs of עָפַל which has a base meaning of "swell." For a detailed discussion on the debate on the meaning of עֻפְּלָה, see J.A. Emerton, "The Textual and Linguistic Problems of Habakkuk II. 4-5," *Journal of Theological Stud-*

the righteous (וְצַדִּיק) in his faithfulness (בֶּאֱמוּנָתוֹ) will live (יִחְיֶה)."[153] This is the key verse of the book and its significance cannot be overstated.[154]

The translation of this verse is not without difficulty. The first line of the verse describes the arrogant one (the "puffed up" עֻפְּלָה) whose soul is not upright in him. The verb עֻפְּלָה "inflated" is ambiguous because it lacks a subject. The closest feminine noun is נַפְשׁוֹ "his soul." Thus נַפְשׁוֹ can be the subject for both the 3fs verbs of עֻפְּלָה and לֹא־יָשְׁרָה "not upright."

In the second line the ambiguity lies in the word בֶּאֱמוּנָתוֹ. There is a debate as to whose faithfulness (בֶּאֱמוּנָתוֹ) does the writer have in mind. There have been three proposals. The first one is God's faithfulness. This is supported by LXX, since it renders this clause: ὁ δὲ δίκαιος ἐκ πίστεώς μου ζήσεται "but the just shall live by my (God's) faith."[155] Some scholars, following the lead of Janzen, argue that it is the reliability of the vision that the righteous shall live by it.[156] However, as A. Jepsen explains, in the passages where אֱמוּנָה appears, it refers mostly to the conduct of a person, either of God or of human, whose behavior may be defined as "genuineness, reliability, conscientiousness."[157] The third view is that the faithfulness of the righteous is in view since the closest antecedent is the substantive use of the adjective צַדִּיק "the righteous."[158] Reading it this way, it gives the contrast between the arrogant one who is not

---

*ies* 28 (1977): 13-6. *BHS*, 1051, suggests reading it as עֻפַּל (Pual perfect 3ms) or עֻפָּל.

[152] Haak does not think that יָשַׁר in the present context has any moral connotation, and sees that it is used to describe the (lack of) smoothness of the throat (נַפְשׁוֹ). See Haak, *Habakkuk*, 58-9. But the close proximity of this word with the word וְצַדִּיק indicates that the writer may have ethical connotation in mind.

[153] The Greek text differs significantly from the MT. LXX renders this clause, "If he who should draw back (ἐὰν ὑποστείληται), my soul has no pleasure in him (οὐκ εὐδοκεῖ ἡ ψυχή μου ἐν αὐτῷ)." *BHS*, 1051, states that the word for εὐδοκεῖ is probably from the Hebrew word רָצְתָה (Qal perfect 3fs of רצה). The difference may due to the variant recensions that the MT and LXX are based on.

[154] For a brief discussion on the importance of this verse in Christian and Jewish theology, see Patterson, *Nahum*, 211-2.

[155] Some argue that the genitive of πίστεώς μου should be objective—"faith in me." However, the presence of the preposition ἐκ clearly points to the origin/means of the faith, thus it is better to translate the prepositional phrase as "from/by my faith." The noun πίστις also means "faithfulness," hence some translate the clause as "but the just shall live by my faithfulness."

[156] For Janzen's argument, see "Habakkuk 2:2-4," 59-62. Andersen is a bit ambiguous in his opinion. He translates v. 4b, "and the righteous person by its trustworthiness will survive," taking it to mean the trustworthiness of the vision. See Andersen, *Habakkuk*, 5. However, later on in his exposition of this verse, he writes, "The certainty of its fulfillment comes from the reliability of Yahweh ('ĕmûnātô, "his dependability"), who never lies." See ibid., 205.

[157] A. Jepsen, "אָמַן" in *TDOT*, 1:317.

[158] For a discussion of the meaning of צדק, see B. Johnson, "צדק" in *TDOT*, 12:243-46.

upright and the righteous one who trusts in God and lives in accordance to God's righteous standard.[159] The divine promise that the righteous will live by his faithfulness becomes the turning point of the book.

I divide 2:5 into two strophes because the first part of this verse consists of a *waw* (ו) + asyndeton + asyndeton,[160] while the second part of the verse consists of three *waw* (ו) clauses.[161] These two strophes further describe the arrogant one mentioned in the first strophe: strophe 2 portrays him as a boastful drunkard and strophe 3 gives a political assessment of him.

Strophe 2 depicts him as a drunkard who is conceited and greedy, "And furthermore,[162] wine is treacherous;[163] a man is haughty and will not abide,[164] who enlarges his throat like Sheol." The phrase "wine is treacherous" (הַיַּיִן בּוֹגֵד) appears to be out of place.[165] Some scholars follow the Qumran text and change הַיַּיִן to הוֹן "wealth," and translate הון יבגוד as "wealth deceives the arrogant man,"[166] or "wealth is treacherous."[167] However, the MT reading of "wine" has the advantage of keeping the imagery of "puffed up" as in 2:4a. In Prov 20:1, wine is said to be a scorner (לֵץ הַיַּיִן), and has the potential of leading astray (שָׁגָה) those who depend on it. And in Isa 28:7, the Israelite leaders, specifically the priests and the prophets, are accused of their indulgence in wine and their erroneous judgment under the influence of alcohol. Thus a man who is under the treacherous effect of wine can become haughty and boastful, and therefore does not last. Moreover, "the cup of the wine of wrath" is used to describe God's judgment in Jer 25:15. Later in this chapter, the image of wine and drunkenness is used in the fourth oracle which talks about the eventual divine punishment on the conqueror, so it is quite possible that the message is presaged here.[168] "He will not abide/endure" (וְלֹא יִנְוֶה) further describes the "haughty man" (גֶּבֶר יָהִיר). Armerding explains that יִנְוֶה has the meaning "to be

---

[159] Patterson, *Nahum*, 217-23.

[160] A rhetorical term that means omission of conjunction between words, phrases, or clauses.

[161] I am indebted to my late thesis advisor Professor Brian Peckham for pointing this out to me. According to him, strophes are defined by the number of lines they have and distinguished from each other by the use and non-use of *waw* and by the conjugation (*qtl* / *yqtl*) of their verbs. Private communication with him.

[162] Emerton, "Textual," 1, points out that the phrase "And furthermore" (וְאַף כִּי) that begins verse 5 links this verse to the previous one.

[163] The Qumran text has הון יבגוד "wealth deceives."

[164] The MT pointing for the verb "endure" (יִנְוֶה) is Qal imperfect 3ms of נָוֶה which has the meaning of "dwell, abide." It was proposed by Wellhausen to emend it to יִרְוֶה "he will not be satiated." But that is not necessary.

[165] Andersen, *Habakkuk*, 217, quotes Wellhausen and Nowack who dismissed this phrase as "impossible." Roberts, *Nahum*, 113, thinks that "one can do nothing" with the MT's version.

[166] Roberts, *Nahum*, 113.

[167] Emerton, "Textual," 8-10.

[168] Andersen, *Habakkuk*, 217.

at home," which fits the description of the rest of this verse that the conqueror is not going to be satisfied staying home but would invade other nations.[169] This clause can also be taken to mean the eventual downfall of the conqueror such that "he does not last." Thus this strophe describes the puffed-up man, who is a drunkard and is never satisfied and who opens his throat like Sheol to consume other nations. It is noteworthy that the mention of the "righteous" and the "puffed-up one" as well as the imagery of opening up the throat to swallow is reminiscent of Habakkuk's complaint in 1:13 that the "wicked" swallows the one more "righteous" than him.

The third strophe has three lines which all begin with the consonant ו, and depicts the conqueror as death swallowing down the nations, "and he is like death and he is not sated, and he gathers to himself all the nations, and he collects to himself all the peoples." The political assessment of the conqueror here fits the earlier description of the Chaldeans in 1:9-11 and 15-17. The repetition of the word "gather" (וַיֶּאֱסֹף) and its synonym "collect" (וַיִּקְבֹּץ) here, which appears in 1:9 and 1:15, links this section to the previous ones. Moreover, the repetition of words such as "nations" (הַגּוֹיִם) and "peoples" (הָעַמִּים) in the following sections links this verse to the woes that follow. Thus this strophe serves to identify this haughty man to be the Chaldeans, as well as an introduction for the ensuing woe oracles.

The last strophe of this stanza serves as a transition from the vision to the woe oracles section, "Will not these, all of them raise a proverb against him, and a satire, mocking riddles about him? And it will say." The antecedents of אֵלֶּה "these" are the "peoples" and the "nations," so it is likely that they are the ones who would raise the taunt-song against the conqueror. The construction "these—all of them" is unusual and is for emphatic purpose.[170] Both Qumran and Greek texts have the plural form of the word וְאָמְרוּ instead of the singular וְיֹאמַר as in MT.[171] But MT still makes sense, for it can refer to the content of the taunt-song, "and it will say."

### Stanza 3 The first woe oracle (2:6b-8)

This new stanza begins the five woe oracles section, which is characterized by the word הוֹי. According to Richard J. Clifford, the word הוֹי appears 53 times in the Old Testament and has three basic uses: (1) to describe actual funeral laments; (2) a cry to get attention; (3) a word used by prophets to introduce announcements of doom.[172] He also speculates that הוֹי originates from funeral laments. Its syntax then develops in the prophetic books, especially in Jeremiah and Habakkuk, to be a curse-like formula.[173] If this is the case, then the follow-

---

[169] Armerding, "Habakkuk," 515.

[170] Andersen, *Habakkuk*, 230.

[171] The Qumran text lacks the needed א, and spells the word וְיֹזְמְרוּ. See Brownlee, *Midrash*, 131.

[172] Clifford, "The Use of *Hôy* in the Prophets," *CBQ* 28 (1966): 458.

[173] Ibid., 459-61.

ing woes are the prophetic announcements of divine judgment presented in a sarcastic tone: they are set in "proverbial saying" (מָשָׁל), "satire" (מְלִיצָה), and "mocking riddles" (חִידוֹת) raised by the persecuted nations. It is interesting to note that at the beginning of every woe, a participial form of the verb always follows the word הוֹי. The participle is used substantively to indicate the group of people committing that particular crime.[174]

The first woe oracle is pronounced against the group who engages in financial extortion, "Woe to the one who increases what is not his. Until when? And making heavy pledges[175] on himself." The phrase "making heavy upon himself pledges" (וּמַכְבִּיד עָלָיו עַבְטִיט) has a double meaning here. On the one hand, it means that the oppressor is making himself rich by means of extortion.[176] On the other hand, it signifies that the oppressor is increasing his own debt to others as he incurs his guilt by unlawful means, and hence bringing upon himself the judgments pronounced in the next two strophes.

Strophe 2 begins with the word הֲלוֹא which links this to 2:6 and creates an ironic twist, "Will not your creditors[177] suddenly arise? And those who make you tremble[178] will wake up, and you will become booties for them." The rhetorical question is meant to create an ironic twist, especially when the word for creditors (נֹשְׁכֶיךָ) has both the meaning of "creditors" and "debtors." Patterson explains that a trope of meaning is intended here: that the debtors accumulate an obligation from the creditor and become creditors themselves.[179] Hence the rhetorical question achieves the irony that is intended by reversing their roles: the debtors become the creditors, and the creditors become the debtors.

Strophe 3 then gives the reason for the judgment. The repetition of the verb "plunder" (שָׁלַל) is used to explain the just punishment that is meted out: he who plunders many nations will in turn be plundered by the remnants of these nations. In the second part of this strophe, the phrase "Because of human bloodshed and violence to the land, to the city and all its inhabitants" is a refrain that also appears in 2:17b. The words "land" (אֶרֶץ) and "city" (קִרְיָה) are all in singular form and the word "violence" recalls 1:3 and 1:9. The purpose of

---

[174] Westermann, *Basic Forms*, 191.

[175] The word "pledges" (עַבְטִיט) is a *hapax legomenon* from the root עבט. Andersen, *Habakkuk*, 236, thinks that it has to do with using property as mortgage and may even mean that the creditor has usufruct as interest. If that is the case, then the land owner would be totally deprived of his livelihood.

[176] The word עָלָיו can also be translated "on it" meaning, "making heavy on the mortgage."

[177] The verbal root for נֹשְׁכֶיךָ is נָשַׁךְ which has two meanings. One is "to bite," thus נֹשְׁכֶיךָ is literally "the ones who bite you" or "your creditors." The other meaning is "to pay, give interest," hence BDB translates it as "your debtors."

[178] מְזַעְזְעֶיךָ is a Pilpel participle of the root זוּעַ which, according to BDB, has a causative and intensive meaning of "those who make you shake violently." See BDB, 266.

[179] Patterson, *Nahum*, 189-90.

the refrain may be to highlight and to summarize, particularly, the atrocity done to Jerusalem by the Chaldeans.

*Stanza 4 The second woe oracle (2:9-11)*

While the first woe uses the imagery of economic exploitation to denounce the plundering of the nations by the Chaldeans, the second woe portrays them as the home owner who intends to secure his own house by means of unjust gains, "Woe to the one who gains unjust profit[180] evil for his house, to put his nest in the high place[181] in order to be delivered[182] from the hand of evil." Nebuchadnezzar is well known for his building projects in the ancient world, especially for fortifying and raising the city of Babylon, his capital, to the summit. Here the imagery of an eagle trying to secure its nest in a high and inaccessible site where it is kept from harm's way fits the historical description of Nebuchadnezzar. Hence this strophe shows how the Chaldeans try to secure themselves by means of unjust profit, but it is false security for they are only securing "evil/harm" (רַע) for their house.

Strophe 2 continues using the "house" imagery but while the previous strophe is a general statement against the one who exploits others, here it is a direct address to the oppressor by using the second person,[183] "You have devised shame for your house, cutting off[184] many people and bringing sin to your soul. For a stone cries out from the wall and a rafter[185] answers it from the wood-

---

[180] The use of the two words of the same root בֹּצֵעַ בֶּצַע "gain by violence, unjust profit" is to emphasize that the gain is made by unjust means. Andersen, *Habakkuk*, 240, suggests reading בֹּצֵעַ בֶּצַע as a complete statement and "evil to his house" as a parenthetical, so that it parallels the corresponding imprecation "shame to your house" in the next strophe.

[181] In Jer 49:16 and Obad 4, Edom is described to have put his nest (קֵן) in such a mountainous site but the Lord, through the prophets, has prophesied that he will bring him down. Here the imagery is applied to the Chaldeans.

[182] The word לְהִנָּצֵל is a Niphal infinitive construct of נָצַל (to be delivered) with a preposition לְ. The preposition לְ can have a purpose meaning "in order to," especially when it is used with infinitive construct. See Williams, *Hebrew Syntax*, §277. Cf. also GKC §114g.

[183] D.R. Hillers, "*Hôy* and *Hôy*-Oracles: A Neglected Syntactic Aspect," in *The Word of the Lord Shall Go Forth: Essays in Honor of David Noel Freedman in Celebration of His Sixtieth Birthday*, ed. C.L. Meyers, and M. O'Connor (Philadelphia: American Schools of Oriental Research, 1983), 185-88, argues that the use of second person in a woe-oracle is to show the vocative element and that woe oracle is not as "impersonal" as first thought.

[184] Both *BHS*, 1051, and BDB, 891, note that some versions have the finite verb קָצוֹתָ (Qal perfect 2ms of the verb קצץ) instead of קְצוֹת (Qal infinitive construct of קצה). Since both verbs have the same meaning of "cutting off" and the MT reading is just as good, I opt to retain the MT reading.

[185] The word for "rafter" (כָּפִים) is a *hapax legomenon*. Apparently this is a technical term used to describe the wood beam which is used to reinforce the brick walls in ancient Mesopotamia. See the discussion in Patterson, *Nahum*, 193.

work." The Chaldeans are infamous for their brutality—they kill and remove any nation that is in their way. The sin of the Chaldeans is so grave that even the building materials, the stone and the rafter, are crying foul. The use of inanimate objects to be the witness against human behavior is well attested in the Old Testament, e.g., Moses called on heaven and earth to witness against the Israelites in Deut 30:19; and in Josh 24:27, Joshua used a large stone as a witness for the covenant renewal ceremony in Shechem.[186] Here the imagery of the rattling of the house as the wind passes by (the crying of the stone and the echoing of the rafter) serves to testify against the unjust gains of the Chaldeans. This is an apt description for earlier in 1:11 the Chaldeans are described to be like wind sweeping through. It is noteworthy to see that Jeremiah pronounces a woe to condemn Jehoiakim for building himself luxury homes through extortion and oppression by using similar language (Jer 22:13-17). But in our strophe the pronouncement is definitely on the Chaldeans, for Jehoiakim can hardly fit the description of "cutting off many peoples." So the pronouncement here on the Chaldeans shows the universal principle of retribution: whoever practices oppression and extortion, whether a Judean king or a foreign power, would have to reap the consequence of his own action, which is bringing shame and sin to himself.

*Stanza 5 The third woe oracle (2:12-14)*
Stanza 5 seems to be a collection of quotations from other prophets (Mic 3:10; Jer 51:58; and Isa 11:9). But in the present context, it depicts the Chaldeans as a builder who engages in building towns and cities. This portrayal fits the historical description of the Chaldeans who are preoccupied with building projects.[187] The first strophe describes the "builder" (בֹּנֶה) and "founder" (כּוֹנֵן) who build city and town with bloodshed and injustice. In Mic 3:10, the prophet accuses the Judean leaders of building Zion with bloodshed (בְּדָמִים) and Jerusalem with injustice (בְּעַוְלָה). Here Habakkuk is either using the same stock language or paraphrasing Micah to accuse the Chaldeans of the same crime.

In the second strophe, Habakkuk uses a rhetorical question and prophesies the destruction of Babylon, "Is it not indeed[188] from Yahweh of hosts that the peoples toil only for fire[189] and nations grow weary only for nothing?"[190] In Jer

---

[186] It may be argued that heaven and earth, as well as stones may not be considered inanimate objects in Habakkuk's time. But to a monotheistic Israelite, these elements are only part of God's creation and are not given deity status.

[187] Patterson, *Nahum*, 194.

[188] The particle הִנֵּה, which directly follows the interrogative particle הֲלוֹא, is used to emphasize that indeed the statement that follows is from Yahweh of Hosts ( יהוה צְבָאוֹת). *BHS* suggests to read הֶנָּה "this," with LXX, Syriac, and Vulgate. But MT reading is more meaningful.

[189] BDB, 191, states that the phrase בְּדֵי־אֵשׁ "for fire" has the meaning of "only to satisfy the fire."

51 the prophet gives a detailed description of the destruction of Babylonian empire, and particularly the torching of the city of Babylon in Jer 51:58 (cf. Jer 50:32). Jeremiah's passage specifically mentions that Yahweh is the one who destroys Babylon (Jer 51:55), so if Habakkuk is quoting Jeremiah, in the present context, it is a reminder to Babylon that Yahweh will bring all its building projects, which are built on bloodshed and violence, to be destroyed by fire. Contrary to Roberts' comment that there is no judgment pronounced in this woe,[191] the statement that "peoples toil only for fire and nations grow weary only for nothing" gives an apt warning to all those who participate in building city and town in bloodshed and violence.

In contrast to the transient grandeur of Babylon, the glory of the Lord will one day fill the earth, "For the earth will be filled with the knowledge of the glory of Yahweh as the waters cover over the sea." Thus this last strophe of stanza 5 portrays an up-beat future and provides hope for those who are suffering under the brutal rule of the Chaldeans. This strophe has long been suspected as an editorial addition due to its similarity to Isa 11:9.[192] But one needs not consider it a later gloss, for it is not unusual for prophets to use well known sayings[193] and incorporate them into their preaching. Also, citing the other prophets gives authority to Habakkuk's logical argument concerning late retribution.

*Stanza 6 The fourth woe oracle (2:15-17)*
This stanza employs the imagery of drinking to portray the immorality of the Chaldeans, "Woe to the one who makes his neighbor drink, pouring out[194] your

---

[190] This part of the verse (2:13b) is almost identical to Jer 51:58b, "And the peoples toil for *nothing*, and the nations grow weary for *fire*." According to Seidel's law, the change of word order indicates quotation. However, Andersen, *Habakkuk*, 245, suggests that the affinity of Jeremiah and Habakkuk texts may mean that both of them are quoting a byword, instead of one quoting the other.

[191] Roberts, *Nahum*, 122-24, thinks that a glossator, who is influenced by Jer 51:58 and who does not understand the whole text of Habakkuk, glosses over the original saying of Habakkuk, which does not have a judgment. However, the final text is all that we have, and I only seek to understand the message of the text in its final form.

[192] *BHS*, 1052. See the discussion in Roberts, *Nahum*, 123-24.

[193] Anderson, *Habakkuk*, 245, thinks that this verse sounds like a slogan that could be put anywhere.

[194] There are two meanings for the word מְסַפֵּחַ: (1) it is a Piel participle from the root ספח which has the basic meaning of "join," "attach to." Hence some translate it as "mix" (e.g., NASB); (2) ספח has an Arabic cognate *safahha*, meaning "to pour out." See BDB, 705. (3) There is still a third choice, whereby some scholars prefer to emend this to מִסַּף "from the cup of," taking the final ח as a dittograph with the next word. This is first proposed by Wellhausen; one of the modern scholars who follow this view is Roberts. See his translation, *Nahum*, 113. But Andersen, *Habakkuk*, 248, suggests to reject this view because in each of the five woes, two participles are parallel to each other, and so מְסַפֵּחַ should be retained in order to parallel מַשְׁקֶה.

wrath[195] and even[196] make them drunk[197] so as to gaze upon their nakedness."[198] In the first strophe of this stanza, the Chaldeans are described as a host who gives drinks to his friend, with the intention of intoxicating the unsuspecting victim so as to exploit and shame him. The meaning of the phrase מְסַפֵּחַ חֲמָתְךָ has some ambiguity. But since "pouring out wrath" is a common usage in Old Testament,[199] and that it would make a good ironic contrast when the oppressor would be forced to drink from "the cup from the right hand of the Lord" in verse 16, I translate it as "pouring out your wrath." The purpose of Babylon pouring out drink to his neighbors is to get them drunk[200] so as to humiliate them. To gaze at others' nakedness is to humiliate and to shame them. In Gen 9:20-24, the word "nakedness" (עֶרְוַת) is used three times to describe Noah's condition when he gets drunk. And as a result of Ham's indecent act (or lack of action), it brings on a curse to Canaan. This incident shows the seriousness of the offense of gazing at another's nakedness. Andersen thinks that it is not just humiliation, "but something closer to sexual licentiousness seems to be in mind."[201]

The second strophe continues the imagery of drinking, but this time it is the Chaldeans who are forced to drink from the cup of wrath from God, "You are sated with dishonor rather than glory. Drink! Even you, and be counted uncir-

---

[195] The word חֲמָתְךָ also has various translations: (1) it is the noun חֵמָה "heat, rage," (which is derived from the verb יחם) with 2ms pronominal suffix, meaning "your wrath, anger." 1QpHab has חֲמָתוֹ "his wrath." See Brownlee, *Midrash*, 179; (2) Following the meaning of "heat," it also has a derived meaning of "venom, poison" such as that in Deut 32:24. See NASB version; (3) A third view is to take the meaning of the word from חֵמֶת "waterskin," and thus translate it as "wineskin." See Haak, *Habakkuk*, 69. See also translation in NIV; (4) C.F. Whitley, "A Note on Habakkuk 2:15," *Jewish Quarterly Review* 66 (1975/76): 143-7, proposes that חֵמָה is a cognate to Aramaic חמא and is also used to refer to wine. He cites several passages where this term is associated with wine (e.g., Hos 7:5; Jer 25:15). The most interesting one is from Isa 27:4, which he translates, "I have no wine," rather than the traditional "I have no wrath" which does not make much sense in that context.

[196] Although the word וְאַף is generally regarded as a conjunctive particle "and also, and even, and indeed," some see that it can also be interpreted as a parallel noun to the preceding noun חֲמָתְךָ "your wrath" and render it "your wrath and your anger." See Armerding, "Habakkuk," 519. But as Patterson, *Nahum*, 203, suggests, the fact that וְאַף is used as a conjunction in 2:5 makes this suggestion unlikely.

[197] שַׁכֵּר is the Piel infinitive absolute, which has the meaning of "make drunken," but here it is used as a finite verb, "you make drunk."

[198] The word מְעוֹרֵיהֶם "their nakedness" has a masculine plural pronominal suffix which indicates that the antecedent noun רֵעֵהוּ "his neighbor" is a collective singular noun or it may refer to the "nations, all of them" as in 2:5-6.

[199] Patterson, *Nahum*, 202.

[200] In Jer 51:7, Babylon is portrayed as the golden cup in the hand of the Lord, making all the earth drunken (מְשַׁכֶּרֶת כָּל־הָאָרֶץ).

[201] Andersen, *Habakkuk*, 249.

cumcised.[202] The cup of the right hand of the Lord will turn upon you, and emetic shame[203] will be upon your glory." This strophe gives a vivid description of the notorious Babylonian drinking party whereby participants often get drunk and expose themselves. This description also gives an ironic twist: the oppressor, who makes others drunk and gazes at their nakedness, is in turn getting drunk and being exposed as uncircumcised. And the cup they are drinking from is the one that comes from the Lord. "The cup," especially when it comes from the Lord, usually symbolizes divine judgment (e.g., Ps 75:9 [Eng 75:8]; Isa 51:17, 22; Jer 25:15; 51:7; Lam 4:21; Ezek 23:32-33).[204] The cup is often described as containing הַיַּיִן הַחֵמָה "wine of wrath" (Jer 25:15),[205] which passes around the nations (Jer 25:15; 49:12), and whoever drinks of it would רָעַל "stagger" (Isa 51:17-22; cf. Jer 25:15), יִתְהֹלָלוּ "go mad" (Jer 51:7), and עָרָה "be naked" (Lam 4:21). In this verse the cup is further described to be "from the right hand of the Lord," which symbolizes "power."[206] The last phrase וְקִיקָלוֹן עַל־כְּבוֹדֶךָ "and emetic shame will be upon your glory," together with קָלוֹן מִכָּבוֹד "dishonor rather than glory" from the beginning of verse 16, forms a strophic *inclusio*.[207]

The final strophe gives the reason for the divine judgment to turn upon the Chaldeans, "For the violence of Lebanon will overwhelm you and the devastation of beasts will terrify you;[208] because of human bloodshed and violence to

---

[202] The Qumran and Greek texts, as well as the Syriac and Vulgate read וְהֵעָרֵל "and be uncircumcised" as וְהֵרָעֵל "reel, shake, stagger." However, MT reading makes good sense, especially when it echoes with מְעוֹרֵיהֶם "their nakedness" in verse 15.

[203] The word קִיקָלוֹן is ambiguous. Some hold that it arises from progressive assimilation from the root קָלַל. See Patterson, *Nahum*, 203 n. 103. Others suggest that it is a compound word constructed "to intensify the concept of disgrace to be experienced by the Chaldeans." Robertson, *Nahum*, 204. But Andersen, *Habakkuk*, 250, is not satisfied with either suggestions and prefers to see קִי as a distinct word, from קיא or קא "vomit." Hence he translates verse 16bβ "Vomit shame over your glory," which would parallel verse 16aβ "Drink, you too, and stagger," emending וְהֵעָרֵל to וְהֵרָעֵל. Taking all these into consideration, I translate קִיקָלוֹן "emetic shame," to describe the shame that the Chaldeans will experience.

[204] There are only a few incidents where "cup" is associated with blessing or salvation, and they all occur in Psalms (e.g. Pss 16:5; 23:5; 116:13). See Patterson, *Nahum*, 204.

[205] The affinity of Hab 2:15-16 to Jer 25:15-29 may mean that the writer of the Habakkuk passage presupposes his audience to have read Jeremiah.

[206] Bailey, *Micah*, 343.

[207] For a discussion on strophe *inclusio*, see Watson, *Classical Hebrew Poetry*, 285.

[208] The verb יְחִיתַן is perplexing; according to BDB, 369, it is a Hiphil imperfect 3ms with 3fp pronominal suffix of the verb חָתַת "he/it will terrify them." But it raises the question, "who is the object of the verb?" It is also possible that the final ן is a paragogic ן. Most versions read, along with Greek (πτοήσει σε) and Syriac, יְחִתֶּךָ "he/it will terrify you." The subject of the verb is "devastation" (שֹׁד) of the beasts. The 2ms suffix from the previous line could be doing a double duty in the MT.

the land, to the city and all of its inhabitants." Throughout the ages, the mountains of Lebanon have been well-known for their forests which give abundant supply of wood for construction in the ancient world.[209] According to Babylonian royal annals, Nebuchadnezzar ordered his army to build a road for the transport of the cedars from Lebanon to Babylon for the construction of his palace and the temple of Marduk; and he did this in the name of freeing the land from its enemies.[210] This exploitation of Lebanon's natural resources is confirmed in Isaiah's taunt against Babylon (Isa 14:8), when the cypress trees and cedars of Lebanon are said to rejoice over the fall of Babylon for they are not able to cut them down anymore. Their wanton exploitation of the natural resources undoubtedly brings suffering to the wild animals there for the workers probably need to hunt for food.[211] Thus verse 17a gives a vivid description of the crime of Babylon that is done to the created world and to the animals.[212] The second half of verse 17, which is a refrain (cf. 2:8b), consists of nominal clauses coordinate to 2:17a. This final strophe does not seem to have an apparent link with the metaphor of drinking in this stanza. The fact that the theme in verse 17 seems to correspond well with the building projects in the third woe, along with the repetition of key words such as "cover" (כסה), "blood" (דם), and "town" (קריה), prompt some to propose that this verse is probably transposed from after verse 13.[213] However verse 17a, with the imagery of stripping other nation's natural resources to a point of "nakedness" seems to give a concrete description of the crime that is committed by the Chaldeans of "making the neighbor drunk so as to gaze at their nakedness" in 2:15.

*Stanza 7 The fifth woe oracle (2:18-20)*
The fifth woe begins with a rhetorical question instead of the usual word הוֹי "woe." This prompts some to transpose verse 18 after verse 19, thinking that it may be due to an erroneous textual transmission.[214] However, Andersen thinks that there is a logical move from "the manufacture of the idols (v. 18), prayer to the idols (v. 19a), the refutation of the idol (v. 19b), and the affirmation of Yahweh as the only real god (v 20)."[215] Bailey argues that the text, as it stands, is intended to give "a sense of urgency and conveying the prophet's indignation at the abomination of worshiping 'lies.'"[216] My opinion is that the arrangement

---

[209] A.F. Rainey and R.S. Notley, *The Sacred Bridge: Carta's Atlas of the Biblical World* (Jerusalem: Carta, 2006), 28. In 2 Kgs 19:23 Isaiah quotes the Assyrian king Sennacherib of his boast of cutting down the cedar forest of Lebanon.

[210] Walton, Matthews, and Chavalas, *Background Commentary*, 792.

[211] Ibid., 793.

[212] Some prefer to read בְּהֵמוֹת as the mythic beastly man *Humbaba* in the *Gilgamesh* epic. Private communication with Peckham; cf. also Andersen, *Habakkuk*, 251.

[213] See textual apparatus in *BHS*, 1052.

[214] For a discussion on various scholarly proposals, see Roberts, *Nahum*, 126.

[215] Andersen, *Habakkuk*, 257.

[216] Bailey, *Micah*, 346.

of the present text is to delimit and to form a chiastic structure of the whole "woe oracles" section from 2:6b to 2:19. 2:6b starts with the word הוֹי (A), followed by a rhetorical question at 2:7 "הֲלוֹא" (B), while 2:18 starts with a rhetorical question "מָה" (B'), then followed by a woe הוֹי (A') at 2:19, thus forming a chiastic structure of A B//B'A' to encompass the whole section.[217]

The indictment against the Chaldeans comes to a climax in the last woe oracle when the religious practice of the Chaldeans is under examination, "What profit is an idol? For the one who forms it has carved it[218]—a molten image[219] and a teacher[220] of falsehood. For he who forms his graven image trusts in it to make dumb worthless gods.[221]" The author begins his argument with a rhetorical question, and argues that an idol is only made by man and whoever trusts in it is doomed to be deceived. The use of literary devices to describe "idol" in this strophe is remarkable: the use of wordplay פְּסָלוֹ "he carved it" is a pun on פֶּסֶל "idol." This is to emphasize that the idol is only man-made. The root יצר "form, shape" appears three times in this verse to emphasize the foolishness and the futility of those who form and shape the idols to trust in their own creation. The use of אֱלִילִים "worthless gods" may have been a deliberate pun on אֱלֹהִים/אֵל in order to show the contrast between Yahweh and the pagan idols. Then the author employs a paronomasia[222] by using the word אִלְּמִים "dumb"[223] to describe the אֱלִילִים. This repetition of similar sound emphasizes the dumbness and worthlessness of the idols.

The second strophe resumes the pronouncement of "woe" to those who worship idols and molten images, "Woe to the one who says to the wood 'Awake!'[224] 'Arouse!' to a silent stone. He will teach?[225] Behold he is encased

---

[217] For a discussion on closure in Hebrew poetry, see Watson, *Classical Hebrew Poetry*, 62-65.

[218] The verb פְּסָלוֹ is Qal perfect 3ms with 3ms pronominal suffix.

[219] In this verse and in Jer 10:14 (same in 51:17), molten image (מַסֵּכָה) is said to be a deception, that is, the thing that deceives, disappoints, and betrays people. Note that both מַסֵּכָה and נֶסֶךְ "molten image" from Jer 10:14 are from the same root נסך. See BDB, 651. In Isa 42:17 the ones who put their trust on an idol (פֶּסֶל) and a molten image (מַסֵּכָה) are condemned.

[220] The word מוֹרֶה is the substantive use of a Hiphil participle ms of ירה, which means "the one who teaches, or teacher." In Isa 9:14, the prophet who teaches lies (מוֹרֶה־שָׁקֶר) is condemned.

[221] The word אֱלִילִים is the plural form of אֱלִיל which has the meaning of "insufficiency, worthlessness." אֱלִילִים usually refers to worthless gods and idols.

[222] Paronomasia is the use of two (or more) different words which sound nearly alike. See Watson, *Classical Hebrew Poetry*, 242-3.

[223] In the ancient near eastern world (e.g. Egypt and Mesopotamia), there was an "Opening of the Mouth" ceremony whereby life was symbolically imparted to the statue or image of the deity, and thus inaugurating or consecrating that statue. See Walton, Matthews, and Chavalas, *Background Commentary*, 629.

[224] The word הָקִיצָה is a Hiphil imperative of the verb קיץ "awake."

in gold and silver; and there is no breath inside him." Andersen speculates that there must have been something in Canaanite religion about a sleeping god, for Elijah told the prophets of Baal to wake him up "יָקַץ" (1 Kgs 18:27).[226] But in the Psalter (Pss 44:24; 59:5-6), the psalmist laments to God and implores him to "wake up" (הָקִיצָה) and "arouse" himself (עוּרָה). Thus it is not a comparison of the soberness of the deities that is in view, but rather, it is the ones being addressed that trouble the prophet. As Andersen aptly puts it, "the blasphemy lies in addressing sticks and stones with language properly used for Yahweh."[227] The mention of "wood" (עֵץ) and "stone" (אֶבֶן) echoes verse 11 where it is in reversed order. The prophet shows his incredulity that an idol is able to instruct for it is only an inanimate object which has no breath in it.

In contrast to the inanimate idols, the Lord dwells among his people in his holy temple. Also, if we take the mention of "his holy temple" as the temple in Jerusalem, rather than the heavenly abode,[228] then this may indicate that the date of the composition of this book, or at least this section, is before the destruction of the temple of Jerusalem by the Babylonians in 586 BCE. The interjection הַס[229] "hush! keep silence" is used here and also in Zeph 1:7 and Zech 2:17, where everyone is called to keep a reverent silence before the Lord and wait for the Lord's action.[230] This verse also serves as a fitting end to the woe oracle section and shows that God as the king and judge of the whole earth is in full control.

## Scene three

*Superscription (3:1)*
The superscription gives chapter 3 the title of "A prayer of Habakkuk the prophet; upon *Shigyonoth*." The title תְּפִלָּה "prayer"[231] is associated with sever-

---

[225] Andersen, *Habakkuk*, 253, notices a chiastic structure from 2:19aα to 2:19bα. Patterson, *Nahum*, 209, points out that the accents of the MT prevent the clause הוּא יוֹרֶה "he will teach" to be read with the previous clause. And though this clause can be taken as a statement, usually it is translated as a rhetorical question, "Will it instruct?" O'Neal, *Interpreting Habakkuk as Scripture*, 44, translates it as a statement but in a sarcastic way, "Surely, it will instruct!"

[226] Andersen, *Habakkuk*, 255.

[227] Ibid., 255.

[228] Andersen mentions that "it is likely that the Temple in Jerusalem, not its heavenly counterpart, is in mind." See his commentary, 256. The Greek version of 3:2 ἐν μέσῳ δύο ζῴων γνωσθήσῃ "Between the two living creatures, you will be known" seems to confirm that the Jerusalem Temple is in view.

[229] Wendland, "The Righteous," 600, notices the use of onomatopoeia for this word.

[230] Roberts, *Nahum*, 128, comments that this verse serves as a transition to the vision in chapter 3.

[231] Balentine, "Prayers for Justice in the Old Testament," 598, understands that "one of the principal functions of OT prayer is to address, clarify, and sometimes resolve theodicean issues."

al psalms (Pss 17; 86; 90; 102; 142), which are personal lament psalms. Several elements that are present in a typical lament psalm can be found in this chapter: petition (v. 2); a hymn of praise of God's theophany (vv. 3-15); and a confession of trust (vv. 16-19a). The presence of the musical term שִׁגְיֹנוֹת "Shigyonoth" further links it to the psalmic literature.[232] Although no one is certain about the etymology and the meaning of this term, some speculate that it may have derived from the root שגה "go astray, reel," and that it is a wild, passionate song with rapid changes of rhythm.[233] The presence of a separate superscription and musical term may indicate that scene three may have been used as a hymn in worship by the later generation.[234]

*Stanza 1 Habakkuk's petition (3:2)*
The first stanza in the third scene records Habakkuk's petition to Yahweh. This is a logical progression from 2:20 when the prophet calls on all the earth to be silent before the Lord. Then the prophet offers this petition on behalf of the people to the Lord. In the first strophe Habakkuk recalls God's past deeds in Israel's history, "O Yahweh I have heard of your report (שִׁמְעֲךָ);[235] I fear, O Yahweh, your work." It is typical for a lament psalm to include a review of God's acts in the past.[236] The recollection of the divine past deeds helps the lamenters to correlate their current situation with the past, as well as to know that their history relies on God's action alone.[237]

The three lines of the second strophe all begin with בְּ which gives this strophe a certain rhythm, "In the midst of the years revive it, in the midst of the years make it known. In turmoil,[238] remember compassion." In fact, the first

---

[232] Ps 7 also has the corresponding word שִׁגָּיוֹן "Shiggaion" in its title; see Armerding, "Habakkuk," 523. Reading the Book of Habakkuk canonically, Christopher R. Seitz suggests that the presence of the psalmic terms such as "Shigyonoth" and "For the director of music. On my stringed instrument" at the end of the prayer, is meant "to direct the reader to that 150-prayer book [the Psalter]." See his book, *Prophecy and Hermeneutics: Toward a New Introduction to the Prophets* (Grand Rapids: Baker, 2007), 215.

[233] BDB, 993. For a detailed discussion, see Patterson, *Nahum*, 227-28.

[234] Some scholars see this as evidence that this psalm is not original to the book of Habakkuk. But that is not necessarily the case. And even if it is not original, this book only concerns the final text and seeks to understand how this prayer fits in the larger context of the whole book of Habakkuk.

[235] Armerding, "Habakkuk," 523, suggests that the use of the word שִׁמְעֲךָ "your fame" indicates "a remoteness from the hearer's experience to the persons or events referred to."

[236] C. Westermann, *Psalms*, 39.

[237] Ibid., 40.

[238] The preposition בְּ "in" attached to רֹגֶז is considered to be a "reversed ballast preposition" to בְּקֶרֶב "in the midst of" in the previous two cola. See the discussion in Watson, *Classical Hebrew Poetry*, 345. Also בְּרֹגֶז is parallel to בְּקֶרֶב שָׁנִים.

two lines form a staircase parallelism (abc//abc').[239] The dubious phrase בְּקֶרֶב שָׁנִים "in the midst of years" has generated many interpretations and emendations.[240] This phrase is peculiar to this passage. But this does not make it an improbable reading, and the difficulties may be overstated. Contrary to Andersen's view that the "more abstract idea of a stretch of time is expressed by the feminine plural,"[241] the masculine plural form of the word שָׁנִים "years" occurs at least eleven times to express a period of time, and some of them are quite abstract (Eze 38:17; Zech 7:3; Job 15:20; 32:7; Eccl 11:8; 12:1; Dan 11:6, 8, 13; Neh 9:30; 2 Chr 18:2), whereas the feminine form only occurs seven times. Secondly, it is precisely during the years of suffering, "in the midst of the years," that the prophet would plead to the Lord to revive his deeds and to make them known.[242] Then by using the two highly emotionally charged words רֹגֶז[243] and רַחֵם[244] the prophet pleads with God to remember to be compassionate (רַחֵם) during the time of turmoil (רֹגֶז). Hence the force of this strophe is to plead to God to revive his deeds of salvation during the years of suffering that are going to come, so as to make his work known to the world. Habakkuk also urges Yahweh to remember his compassion during the time of disturbance.

---

[239] Watson, *Classical Hebrew Poetry*, 150-56.

[240] For a detailed discussion of the various interpretations in history, see Copeland, "The Midst of the Years," 91-105. LXX presumes a different vocalization of שָׁנִים in the first occurrence, and understands it as δύο "two" (from שְׁנַיִם). The Greek version also has a different translation on חַיֵּיהוּ, taking it to mean ζῴων "living creatures" (from חַיּוֹת). Thus the Greek rendition for the first clause is: ἐν μέσῳ δύο ζῴων γνωσθήσῃ "Between the two living creatures (cherubim), you will be known." However, as attractive as it is, the Greek rendition fails to have a consistent translation for the two identical phrases of בְּקֶרֶב שָׁנִים. The second one is translated as "when the years draw near," repointing בְּקֶרֶב to בִּקְרֹב, and taking שנים as "years."

[241] Andersen, *Habakkuk*, 278.

[242] Recently, Pinker, who observes the affinity of Hab 2:20-3:2 to Ps 138, proposes to emend שָׁנִים to שֹׁבִים, and translates verse 3 as "O Lord, I heard Your renown, I fear Your deed, among his captors make him survive, [when] among his captors announce, in anger mercy You will remember." See A. Pinker, "'Captors' for 'Years' in Habakkuk 3:2," *RB* 112 (Jan 2005): 20-26. His speculation, however, does not have any support from ancient manuscripts.

[243] The words רֹגֶז "agitation, excitement, raging," portrays the situation of disturbance or turmoil that is coming. Many translators prefer to see רֹגֶז as God's wrath, but as Andersen, *Habakkuk*, 282, argues it is best to read this word as it appears in v. 2 and v. 16 as the agitation experienced by a human rather than by God's wrath.

[244] רַחֵם "compassion" is derived from the noun רֶחֶם meaning "womb."

*Stanza 2 Theophany: the coming of Yahweh (3:3-5)*

Stanza 2 of the third scene describes the movement of God and his theophanic splendor; "God[245] came[246] from Teman[247] and the Holy One from Mount Paran.[248] Selah.[249] His splendor covered heavens and his praise filled the earth." This poem contains many archaic features, which prompts some scholars to think that Habakkuk is probably using one of the ancient Israelite theophanic poems.[250] Andersen points out that the use of the ancient divine names אֱלוֹהַ and קָדוֹשׁ "point to a stage before the widespread or at least dominant use of Yahweh."[251] The archaic features and motifs of the psalms are similar to other passages recalling Yahweh's great deeds in Israel's history, such as Deut 33:2-5; Judg 5:4-5; Ps 68:8-9 [Eng 7-8]. The marching of Yahweh from Teman and Paran, the regions south of Judah, alludes to Yahweh's leading of Israel through the wilderness. Yahweh's majesty (הוֹדוֹ),[252] is described as a storm cloud that covered[253] the heavens and his glory (תְהִלָּתוֹ),[254] is said to fill the earth. These two clauses in v 3b are arranged in a chiastic form, focusing on God's splendor and glory. Moreover, Watson observes that there is a "gender-matched synonymous parallelism" in this clause, for both "heaven" (שָׁמַיִם) and

---

[245] The word for "God" (אֱלוֹהַ) is an archaic name which is used in ancient poems such as Deut 32:15, 17, and Ps 18:32. This is one of the many archaic elements that are present in this poem.

[246] The verb form יָבוֹא "come" is a preterite form, the use of alternating preterite and perfect form of the verb is a feature of ancient Hebrew poetry. See Patterson, *Nahum*, 233-34.

[247] Teman generally refers to the kingdom of Edom, southeast of Judah. Yahweh's association with Teman is further confirmed by the inscriptions found in Kuntillet 'Ajrud which lies about forty miles south of Kadesh Barnea. One of the inscriptions reads, "I bless you by Yahweh of Teman and by his asherah." See J.M. Hadley, *The Cult of Asherah in Ancient Israel and Judah: Evidence for a Hebrew Goddess* (Cambridge: Cambridge University Press, 2000), 125.

[248] Mount Paran is the general region southwest of Judah in the Sinai Peninsula (cf. Deut 33:2).

[249] סֶלָה "Sela" is a term that associates with the psalms. The etymology of the term and its meaning is not certain. It is widely believed that it is probably a musical term that associates with worship, either as a "musical interlude" or "pause." For a detailed discussion, see P.C. Craigie, *Psalms 1-50*, 2d ed. WBC 19 (Nashville: Nelson, 2004), 76-77.

[250] Albright opined that this poem "was probably taken with little alteration from a very early Israelite poem on the theophany of Yahweh as exhibited in the south-east storm, the *zauba'h* of the Arabs." See Albright, "The Psalm of Habakkuk," 8.

[251] Andersen, *Habakkuk*, 289.

[252] Amerding, "Habakkuk," 525, says that הוֹד can be used to describe kingly authority (e.g. Num 27:20; 1 Chr 29:25; Ps45:3; Zech 6:13).

[253] Roberts, *Nahum*, 152, points out that the verb כָּסָה "cover" suggests that a storm cloud has covered the sky, leaving no area unaffected.

[254] תְהִלָּתוֹ also has the meaning of "splendor, glory," from another meaning of the root הלל "to shine."

"his splendor" (הוֹדוֹ) are masculine, meanwhile "his praise" (תְּהִלָּתוֹ) and "the earth" (הָאָרֶץ) are feminine.[255] This type of parallelism functions as *merismus*[256] to convey the idea of completeness.

The second strophe uses the brightest light to describe Yahweh's splendor, "And the brightness[257] was like the sunlight;[258] he had rays[259] [coming] from his hand,[260] and there was the hiding place[261] of his strength.[262]" The theophany of Yahweh is often associated with thick cloud, lightning, fire, and thunder (cf. Exod 19:16-19; Deut 5:20-23; 33:2; Ps 18:8-16[Eng 7-15]; Ezek 1:4-28). Here the brilliance of Yahweh's glory is portrayed as bright sunlight radiating from the thick cloud which is the hiding place of his presence. This seems to be in

---

[255] Watson, *Classical Hebrew Poetry*, 31.

[256] The term *merismus* means that the two opposite images are used to convey a totality. See ibid., 321-4.

[257] The word נֹגַהּ "brightness" usually refers to "the shining of celestial luminaries" (2 Sam 23:4; Isa 13:10; Joel 2:10; 4:15[Eng 3:15]) as well as the glory of God (Ezek 1:4, 28; 10:4; Ps 18:13, 29[Eng 18:12, 28]). See Patterson, *Nahum*, 233.

[258] אוֹר "light" can refer to the "sunlight" (Isa 18:4) or even the "sun" itself (Job 31:26). Professor Taylor comments that אוֹר in Job 31:26 likely refers to the sun. See J.G. Taylor, *Yahweh and the Sun: Biblical and Archaeological Evidence for Sun Worship in Ancient Israel*, JSOTSup 111 (Sheffield: JSOT, 1993), 217. Andersen, *Habakkuk*, 295, also prefers the "sun."

[259] The noun קַרְנַיִם "horns" is a dual form meaning "two horns." The meaning of "rays" can be found in Exod 34:29-30, when Moses came down from Mount Sinai, his face was said to be "sending out rays" (קָרַן) or "shining." The reason for the noun to be in dual form may indicate that rays were coming out from both of his hands. Moreover the Egyptian iconography usually displays rays from the sun in the form of a "two pronged" fork that was shaped like a hand. As Tsumura suggests, קַרְנַיִם may have a dual meaning of both "rays" and "horn" so as to function as a "Janus parallelism," corresponding to "brightness" (נֹגַהּ) in the previous colon with the meaning of "rays" and to "his strength" (עֻזֹּה) with the meaning of "horns" in the following colon. See D.T. Tsumura, "Janus Parallelism in Hab. III 4," *VT* 54 (2004): 124-6.

[260] The word "hand" (יָד), which is used as a metonymy, has the meaning of "power" which anticipates the word "strength" in the next line.

[261] The word חֶבְיוֹן "hiding-place" is a *hapax legomenon*. This prompts some scholars to emend the text unnecessarily. An example of emendation is Hiebert's emendation and rearrangement of consonants to yield ישמח ביום עזה "He rejoiced in the day of his strength." See Hiebert, *God of My Victory*, 4-5. But the meaning of the text is clear enough, as Keil said, "In the sun-like splendour, with rays emanating from it— is the hiding place of His omnipotence, i.e., the place where His omnipotence hides itself; in actual fact, the splendour forms the covering of the Almighty God at His coming, the manifestation of the essentially invisible God." See Keil, *Twelve Minor Prophets*, 100.

[262] According to Albright, the spelling of the pronominal suffix of the third person masculine singular with ה on the noun עֻזֹּה "his strength" reflects an orthography of the early sixth century BCE. See his essay, "The Psalm of Habakkuk," 10.

agreement with the wilderness narration where the cloud covering the Tabernacle appears as fire by night (Num 9:15-23).

Strophe 3 describes Yahweh's entourage, "Before him went pestilence, and plague came forth at his feet." The word for "pestilence" (דֶּבֶר) is also the name of a nocturnal demon "Deber" (Ps 91:6), which is the personification of illnesses as demon.[263] The word for "plague, or flame" (רֶשֶׁף) is also the name of a popular West-Semitic god "Resheph," who was venerated in Syria, Palestine and Egypt.[264] Resheph is identified with Nergal and attested as a plague-god in the Ugaritic literature. Roberts thinks that the Hebrew use of the term for "flame" may derive from this god's association with fever,[265] although the etymology of the name is still uncertain.[266] The presence of "Deber" and "Resheph" in the entourage of Yahweh follows the ancient Near Eastern tradition, which portrays the coming of the major deity accompanied by minor deities.[267]

*Stanza 3 The arrival of Yahweh (3:6-7)*
This new stanza describes the arrival of God. In the first strophe of this stanza, God is portrayed as an architect who stood and measured the earth, but the purpose of measuring is for destruction rather than construction,[268] "He stood and he measured[269] the earth, he looked and he startled[270] nations." Elsewhere in Isa 65:7, Yahweh says that he is going to "measure" (מָדַד) the Israelites' sinful works so as to mete out their well-deserved judgment into their bosom. However, some think that the root is מוד, "set into motion, shake, convulse."[271] The first meaning seems to have divine judgment in mind, whereas the second meaning emphasizes the effects of divine action.[272] The first two cola of this strophe parallel each other: they both begin with a perfect conjugation of the verb, followed by a preterite conjugation; and "land" (אֶרֶץ) parallels with "na-

---

[263] G. Del Olmo Lete, "Deber," in *Dictionary of Deities and Demons in the Bible*, ed. K. Van der Toorn, B. Becking, P.W. Van der Horst (New York: Brill, 1995), 231-32.

[264] P. Xella, "Resheph," in *Dictionary of Deities and Demons in the Bible*, ed. K. Van der Toorn, B. Becking, P.W. Van der Horst (New York: Brill, 1995), 701-703.

[265] Roberts, *Nahum*, 135.

[266] Xella, "Resheph," 701.

[267] For a detailed discussion of the attendants accompanying the deity, see Andersen, *Habakkuk*, 300-306.

[268] "Measuring" can have both constructive and destructive purposes; the former can be found in Isa 40:12 and the latter in Isa 65:7.

[269] The verb וַיְמֹדֶד is a Polel stem of the verb מדד "measure." See BDB, 551. Andersen, *Habakkuk*, 307, speculates that the choice of this verb may be due to the striking sound effect achieved by the repetition of the consonants מד in the first two verbs (עָמַד וַיְמֹדֶד).

[270] The verb וַיַּתֵּר is a Hiphil of the root נתר "startled, spring due to fear" (cf. Job 37:1).

[271] W.L. Holladay, *A Concise Hebrew and Aramaic Lexicon of the Old Testament* (Grand Rapids, Eerdmans, 1988), 185.

[272] Armerding, "Habakkuk," 526.

tions" (גּוֹיִם). As a result of Yahweh's action, standing and measuring the earth, the nations are startled and the mountains are thrown into convulsion. The next two cola of this strophe again form another synonymous parallelism, "and ancient mountains were shattered, eternal hills were prostrate." The verbs used are both geminate verbs, i.e., וַיִּתְפֹּצְצוּ "be shattered" (from פצץ) and שַׁחוּ "prostrate" (from שׁחח). Then the term "ancient mountains" (הַרְרֵי־עַד) parallels with "eternal hills" (גִּבְעוֹת עוֹלָם). Hence the two sets of synonymous parallelisms highlight divine arrival (the first two cola) and cosmic reaction (the next two cola). The last colon of this strophe is somewhat ambiguous, "The ancient pathways before him." There is a debate on whether the word הֲלִיכוֹת "pathways" indicates paved tracks on earth or cosmic "orbits."[273] The fact that this verse mentions "earth," "nations," "mountains," and "hills," makes it more likely that geographic pathways are in view. Since this word also has the meaning of "goings" or the "marching" of Yahweh (cf. Ps 68:25 [Eng 68:24]), it is very probable that the prophet is talking about the ancient routes that the Lord marched before his people in the wilderness (cf. Ps 68:8 [Eng 68:7]). If this reading is accepted then this colon serves as a link to the previous stanza.

In the last strophe of this stanza, Habakkuk witnesses seismic activity in the Cushan and Midian areas; "I saw the tents of Cushan under distress,[274] the curtains of the land of Midian quivered." Although the identity of Cushan is uncertain,[275] the mention of "the tents of Cushan" indicates that they may be nomads. Most scholars believe that Cushan could either be an alternative name for Midianites, or a subgroup of them.[276] The Midianites are believed to be the descendants of Abraham and Keturah, who live in the southern portions of the Transjordan region. The mention of "the curtains" (יְרִיעוֹת) accords well with their semi-nomadic living. The verb for "quivered" (יִרְגְּזוּן) has the same root as "wrath" (בְּרֹגֶז) in verse 2. The repetition of this root, along with the mention of the two places "Cushan" and "Midian," which parallels with "Teman" and "Paran" in verse 3, form an *inclusio* for this section.

*Stanza 4 Yahweh as warrior (3:8-9)*
Stanza 4 begins a new section that portrays Yahweh as a warrior. The rhetorical question that begins this stanza is directed to the Lord, "Did Yahweh rage

---

[273] Albright, who based his opinion on Akkadian and Ugaritic usage, understood it to be "orbits of the stars;" see his article, "The Psalm of Habakkuk," 14 note t.

[274] Albright, "The Psalm of Habakkuk," 11, attached the first two words of this verse (תַּחַת אָוֶן) to the last word of verse 6, and emended the word to be לְתִתְאָן "were shattered," taking the preposition to be emphatic, and the verb to be a Niphal Imperfect of a conjectured root חתא. But this emendation is not necessary. אָוֶן has the meaning of "trouble, sorrow." Hence I translate, with others, "under distress," which parallels with יִרְגְּזוּן "quivered."

[275] Peckham thinks that כּוּשׁ may be Nubia or Mesopotamia (cf. Judges 3:8), and the last part of the word –an may mean "one of Cush." Private communication with him.

[276] For a more detailed discussion, see D.W. Baker, "Cushan," *ABD*, 1:1219-20.

against the rivers[277]? Or was your anger against the rivers?[278] Or your fury against the sea when you mounted[279] your horses, your chariots of salvation?" This strophe refers to the exodus event by mentioning God's wrath against the literary pair "rivers" and "sea,"[280] and recalls Exod 15:1-21 by words such as "horses," "chariots," "salvation." The word יְשׁוּעָה "salvation" is sometimes rendered "victory" when it is used in a military context, despite Keil's strong objection.[281] Keil commented that by portraying God's chariots as "chariots of salvation," the prophet points at the outset that God's riding was for the salvation or deliverance of his people.[282] But even if it is translated "victory," it still fits the context of portraying God as a victorious warrior, who comes to deliver his people.

While the first strophe of stanza 4 describes Yahweh's action against the rivers and the sea, the second strophe focuses on his weapon and his readiness to engage in warfare against his enemy, "You exposed the nakedness of your bow; arrows fulfilling your word. Selah. You cleaved the rivers of the earth." This strophe is notoriously difficult to translate, not only are the meanings of certain words ambiguous, the sentence structures are peculiar because all the construction chains are broken: literally the strophe reads, "[the] nakedness—you exposed—your bow, fulfilling—arrows—[your] word. Selah. Rivers—you cleaved—earth." The ambiguity of the first colon is due to the uncertainty of the meanings of the first two words. LXX understands עֶרְיָה "nakedness" to be an infinitive absolute with a finite verb (עָרֹה תֵעֹרֶה),[283] and thus renders it ἐντείνων ἐντενεῖς "Surely you bend your bow." The verb תֵעוֹר can be taken as Niphal imperfect 3fs or 2ms of the root עוּר which has two meanings: "to rouse oneself, awake" or "to be exposed, bare." But some scholars, following LXX's

---

[277] The masculine plural form of the word "rivers" (נְהָרִים) is rare; more frequently used is the feminine form נְהָרוֹת. The usage of this rare form may allude to the Isaiah passage, where Cush is mentioned and described as "a people feared (נוֹרָא) far and wide, an aggressive nation of strange speech, whose land is divided by rivers (נְהָרִים)" (Isa 18:2, 7).

[278] *BHS* textual apparatus, 1053, suggests to delete אִם בַּנְּהָרִים in the second colon. But that is unnecessary, for the three-fold questions intensify and emphasize divine anger. Moreover, as Watson, *Classical Hebrew Poetry*, 183, points out that in Hebrew poetry, it is common to use a tricolon to mark an opening of a stanza.

[279] The verb רָכַב indicates mounting on a chariot rather than riding on a horse. See Keil, *Twelve Minor Prophets*, 103.

[280] Sometimes "sea" and "rivers" are interchangeable. Some scholars see the two words recalling a mythic tradition of Yahweh, like Baal in the Ugaritic texts opposing Yam, the "sea god." See Andersen, *Habakkuk*, 317; Roberts, *Nahum*, 155. See also Hiebert, *God of My Victory*, 98-99, though he does not think that the waters are Yahweh's enemy. Cf. U. Cassuto, "Chapter III of Habakkuk and the Ras Shamra Texts" in *Biblical and Oriental Studies*, vol. 2 (Jerusalem: The Magnes Press, 1975), 11.

[281] Keil, *Twelve Minor Prophets*, 103-104.

[282] Ibid., 104.

[283] *BHS*, 1053.

lead, think that it is from the root עָרָה "be naked, bare." My translation reflects the understanding that Yahweh is the subject who exposed his weapon. Despite its ambiguity, the sense is that Yahweh is getting his weapon ready for attack.[284] The second colon is even more difficult to decipher and there is no consensus on its meaning.[285] Margulis calls it "patently impossible."[286] Bruce thought that it "requires some violent handling to make it yield sense in the context; most probably it originated as a marginal rubric relating to this psalm."[287] The word שְׁבֻעוֹת, according to MT pointing, means "oaths, curse."[288] The word מַטּוֹת is the plural form of מַטֶּה which has several meanings "staff, rod, branch, arrow, tribe." The word אֹמֶר is a noun, meaning "utterance, word, promise, decree."[289] Day proposes to render this verse, "Utterly laid bare are your bow and seven arrows with a word," with the sense that "simply by the divine word of command Yahweh's bow and seven arrows are brought forth from their respective bow case and quiver."[290] He further argues that this imagery echoes Baal's seven thunders and lightning in the Ugaritic texts.[291] Tsumura argues from Ugaritic and Akkadian literature that מַטּוֹת should not be translated as "arrows" but rather "mace, rods, or sticks," and the plural noun can be explained as a "plural of intensity."[292] However a bow usually is accompanied by arrows as a weapon. My translation shows that Yahweh is getting his weapons ready, the bow and arrows, which are going to fulfill his word.[293] In the third colon, the verb תְּבַקַּע is a Piel imperfect or preterite 3fs or 2ms of the root בקע "to cleave, break open." This creates the problem of identifying the

---

[284] Tsumura, whose grammatical discussion is extensive, comes up with the translation, "Your bow is uncovered (the nakedness);" see his article, "Niphal with Internal Object in Habakkuk 3:9a," *Journal of Semitic Studies* 31 (1986): 11-6.

[285] Andersen lists a dozen different translations, and one can easily add more to the list. See Andersen, *Habakkuk*, 321.

[286] Margulis, "The Psalm of Habakkuk," 420.

[287] Bruce, "Habakkuk," 886-7, appealed to Thackeray's article and suggested that it was a lectionary note that points to the pentateuchal readings for the occasion according to the triennial lectionary. But Andersen, *Habakkuk*, 325, dismisses it as "a case of explaining the obscure by the even more obscure."

[288] Many scholars, however, take it to mean "heptad, sevenfold," or "seven," by emending it to שִׁבְעָה.

[289] Some scholars follow Dahood's suggestion and take it to mean "see." See M.P. O'Connor, *Hebrew Verse Structure* (Winona Lake: Eisenbrauns, 1980), 236. Andersen, *Habakkuk*, 323, expresses hesitation with this suggestion, but he translates this colon, "Seven clubs thou didst bring to view."

[290] Day, "Echoes," 146-47.

[291] Ibid., 147-51.

[292] D.T. Tsumura, "The 'Word Pair' *qšt and *mt! in Habakkuk 3:9 in the Light of Ugaritic and Akkadian," in *Go to the Land I Will Show You: Studies in Honor of Dwight W. Young*, ed. J. Coleson and V. Matthews (Winona Lake: Eisenbrauns, 1996), 353-61.

[293] If this refers to the exodus event, then the word could be the divine promise to Abraham in Gen 15:13-18.

subject and the object of the verb. Andersen credits Cassuto for recognizing Ps 74:15[294] to provide the key to this colon, and argues that rivers is the object of the verb תְּבַקַּע.[295] Since the whole stanza is directed towards Yahweh and the 2ms pronominal suffix in this strophe confirms it, it is likely that Yahweh is the subject. Moreover, in the previous strophe it is asked whether Yahweh's anger is burning against the rivers; then it is only logical that his weapons are launching against them. The *Maqqeph* before the word אֶרֶץ may be a broken construct chain to link with נְהָרוֹת. Thus my translation of this colon "you cleaved the rivers of the earth," completes the picture of Yahweh's attack on the rivers, which is likely to be a reference to the exodus experience of Yahweh's splitting up the water.

In sum, this stanza recalls the exodus event and portrays Yahweh as a warrior mounting his chariot and aiming his arrow at the sea to cleave it open so as to deliver his people and to fulfill his promise to Abraham.

*Stanza 5 Cosmic reaction (3:10-11)*

This stanza focuses on the reaction of the natural elements to the theophany. The first strophe describes the phenomenon on earth, "Mountains saw you and writhed; a downpour of waters passed by. The deep give its voice; it raised its hand on high." Earlier in verse 6, the mountains are said to be "shattered," hills are "collapsed or prostrated;" here they are described as "writhing" (יָחִילוּ).[296] The "writhing" of the mountain may be due to the mudslide after the torrential downpour of the rain. The "downpour" (זֶרֶם) of waters is also associated with theophany. Ps 77:18 [Eng 77:17] has a similar description, "The clouds pour out waters" (זֹרְמוּ מַיִם עָבוֹת).[297] "The deep" (תְהוֹם) seems to be the place where the subterranean waters are held. It is used as a divine means of annihilating the earth in the flood narrative where "all the fountains of the great deep burst open, and the floodgates of the sky were opened" (Gen 7:11). Here it gives a vivid description of the roaring of the bursting out of the subterranean water, lifting up (נָשָׂא) its wave (metaphorically "its hand") high. This may refer to the returning of the water and the drowning of the Egyptians as described in Exod 15:5: "The deeps covered them" (תְּהֹמֹת יְכַסְיֻמוּ).

---

[294] Cassuto, *Biblical and Oriental Studies*, 12, explained that "rivers" should be the direct object of the verb "cleaved" according to Ps 74:15, which says, "You cleaved (בָקַעְתָּ) spring and torrent, you dried up ever-flowing rivers (נְהָרוֹת)."

[295] Andersen, *Habakkuk*, 325.

[296] In Ps 77:17 [Eng 77:16], the same verb is used to describe the reaction of the waters, "when the waters saw you (רָאוּךָ), they writhed (יָחִילוּ)." And in Ps 114:4, the mountains are portrayed as "skipping" (רָקְדוּ) like rams, the hills like lambs.

[297] Hiebert, *God of My Victory*, 30, proposes to emend the present text to read as Ps 77:18, which is unnecessary.

The second strophe continues with the reaction of the celestial bodies, "Sun, moon[298] stopped[299] in their high abode[300] at the light of your arrows as they flew,[301] at the brightness[302] of the lightning of your spear."[303] This strophe portrays God's power as manifested in a severe thunderstorm when the dark cloud covers the sun and moon and causes them to lose their shine and to hide themselves in their lofty place (at their zenith), while the lightning strikes like arrows and spears all around. The mention of "sun and moon stopped in their high abode," may also allude to the incident recorded in Josh 10:12-13, where "the sun (הַשֶּׁמֶשׁ) stood still (וַיִּדֹּם), and the moon (וְיָרֵחַ) stopped (עָמָד)."[304]

*Stanza 6 Purpose of divine coming (3:12-13)*
In stanza 4 God's anger is against the rivers and sea; here in this stanza God's "indignation" (זַעַם) is against the nations: "In indignation you strode[305] the earth, in anger you trampled[306] nations." When the divine indignation is directed against the nations, particularly those who have inflicted suffering on Israel, it means salvation for his people (cf. Isa 10:24-25; 26:20-21; 30:27-28;

---

[298] The presence of word pair יָרֵחַ // שֶׁמֶשׁ without the conjunction "and" is a common technique known as *parataxis*, which, according to Watson, *Classical Biblical Poetry*, 81, is "one of the strongest indications that ancient Hebrew poetry was composed orally."

[299] The verb "stood" (עָמַד) is Qal 3ms, rather than the expected plural form; this prompts some scholars to emend the text. However it is not without precedent that the verb agrees in gender and number with the subject immediately preceding it, when more than one subject is present (e.g. Isa 9:4). In our case, יָרֵחַ "moon" is a masculine noun which precedes the verb, while שֶׁמֶשׁ "sun" is a feminine noun. See GKC, §146e.

[300] The ending of זְבֻלָה "high abode, zenith" can be regarded as the feminine ending, which is in agreement with שֶׁמֶשׁ, a feminine noun. See Patterson, *Nahum*, 245. BHS recommends to repoint it to זְבֻלֹה so as to agree with יָרֵחַ, but that is not necessary. Another explanation suggested by Gesenius: the ending can also be regarded as a directional ending, i.e., "into the high abode." See GKC, §90d.

[301] There is a debate on whether the sun and the moon are the subjects of the verb יְהַלֵּכוּ "go." But the accents of the MT indicate that the subject should be חִצֶּיךָ "your arrows."

[302] נֹגַהּ "brightness" can be used to describe the brightness of a theophany (e.g., 2 Sam 22:13).

[303] Albright emended this clause to read, "The exalted one, Sun, raised his arms, Moon stood <on> his lordly dais." Albright, "The Psalm of Habakkuk," 12.

[304] Patterson, *Nahum*, 244, points out that if this refers to Joshua's passage, then "the Exodus epic must have contained several songs of the conquest period." Others are skeptical that this refers to Joshua's passage at all, since they regard Joshua's passage as late.

[305] In Judg 5:4 and Ps 68:8, God's marching (צָעַד) from the wilderness is celebrated.

[306] The word דּוּשׁ "tread, thresh" is used to describe God's judgment against Israel's enemy in Isa 25:10.

Joel 4:1-21 [Eng 3:1-21]; Zeph 2:8-10). Thus this verse describes God as an enraged warrior marching out to fight against his enemies and to win his battle.

In the second strophe, the purpose of Yahweh's coming is explicitly stated, "You came forth[307] for the salvation of your people, for the salvation of your anointed.[308]" The first two cola are linked together by the repetition of the word לְיֵשַׁע "for the salvation," which emphasizes the divine purpose of coming to deliver his people and his anointed. The mention of "salvation" also reminds us of the prophet's initial complaint at 1:2b that Yahweh does not save. Thus this serves as an answer to his lament on the inactivity of Yahweh. The most common use of the noun מָשִׁיחַ "anointed one" is the king of the Davidic dynasty. This phrase "for the salvation of your anointed" then serves as a transition from the exodus imagery to the contemporary situation of the prophet. The wordplay between מְשִׁיחֶךָ and מָחַצְתָּ makes a smooth transition to describe the vivid details of the divine warfare in the third colon: "You shattered the head from the house[309] of the wicked, laying bare[310] from foundation to neck. Selah." The ambiguity of this colon lies in the identification of the "head" (רֹאשׁ).[311] The mention of the "house of the wicked (רָשָׁע)" seems to indicate that the king of the Chaldeans, Nebuchadnezzar, is the most likely candidate, since the Chaldeans are referred to as the "wicked" earlier in 1:12-13. Another uncertainty is the vagueness of the meaning of the imagery. If the "house" imagery is maintained here, and יְסוֹד is taken to mean "foundation," then עָרוֹת would mean "to demolish it and tear out its foundation." However the last word of the strophe צַוָּאר "neck", along with the word רֹאשׁ "head," seem to indicate that a "person" is in view. Thus the prophet uses both the imagery of the destruction of a house

---

[307] The verb יָצָא "go, come forth" can be used to describe an army marching out to the battlefield (e.g., 1 Sam 8:20; 17:20; 2 Sam 11:1).

[308] Although מָשִׁיחַ "anointed one" sometimes refers to the high priest (e.g. Lev 4:3) or individuals chosen by God to be leaders (e.g., 1 Kgs 19:16; Isa 45:1), in the present passage the Davidic king best fits the context.

[309] The preposition in מִבֵּית appears to be intrusive. See Bruce, "Habakkuk," 890. This prompts some scholars to emend this word. Albright, "The Psalm of Habakkuk," 11-13, suggested emending this to מָוֶת "Death," and thus rendered this colon, "Thou didst smite the head of wicked Death." This does not seem to be necessary or desirable. Ferris J. Stephens' suggestion of emending this term to "Behemoth" (בְּהֵמוֹת) does not fare any better. See F.J. Stephens, "The Babylonian Dragon Myth in Habakkuk 3," *JBL* 43 (1924): 290-93. Hiebert appeals to Ugaritic cognate "*bamtu*" and emends this word to בָּמַת, the fs construct form of בָּמָה with the unusual meaning of "back" rather than "height." See Hiebert, *God of My Victory*, 8-9, and his discussion, 36-40. But the "house" imagery continues in the next colon with the use of the word יְסוֹד "foundation." Thus it is better to retain the MT reading. JPS translates it as: "You will smash the roof of the villain's house."

[310] "To be naked" usually denotes a state of vulnerability, or emptiness.

[311] Patterson gives a succinct summary of various proposals, ranging from a mythological figure to the Chaldeans. See his commentary, 248. For the rare occurrences of the Dages in ר, see GKC, §22s.

and a person to portray the utter demolition of the Babylonian empire—both its king (the head) and his kingdom (the house).

*Stanza 7 Divine warfare (3:14-15)*

This new stanza continues the imagery of the divine warfare. The first strophe (v. 14) is so difficult that some scholars, such as Albright and Hiebert, consider it as corrupt and simply ignore most parts of it.[312] The first problem appears to be the division of the first colon, "You pierced with his own arrows (בְּמַטָּיו) the head (רֹאשׁ) of his warriors (פְּרָזָיו)." Hiebert stops at רֹאשׁ rather than including פְּרָזָיו, because he thinks that "the addition of another word would overload the line."[313] But his conjecture lacks support from the manuscripts, and the division of the MT still makes sense. Another problem that puzzles most scholars is the 3ms pronominal suffix of the word בְּמַטָּיו, as well as the meaning of the word. *BHS*, along with many scholars, suggests to change it to 2ms suffix instead, i.e., בְּמַטֶּיךָ "your arrows/maces/clubs". But some follow the MT reading and understand it to mean that the "troops will slay one another in consequence of the confusion,"[314] similar to what is described in 1 Sam 14:20 and 2 Chr 20:23, 24. It is quite possible that such "friendly fire" may happen, and that may have been the irony that the poet wanted to portray.[315] Hence the first colon of this strophe shows that Yahweh uses the enemies' own weapons to smash their head. The next two cola also invite many emendations by the scholars, "They had stormed to scatter me. Their exultation[316] resembled devouring[317] the helpless in secret." Some scholars, such as Bruce, following the lead of Driver, propose to repoint the verb יִסְעֲרוּ "they storm along" to a Pual יְסֹעֲרוּ "they were blown away," and emend כְּמוֹ "as" to כְּמֹץ "like chaff," appealing to the example of Hosea 13:3.[318] But this makes too many unnecessary changes. Others, such as Patterson, see that the problem lies with the word לַהֲפִיצֵנִי, and propose to divide it into two words: פוּץ "to scatter" and צָנִיעַ[319] "humble,"[320] thus ren-

---

[312] Andersen laments that "this verse is largely unintelligible, and the second part is best left untranslated." Andersen, *Habakkuk*, 338.

[313] Hiebert, *God of My Victory*, 44.

[314] Keil, *Twelve Minor Prophets*, 111.

[315] A. Pinker, "On the Meaning of מטיו in Habakkuk 3,14a," *Biblica* 86 (2005): 376-86, relying on the drawing that depicts the typical hairstyle of the Assyrian/Babylonian warriors, proposes to emend the word במטיו into במטוי (construct state) "into the spun," which he refers to the locks and braids at the back of the head of the warriors, and depicts the Lord smashing the heads of the fleeing army. His suggestion is interesting, but the root טוה "to spin" is not attested in the Hebrew Bible.

[316] The noun עֲלִיצָתָם "their exultation" is a *hapax legomenon* from the verb עָלַץ "rejoice, exult." This word also denotes "gloating and boasting."

[317] לֶאֱכֹל has the meaning of "to devour, consume."

[318] Bruce, "Habakkuk," 891.

[319] *BHS* suggests עָנִי "the poor," which seems to be less intrusive than Patterson's suggestion.

[320] See Patterson's discussion in his commentary, 254.

dering it "to scatter the humble." I prefer to follow the MT reading, and understand the 1cs suffix to be the prophet's personal identification with his people.[321] Robertson also argues that the prophet has played an important role in this poem, and so it is likely that he is referring to himself.[322] Peckham suggests that this may have been the "Messiah" (מָשִׁיחַ) who is talking here. But other than in 3:13aβ, there is no mention of him in the book, and it is hard to establish that this is his speech here. Hence the second colon depicts the enemies storming to invade Judah and causing the people to scatter and run for their lives. The third colon portrays the exuberance of the enemies when they find their victims in their hiding place.[323] The insertion of the description of the enemies' arrogance and fierceness here serves to justify the divine anger against them.

In the last strophe of stanza 7, the portrayal of God riding on horses and treading upon the sea echoes verse 8, and forms an *inclusio* for this section that depicts God as a warrior, "You trod on the sea with your horses, the foaming of many waters." The word חֹמֶר "heap" is actually from the verb חָמַר "to foam up" (cf. Ps 46:4 [Eng 46:3]), or the surging of the waters. It may even have the connotation of "heaping up" water, which may allude to Exod 15:8 where water is said to have "piled up" and stood like a "heap."[324]

*Stanza 8 Habakkuk's reaction: lament (3:16-17)*
The last section of this chapter records Habakkuk's reaction to the theophany and his resolution. I divide this into two stanzas; the first one (stanza 8) describes his condition and the second one (stanza 9) his trust in the Lord.

Habakkuk gives a vivid description of his physical reaction to the theophany, "I heard and my belly churned;[325] at the sound my lips quivered.[326] Rottenness entered into my bones,[327] and underneath me I trembled, that[328] I must wait[329]

---

[321] So Pinker, "On the Meaning," 384.

[322] Robertson, *Nahum*, 241.

[323] Pinker, "On the Meaning," 385.

[324] So Andersen, *Habakkuk*, 339.

[325] The verb רָגַז means "be agitated, quiver, be excited, perturbed."

[326] The verb צָלַל "tingle, quiver" usually refers to the tingle of ears due to dreadful news (cf. 1 Sam 3:11; 2 Kgs 21:12; Jer 19:3).

[327] The phrase "rottenness of bones" is used to describe the internal decaying power (cf. Prov 12:4; 14:30).

[328] Many scholars, agreeing with *BHS*, argue that the word אֲשֶׁר should be emended to אֲשֻׁרַי "my steps" and be put together with אֶרְגָּז "I trembled," for the relative pronoun is out of place and the poem is off-balance. See Andersen, *Habakkuk*, 344-45. However the MT still makes sense for אֲשֶׁר can be used as a conjunction "that" (see BDB, 83), and is to be read with the next colon. I follow the accent in the MT. So Keil, *Twelve Minor Prophets*, 113.

[329] The verb נוּחַ usually means "rest," but here it has the peculiar meaning of "to wait quietly." See BDB, 628. This peculiarity prompts BHS, 1054, to suggest to emend it to אֲחַכֶּה "I will wait," and some scholars, such as Hiebert, propose אָאֱנַח "I groaned." See his emendation and translation in his book, *God of My Victory*, 8-9,

for the day of distress[330] when he who will attack us will come up[331] against the people." In the opening strophe of the last section of the book, Habakkuk again refers to what he has heard (cf. 3:2). He uses the verb רָגַז[332] twice to describe his great anguish and to form an *inclusio* for the first part of this strophe so as to highlight his emotive reaction to the theophany. Habakkuk's terror is described in the most vivid terms: his belly is agitated and his lips quiver. The great fear and anguish make him feel like his life is ebbing away and his feet lose strength and he nearly collapses. Despite his fear, he must wait for the coming of the "day of distress." There is a debate on whether the "distress" is upon Israel or the Chaldeans. The confusion lies on the ambiguity and the relationship of the three words in the last colon. I follow Keil to see that לַעֲלוֹת is co-ordinate to יוֹם צָרָה and that יְגוּדֶנּוּ "he will attack us" is the subject of "to come up" (לַעֲלוֹת).[333] The next problem is the identification of the "people" (לְעָם). If we take it to mean "the Judean," with the word יְגוּדֶנּוּ as the subject, then the last two cola of this strophe can be translated, "that I must wait for the day of distress, when he who will attack us will come up against the people (the Judean)." The word order in the Hebrew text is to emphasize the "coming up of the enemy." That may also explain the emotional and involuntary physical response of the prophet in the first part of this verse. His great fear is not just due to the awe of theophany, but also the imminent coming of the Babylonian invasion. The next strophe confirms this observation.

While the first strophe of this stanza describes Habakkuk's reaction when he hears the coming of the calamity, the second strophe further describes the situation in the day of distress. The first part of this strophe deals with the agricultural produce from the ground, "Though the fig tree does not blossom, and there is no produce on the vines; the yield of olive fails, and fields do not yield food."[334] The list of produce, i.e., figs, grapes, olives, are crops that are vital to

---

and his discussion, 52. But Roberts, *Nahum*, 146, quotes 1 Sam 25:9 and comments that the verb נוּחַ is used in the sense of "to cease speaking while waiting for an answer."

[330] The phrase "day of distress" (יוֹם צָרָה) usually refers to the time when Israel is facing calamity, particularly being attacked by a foreign power (e.g., 2 Kgs 19:3; Isa 37:3; Jer 30:7; Obad 1:12, 14; Zeph 1:15).

[331] The word לַעֲלוֹת is an infinitive construct of the verb עלה with the preposition לְ. This word can be translated as "to go up." But since "going up" has the connotation of "going to war," especially when it is followed by a preposition לְ which could mean "against," so לַעֲלוֹת can be taken to mean "the coming up of the enemy," or "the attack."

[332] The verb רָגַז is used earlier in 3:7 where the curtains of Midian were trembling due to earthquake.

[333] Keil, *Twelve Minor Prophets*, 114.

[334] When the syllables are counted, both lines yield the same total number of 15 syllables, i.e., 7+8 and 6+9. Each line also forms a chiastic parallelism of its own, e.g., *fig tree* (a) *does not blossom* (b); *no produce* (b') *on the vines* (a'). The second colon of

Israel's agricultural economy.[335] The failure of agricultural production is probably due to foreign military invasion and the absence of divine blessing. The second part of this strophe deals with the disappearance of livestock due to the desolation of the land; "Cut off[336] from the fold are the sheep, and there are no cattle in the stables." In this strophe Habakkuk imagines the worst possible scenario that even if all the necessities of life are deprived, he still resolves to trust in the Lord.

*Stanza 9 Habakkuk's resolution: trust (3:18-19a)*
The last stanza of this chapter demonstrates Habakkuk's resolve to trust in the Lord despite all the calamities that might befall the land around him, "Yet I, in Yahweh, I *will* exult.[337] I *will* rejoice[338] in the God of my salvation." In the first strophe, the personal pronoun with an adversative וַאֲנִי "but I" is to emphasize the nominative subject, the prophet himself.[339] The use of the cohortative form of the verbs אֶעְלוֹזָה and אָגִילָה, along with the chiastic pattern of the two cola, highlight his resolution to rejoice in the Lord. The genitive 1cs pronominal suffix at the end (יִשְׁעִי), along with the subjective independent 1cs pronoun (אֲנִי) at the beginning form an *inclusio* for this verse. The verb אֶעְלוֹזָה recalls verse 14, where the enemies exult (עֲלִיצֻתָם) over the finding of their victims.[340] Meanwhile the verb אָגִילָה recalls 1:15, where the Chaldeans are rejoicing over their catch of many nations. But here, the prophet would have the last laugh and joy, for his exultation is in the Lord and his salvation.

In the second strophe of this last stanza, Habakkuk celebrates the Lord as his strength; "Yahweh, the Lord[341] is my strength, and he will make my feet like

---

the second line has a ballast variant "to maintain the balance of colon length," i.e., *fails* (a) *the yield of olive* (b); *the fields* (b') *do not yield food* (a'). For a discussion on ballast variants, see Watson, *Classical Hebrew Poetry*, 346.

[335] Armerding, "Habakkuk," 533, helpfully comments that the prosperity of Israel depends on her obedience to God's covenant (Lev 26:3-5, 10; Deut 28:2-14).

[336] *BHS* suggests to read the verb גֻּזַר as a Niphal נִגְזַר "be cut off." Hiebert thinks that it is more likely to be read as an internal Qal passive גֻּזַר, "an archaic form with which the Masoretes were no longer familiar." See Hiebert, *God of My Victory*, 55. Eaton suggested that it can also be pointed as a Qal passive participle גָּזֻר. But since גָּזֻר may have the indefinite subject, he translated this colon as "Cut off the flocks from the fold." See his article, "The Origin and Meaning of Habakkuk 3," 157. Albright, "The Psalm of Habakkuk," 13, translated this clause "Cut off from the fold are the sheep." My translation tries to retain the word order of the MT and follows Albright's lead.

[337] Qal cohortative 1cs of the verb עלז "to exult, triumph."

[338] Qal cohortative 1cs of the verb גיל "rejoice."

[339] Williams, *Hebrew Syntax*, §106.

[340] The similarity of the two roots עלז and עלץ can hardly be missed.

[341] There is a debate on whether to translate אֲדֹנִי "my Lord," or "the Lord." LXX renders it "God" (ὁ θεῷ) but Barberini renders it with a pronominal suffix "my God" (ὁ θεός μου). For a succinct discussion, see G.P. Hugenberger, "The Name אֲדֹנִי" in *Basics of Biblical Hebrew Grammar*, G.D. Pratico, and M.V. Van Pelt (Grand Rapids:

the hinds, and upon my high places he will make me tread." The close resemblance of the second line of v. 19a to Ps 18:34 [Eng 18:33] (=2 Sam 22:34) has been well noted. The simile "feet like hinds" is a phrase that David used to describe his deliverance from his enemies (Ps 18:34). Hinds are female deer that are well-known for their swiftness,[342] and their surefootedness on the rough mountainous terrain.[343] The second colon, "and upon my high places he will make me tread" (וְעַל בָּמוֹתַי יַדְרִכֵנִי) brings to mind Deut 33:29, "and you will tread (תִדְרֹךְ) upon his high places (בָּמוֹתֵימוֹ)." בָּמוֹתַי "my high places" also has the meaning of "the land of victory, dominion."[344] Thus here Habakkuk is celebrating Yahweh who is his strength and who is the one who enables him to traverse with confidence through life's rough terrain and to claim victory despite the dire situation. The verb "tread" (דרך) recalls v. 15, where the Lord is said to have treaded the stormy sea with his horses, and here God is enabling his servant to tread the high places, the land of victory, despite the chaotic situation.

### Subscription (3:19b)

In the subscription, "To the director (לַמְנַצֵּחַ)[345] with my string music (נְגִינוֹתָי)," two terms that are usually present in the Book of Psalms but are peculiar in the prophetic literature, appear. Other than here, the term לַמְנַצֵּחַ occurs 55 times as a superscription in the Psalter. The most common translation is "musical director" or "choirmaster," but the precise meaning is not certain. The term נְגִינוֹתָי "stringed instruments" also accompanied several psalms (4; 6; 54; 55; 61; 67; 76) in their titles. Other than in psalms, Isa 38:20 records Hezekiah's thanksgiving song after he was healed by God, saying, "So we will play (נְנַגֵּן) to my stringed instrument (וּנְגִינוֹתַי)." The presence of musical notations at the end of this psalm, as well as at the beginning of the chapter, forms an *inclusio* to the whole psalm. The fact that these terms are found in the Psalter probably indicates Habakkuk 3 is used liturgically in Israel's worship.

### Conclusion on the structure of the book

Scene 1 contains six stanzas. The first stanza (1:2-4) consists of three strophes, which is characterized by the "I-you" lament, and records Habakkuk's complaint about Yahweh's inactivity in the presence of evil. The change of speaker

---

Zondervan, 2001), 269-70. However, Hiebert, *God of My Victory*, 56, suggests that since the treatment of this term as a holy name is probably a late development; it is better to read the pronoun and to understand the original form to have been אֲדֹנִי. But since MT still makes good sense, I opt to retain it.

[342] Keil, *Twelve Minor Prophets*," 115.

[343] Robertson, *Nahum*, 247.

[344] BDB, 119. Cf. also Crenshaw, "*Wədōrēk 'al-bāmôtê 'āreṣ*," in *CBQ* 34 (1972): 49-50.

[345] The term is a Piel participle of the verb נצח "act as overseer, director." See BDB, 664.

in 1:5 and in 1:12 marks off the second section which contains three stanzas (2 to 4) that record the response of Yahweh. Stanza 2 (1:5-6) gives the surprise answer from Yahweh that he is raising up the Chaldeans to deal with the condition that the prophet is complaining about. Stanzas 3 and 4 (1:7-8 and 9-11) describe the swiftness and the fierceness of the Chaldeans respectively. The last section of scene 1 contains two stanzas (5 and 6) of Habakkuk's second complaint against the divine decision. In stanza 5 (1:12-14) he questions the apparent incongruity of Yahweh's character and his actions, and in stanza 6 (1:15-17) he laments the brutality of the Chaldeans. The use of rhetorical questions in both stanzas is meant to evoke a response from the Lord.

Scene 2 contains seven stanzas. Stanza 1 (2:1-3) consists of two strophes: the first strophe (v. 1) shows Habakkuk's action of going up to the rampart, while the second strophe (vv. 2-3) gives Yahweh's command for him to write down the vision. Stanza 2 (2:4-6a) consists of four strophes related to the vision: the first strophe (v. 4) contrasts the haughty with the righteous; the second strophe (v. 5a) further describes the haughty; and the third strophe (v. 5b) relates the Chaldeans to the haughty. Meanwhile the fourth strophe (v. 6a) gives a voice to the oppressed nations who pronounce a satire against the Chaldeans. Stanzas 3 to 7 (2:6b-8, 9-11, 12-14, 15-17, and 18-20) are the five woe oracles, which detail the crimes of the Chaldeans; each consists of three strophes of various lengths. The first four woe oracles can be demarcated by the particle הוֹי while the refrain at the end of the fourth woe (2: 17b) separates the fifth woe from the previous one.

Scene 3 has its own superscription (3:1) and subscription (3:19b) to define its content. This scene is comprised of nine stanzas: stanza 1 (3:2) consists of two strophes, which contains Habakkuk's plea. The theophany corpus is recorded in six stanzas (stanzas 2-7). Stanza 2 (3:3-5) consists of three strophes which show the coming of Yahweh and the majesty of his appearance. Stanza 3 (3:6-7) has two strophes that depict divine arrival and his action. Stanza 4 (3:8-9), which addresses Yahweh directly, expresses his anger against the rivers and depicts him as a warrior getting ready for war. Stanza 5 (3:10-11) presents the reaction of the cosmic elements to the theophany. Stanza 6 (3:12-13) tells of Yahweh's anger against the nations for the salvation of his people. Stanza 7 (3:14-15) gives the detail of divine warfare and ends with the imagery of Yahweh treading the sea. The mention of key words such as "against sea" (בַיָּם) and "your horses" (סוּסֶיךָ) in this verse and in verse 8 forms an *inclusio* for this section. Finally, the prophet's reaction to the theophany is described in stanzas 8 and 9, with two strophes in each: stanza 8 (3:16-17) describes Habakkuk's physical reaction to the coming of the calamity, and stanza 9 (18-19a) informs the audience of his resolution to trust in the Lord.

## Literary forms of the book

It has long been recognized that the book of Habakkuk includes at least three major genres: lament, woe saying, and a prayer which incorporates elements found in a song of victory. The overall framework of the book is a lament, with an address and initial petition for help in 1:2, and a confession of trust and a vow to rejoice in God in 3:17-19a. According to Westermann, community lament usually consists of the following elements:[346] (1) the address; (2) the complaint, usually in three parts—accusation against God (you), we-complaint, and complaint about enemies (they); (3) review of God's past saving acts; (4) the petition for help; (5) divine response;[347] and (6) a vow to praise. Wendland identifies all these six elements of a communal lament in the book of Habakkuk:[348]

(1)  Opening address with an initial petition for help 1:2
(2)  Complaint: against God (you) 1:3, 12-13a; description of the righteous suffering (we) 1:4, 13b; against enemies (they) 1:15-17
(3)  Profession of God's past deeds of deliverance 3:3-15
(4)  Petition for divine intervention 3:2
(5)  Divine response 1:5-11, 2:2-20; 3:3-15
(6)  Vow to praise 3:16-19

Wendland incorporates the third chapter as part of the lament, although he recognizes that its lyric contains "stylistic elements from other psalmic genres, such as a historical recital, a royal eulogy, a profession of trust, and a hymn of divine praise-thanksgiving."[349] Hiebert, on the other hand, rejects the idea that chapter 3 is a lament encompassing a hymn of victory for that is "atypical of classical prophecy."[350] However, as I have argued in chapter one, the prayer of Habakkuk is a song of victory (3:3-15) framed by a lament (3:2, 16-19a). One of the main features in the song of victory is the description of God's epiphany which is very often connected to the exodus event.[351]

Hab 2:6b-19 is one of the three major clusters of prophetic woe oracles in the Old Testaments.[352] The woe oracle was proposed by Westermann to have originated from the cultic curse formula.[353] Gerstenberger, however, challenges this conclusion and proposes that the woe sayings, along with the bliss-formula,

---

[346] Westermann, *Psalms*, 35-43.
[347] Westermann mentions that divine response, though suggested in many psalms, is not actually recorded in the Psalter. See *Psalms*, 35.
[348] Wendland, "The Righteous Live by Their Faith," 601-602.
[349] Ibid., 602.
[350] Hiebert, *God of My Victory*, 134.
[351] Westermann, *Psalms*, 49-50.
[352] R.F. Clements, "OT 'Woe' Oracles," in *ABD*, 6:946. The other two clusters are in Isaiah 5:8, 11, 18, 20, 21, 22; 10:1; and Amos 5:18; 6:1, 4.
[353] C. Westermann, *Basic Forms of Prophetic Speech*, 190-98.

originated as didactic tools of the sage to guide the people to the proper conduct.[354] Another suggestion for the origin of prophetic woe oracle is that its use
is adapted from the funeral rite, which uses the identical cry הוֹ, and is later
developed to a curse-like formula in the prophetic literature.[355] The features of
woe oracles in prophetic literature include the particle הוֹי, followed by a description of a person or a group (usually appearing in participial form) of their
wrongful activities. Westermann points out that "the woe followed by a participle is by nature concerned with a section of the whole and this section is defined by the participle."[356] In other words, each woe is pronounced for a specific crime done by a specific group of people. That may explain why five woes
are pronounced against the same conqueror—the Babylonians—to cover their
wide range of sins. The indictment then leads to one or more of the following
elements: a threat, a lament, a series of ironical questions, a proverbial saying, a
judgment or its reason, further indictment, and a rhetorical question.[357] It is not
difficult to see that Hab 2:6b-19 follows this pattern: each woe oracle, except
the fifth one,[358] begins with a cry הוֹי and is followed by a participial form of the
verb to describe the wrongdoers; then comes the pronouncement of a threat or a
judgment. I will use the first woe in 2:6b-8 as an example to illustrate these
features:

Indictment: "Woe (הוֹי) to the one who increases (הַמַּרְבֶּה) what is not his."
Lament: "Until when (עַד־מָתַי)?[359] And making heavy on himself heavy pledges."
Threat: "Will not your creditors suddenly arise and those who make you tremble will wake up, and you will become booties for them?"
Reason for judgment: "Because (כִּי)[360] you have plundered many nations, all the
remnant of the peoples will plunder you; because of human bloodshed and violence to the land, to the city and all its inhabitants."

The reason for the eclectic use of genres is for the author to find the most appropriate way to express his feelings and to present his view. There is no better
literary genre than lament, to express the depth of his suffering as he observes

---

[354] Gerstenberger, "Woe-Oracles of the Prophets," 249-63.

[355] Clifford, "The Use of *Hôy* in the Prophets," 458-64. See the assessment of this view
in Clements, "OT 'Woe' Oracles," 946. For a detailed discussion on this view, see also W. Janzen, *Mourning Cry and Woe Oracle* (Berlin: de Gruyter, 1972).

[356] Westermann, *Basic Forms*, 191.

[357] Gerstenberger, "Woe-Oracles of the Prophets," 252-53.

[358] In order to form an *inclusio* for this distinct section, the fifth oracle reverses the sequence of the pattern and begins with the rhetorical question then followed by the
woe saying. See the discussion on stanza 7 of scene 2.

[359] The term עַד־מָתַי appears frequently in lament psalms.

[360] The particle כִּי has the meaning of "because, since." See BDB, 473. Muilenburg also
confirmed its causal use. See J. Muilenburg, "The Linguistic and Rhetorical Usages
of the Particle כי in the Old Testament," *HUCA* 32 (1961): 145.

the violence surrounding him. Hence through his dialogue with Yahweh, presented in the form of lament, the prophet attempts to tackle the hard core issue of the divine role in the midst of human suffering. Though powerless in the face of extreme atrocity, the prophet finds lament his only weapon and hopes to arouse Yahweh to change his situation. The woe oracles, in a bitter "death-mourning-vengeance continuum,"[361] are divine retributions that serve to vindicate God's sovereignty and to warn the wicked of their wrongdoings. Finally, the song of victory, in its highly mythical and metaphorical language, presents aptly the majesty and power of God, and reassures the prophet of God's deliverance.

---

[361] Janzen, *Mourning Cry*, 66. In his study, he concludes that *hôy* originates as a funeral lament, then the mourning for the dead becomes a cursing of the guilty in the case of a violent death. This lamentation-vengeance pattern becomes the basis for the woe-cry. See ibid., 39.

# CHAPTER 3

# Habakkuk and Theodicy

The enigma of human suffering, especially when suffering of the innocent is caused by the prevalence of evil in human society, sometimes makes the belief in a just God who oversees human affairs difficult. The questions raised by Habakkuk indeed give voice to the honest doubters who earnestly seek to reconcile the hard reality of life with belief in a benevolent God. In this chapter I will focus on the issue of theodicy and its resolution in the book of Habakkuk. To meet this end, literary elements such as plot and characterization of the book will be analyzed to find out how the author[1] presents his material and his viewpoint, and the themes of the book will be explored by examining the interaction of various literary devices. By these investigations, I hope to identify Habakkuk's questions and his resolution of the issue.

Since the issue of theodicy is also raised in other biblical passages, such as Job (in Job, I will focus on Yahweh's speech in chapters 38-41), Psalms 73 and 77, as well as Jeremiah's confessions,[2] it is pertinent to investigate how the writers of these passages wrestle with the issue. In order to do that, I will give a brief description of the above passages. Then I will examine the questions raised by these passages, the solutions the biblical writers offer to these problems, and the similarities of these passages to Habakkuk.

## The plot of the Book of Habakkuk

The plot of a story is more than a sequential recounting of events in a story. It tells not only what happens but also why it happens. It shows the causality of events. House says it well, "The key to good plot analysis, then, is to go beyond the events of the story line to the reasons for those events."[3] He offers a working definition for plot: "Plot is a selected sequence of logically caused events that present a conflict and its resolution by utilizing certain established literary devices (introduction, complication, crisis, denouement, etc.). Further, it is

---

[1]  Here "author" is used as a collective singular term, and does not deny the existence of later editorial works.

[2]  Due to the affinity in form and inquisitive spirit between Jeremiah's confessions and Habakkuk, I decide to discuss them in detail in this chapter.

[3]  House, *Zephaniah*, 61.

character-oriented, normally reflects a comic or tragic perspective, and must have an important message to proclaim."[4]

In Habakkuk, the plot is quite simple. In order to propel the plot and to sustain the interest of his audience, the author uses dialogue[5] as a means to create surprises and ironies. In this book I divide the book of Habakkuk into three scenes. The first scene begins with Habakkuk lamenting to God about the widespread violence and iniquity in his society. He employs the conventional complaint formula, "How long, O Yahweh, should I cry for help?" (1:2). He could not understand how God could remain silent in the face of evil and allow Torah to become ineffective and justice to fall away (1:4). At this point, usually the Lord is expected to comfort the prophet or to give a favorable response to his faithful one. But in this case, Yahweh gives a surprise response[6] that he is raising up the Chaldeans to deal with the violence and injustice in the Judean society (1:5-6). And as if this news were not shocking enough, he further describes the swiftness and the brutality of the Chaldeans in the third and fourth stanza (1:7-11). Yahweh's response creates further conflict which propels the plot. Habakkuk is perplexed by this answer, for how can a holy God allow a greater evil to fight evil, and to give the wicked a free rein? (1:13a) With his understanding of God's holiness, he is frustrated by the apparently inappropriate activity of God and raises a second complaint[7] that God allows the wicked to swallow the one more righteous than him (1:13b).

After the prophet's second complaint, there is a delay in the Lord's response.[8] The delay is presented by the change of scene,[9] which describes the prophet taking up the role of a watchman at the rampart to wait for the Lord's response (2:1).[10] The reason for Habakkuk to go up to the rampart is due to God's word that the enemies are coming. Here the interesting point is that instead of looking out for the enemy, Habakkuk is getting ready to challenge God, "and I will keep watch to see (וַאֲצַפֶּה לִרְאוֹת) what he will speak to me (מַה־יְדַבֶּר־בִּי), and what I will reply (וּמָה אָשִׁיב) concerning my reproof

---

[4] P. House, *Unity of the Twelve*, 115.

[5] Speeches are important for the revelation of plot, movement, characterization and themes. See House, *Zephaniah*, 57-8.

[6] The sudden change of speaker in the second stanza helps to dramatize the surprise response from the Lord.

[7] Habakkuk's second complaint can be further divided into two parts: the first part (stanza 5) is against God, and the second part (stanza 6) is against the Chaldeans.

[8] Westermann observes that in lament, usually after the call to God, complaint, and petition, there is a break to wait for the divine response. See Westermann, *Psalms*, 35. Here the delay seems to confirm his observation.

[9] The first stanza of the second scene records the prophet's action and Yahweh's command (2:1-3).

[10] Traditionally, prophets are the watchmen appointed by God to warn the people of the danger or the approaching enemies (Ezek 3:17-21; 33:2-6; Hos 9:8; cf. Isa 21:6-8).

(עַל־תּוֹכַחְתִּי).)." He is expecting to have a debate with God![11] The interjection of the sentence "And Yahweh answered me and he said"[12] is to call attention to Yahweh's second response which is related to the vision (חָזוֹן). Instead of engaging in the debate, the Lord simply commands Habakkuk to write the vision down.[13] The second stanza then records the vision which contrasts the two endings awaiting the righteous and the wicked (2:4-5). The ensuing five woe oracles in stanzas 3 to 7 (2:6b-19), which are attributed to the nations,[14] further explain the fate of the arrogant described in 2:4-5.[15]

The woe sayings help to advance the plot by indicting the actions of the conqueror and by showing the eventual consequences that would befall him. The indictments against the Babylonians move from their economic oppression of others (the first woe) to their scheming against other nations for self-gain (the second woe). Then they intensify to the pillage of many peoples (the third woe), and to the exploitation and stripping naked both people and nature (fourth woe). Finally, the indictment climaxes at idolatry, the root of all crimes (the fifth woe). In addition to advancing the overall plot of the book, each woe oracle in fact contains its own three phases of a plot: conflict, peak, and resolution. The interjection of a doxology in 2:14 serves to contrast the futility of human endeavor by violent means and the eventual manifestation of God's presence. The call to worship in 2:20, which contrasts the uselessness of the idols and the holiness of God, provides a fitting end to the whole woe oracles section as well as prepares the audience for the theophany in chapter 3.

In the third scene, the prophet reflects on the Lord's activities in history and pleads for the manifestation of the divine deeds and mercy in the opening stanza.[16] It is as if while he is meditating on this, he receives a theophanic vision of God coming from the south (3:3). The next six stanzas describe the theophany. He gives a vivid description of the cosmic reaction to the theophany in stanzas 2 and 3 (3:3-7), and portrays Yahweh as a warrior coming to deliver his people in stanzas 4 to 7 (3:8-15).[17] He also records his own reaction and his resolution

---

[11] Wendland, "The Righteous Live by Their Faith," 596, also notices the disputational attitude of Habakkuk.

[12] Cf. Wendland's comment that this sentence marks "the onset of the second, resolutional half of debate." See ibid., 595.

[13] The command to write the vision recalls Isaiah's passage (Isa 30:8ff).

[14] These nations are the ones mentioned in 1:5-11, who suffer devastation under the Chaldeans. The woe oracles are attributed to them to create irony and to give a voice to the oppressed nations.

[15] The woe oracles implicitly show that Habakkuk accepts the inevitable.

[16] Habakkuk's plea to Yahweh shows that he now understands that salvation will come after calamity.

[17] The theophany is not just a replay of the exodus experience but may also have a future dimension. Janzen helpfully points out that by recalling the work in the past Habakkuk revivifies the ancient work of Yahweh, which gives energy for the present and assurance for the future. See J.G. Janzen, "Eschatological Symbol and Existence

in stanzas 8 and 9 (3:16-19a). Though the invasion of Judah by the Chaldeans is inevitable, the memory of the paradigmatic exodus experience lets Habakkuk actualize God's protection and guidance; and the theophanic vision helps him to put all his concern to rest and to give him hope for the future.

In sum, through the twists and turns of the plot, the implied author tries to deal with the difficult issue of theodicy. The plot helps to keep the interest of the audience, and to grasp their attention as the author guides them through his argument. Through the lament of the prophet and the dialogues between the main characters, he exposes the reality of the suffering of the righteous and the prevalence of violence in Judean society, and questions the divine inactivity in the presence of evil. When God reveals his plan to deal with the problem, he further questions the divine solution. The author struggles to reconcile divine nature and law on the one hand, and the reality of evil and human suffering on the other hand. After the divine answer in 2:2-5, he starts to understand that though destruction and suffering is inevitable, there is always hope for the righteous: "the righteous in his faithfulness will live;" meanwhile the wicked will meet their apt judgment at the end. The woe oracles further demonstrate that the principle of retribution[18] is very much at work to deal with human wickedness. The memory of divine activity in history and the theophanic vision confirm the divine power and his concern for the salvation of his people. This gives Habakkuk hope for the future and strength to live out the life of the righteous as prescribed by the Lord.

---

in Habakkuk," 411. Indeed, Habakkuk understands that Yahweh will come to deliver his people and his anointed (3:13-14).

[18] Klaus Koch argues that since the concept of retribution requires a judicial process to take place, the Old Testament, for the most part, does not have a "retribution belief," but rather an "Action-Consequences-Construct" which means that there is a built-in and inherent connection between an action and its consequences and that Yahweh merely ensures that this process takes place. See his discussion in K. Koch, "Is There a Doctrine of Retribution in the Old Testament?" in *Theodicy in the Old Testament*, ed. J.L. Crenshaw (Philadelphia: Fortress, 1983), 57-87. However, his view raises many questions such as: Who sets that "Action-Consequences-Construct" in the first place? Who defines its terms and determines its consequences? What about the prophetic indictments? Are they not a form of judicial process? If this "Action-Consequences-Construct" is set by God to ensure that his justice goes forth, then this could very well be a form of retribution that is divinely ordained to make sure that judgment fits human action. Hence I see his "Action-Consequences-Construct" as a form of retribution. Furthermore, Patrick Miller Jr. argues that in several passages sin and judgment are clearly correlated, and Yahweh is actively involved in setting the connections between act and consequence. See his book, *Sin and Judgment in the Prophets: A Stylistic and Theological Analysis*. SBL Monograph Series 27 (Chico: Scholars Press, 1982), 121-39.

## Characterization in Habakkuk

Characterization, in a nutshell, is the way a writer portrays a character in a story. Thus characterization of a person in a story reveals the true nature of that character.[19] In this section, I will explore characterization by using two methods. The first method is an assessment or description of a character by means of his own word, by what others respond to him or say about him, and by his own actions. The second method is to examine the development of a character as the story unveils.

The two main characters in the book of Habakkuk are Yahweh and the prophet himself. The dialogues between them reveal their personalities and a development in their characters. They discuss other people (e.g., the wicked and the Chaldeans), whose actions are at the center of the topic that propels the plot.[20] Babylon, represented by its king Nebuchadnezzar, is the chief antagonist and a large portion of the book is allotted to characterize him (1:6-11, 15-17; 2:6-19). In fact the advancement of the plot is linked to his characterization. He is epitomized as the wicked conqueror; meanwhile Yahweh is the protagonist and Habakkuk takes up the role of the narrator.

### The Chaldeans

The Chaldeans are the agent raised by Yahweh as a response to the evil in the Judean society as described by the prophet in 1:2-4.[21] Their presence is felt in all three scenes: in scene one, the author uses four stanzas to portray their military might (stanza 2 to 4 in Yahweh's first response, and stanza 6 in Habakkuk's further complaint); in scene two they are the puffed-up ones described in the vision and the object of woe oracles (stanzas 2 to 7); while scene three sees their ultimate destruction (stanzas 6 and 7). They are described as "fierce and impetuous;" their swiftness and their military might are portrayed as having no comparison (1:5-11). In the book of Habakkuk, the Chaldeans are personified

---

[19] House, *Zephaniah*, 68. William Harmon, *A Handbook to Literature: Based on Earlier Editions by William Flint Thrall, Addison Hibbard, and C. Hugh Holman*, 9th ed. (Upper Saddle River, NJ: Prentice Hall, 2003), 88, describes three methods of characterization: (1) through the explicit, direct comment by the author; (2) through the actions of the characters with little or no comment by the author; (3) by exposing the character's inner self through his own words and actions.

[20] To use Berlin's term, they may be called "agent." Berlin describes an agent as a non-person, who is simply part of the plot and whose action is necessary to the plot. See A. Berlin, *Poetics and Interpretation of Biblical Narrative* (Sheffield: Almond, 1983; reprint, Winona Lake: Eisenbrauns, 1994), 27.

[21] "The wicked" in 1:4 are not explicitly named; and that prompts many scholars to think that they are the Chaldeans. However, as argued before, they are best seen as the Judeans here. By identifying different groups as wicked in 1:4 and 13, the author exposes the universality of evil in his world. Moreover, the anonymity of the wicked in 1:4 may have been intentional so as to protect the lamenter from possible reprisal, especially when the wicked are the powerful ones in the community.

or represented by their king, Nebuchadnezzar, although his name is never mentioned and he is not even given a voice in the book. Yet he is the center of discussion between Yahweh and Habakkuk. Although he is the agent of Yahweh, he does not honor him, but worships his own might as his god. Yahweh's comment, "from him his judgment and his dignity go forth" (1:7), seems to be in agreement with the Neo-Babylonian texts that depict Nebuchadnezzar as a law-giver.[22] All of the descriptions of the perpetrator in the woe oracles[23] accord well to the historical account of Nebuchadnezzar. He is well known for his military expeditions and famous for many construction projects, especially in the city of Babylon.[24] Some of his constructions include: the hanging garden, which he built for his wife, and which is regarded as one of the Seven Wonders of the World; the fortification of the city wall of Babylon; and the building of many temples and ziggurats.[25] These gigantic building projects require numerous workers who are the captives brought back from his many military expeditions. Thus it is highly probable that the woe oracles are directed against him: the plundering of the nations by means of financial extortion (first woe),[26] the fortifying of his own house in order to secure himself (second woe), the building of city with blood and injustice by means of forced labor and exploitation of captives (third woe), the exploitation of Lebanon's forestry for his massive building projects (fourth woe), and the worshipping of idols (fifth woe).[27] Even though he might enjoy his success for a while, his kingdom is doomed to destruction.

### Yahweh

Yahweh is the protagonist in the book. He is the one being spoken to and spoken about by the prophet. Most of the characterization of Yahweh is portrayed through the prophet's speeches. At the beginning of the book, he is being called upon by the prophet in a time of distress (1:2). This shows that Yahweh is a God who listens to the cry of his people, and who can be bargained with, as in the case of Abraham (Gen 18:23-32). Yahweh is first described as inactive and oblivious to the violence in Judean society, which leads to the perversion of

---

[22] For a detailed discussion, see P. Coxon, "Nebuchadnezzar's Hermeneutical Dilemma," *JSOT* 66 (1995): 89-91.

[23] The woe oracles address him with the second person masculine singular "you."

[24] In this section, I follow the work of R.H. Sack, "Nebuchadnezzar," in *ABD*, ed. D.N. Freedman (New York: Doubleday, 1992), 4:1058-59.

[25] The implied author of Habakkuk is not being specific about Nebuchadnezzar's building projects, although he pronounces two woes (the second and third woe) directly, and the fourth woe indirectly, to denounce his building works.

[26] The plundering of "many nations" purposefully links this woe to the previous scene where the Chaldeans treats them like fish. For a detailed discussion, see chapter 2 of this book.

[27] The delay of the "woe" (הוֹי) until v. 19 is to serve as an *inclusio* for the section as well as to heighten the final woe; see discussion in chapter 2.

justice (1:2-4). His solution of bringing in the Chaldeans to judge the Judeans (1:5-6) seems illogical and callous, for he is well aware of the impetuous and ferocious nature of his agent (1:6-11). From Habakkuk's perspective, the decision of Yahweh is viewed as incomprehensible, if not outright unreasonable and unjust, for it contradicts the nature of God as he knows it (1:12-13). The prophet gives some direct descriptions about Yahweh's nature: he is the Holy One from of old (1:12a), he is morally pure (1:13aα), but more poignantly, he is the one responsible for appointing the Chaldeans as judgment (1:12b), and making humanity vulnerable before their conqueror (1:14-17). In Habakkuk's lament in the opening scene, Yahweh is being put in quite a negative light—he shows little interest in human affairs,[28] and he does not seem to act according to his nature.[29]

The fact that Yahweh does not defend himself or rebuke Habakkuk for his audacious accusation says something about his character. He seems to be patient with his prophet, for even Habakkuk himself expects a rebuke from the Lord (2:1b). After a long pause, Yahweh finally breaks the silence in scene two and responds to Habakkuk. Yahweh's second answer insists that the vision is going to happen and shows that he intends the righteous to live by his faithfulness, while the haughty men will not endure (2:4-5).[30] This answer serves as a turning point for the plot, and Habakkuk begins to understand how divine justice works. In the ensuing woe oracles, divine justice is presented in a form of retribution. This shows that, as a normal practice, Yahweh prefers to work by means of a "reap what you sow principle," and lets history take its course. While the woe oracles are put in the mouth of the oppressed nations, they nevertheless vindicate God's justice, for he is the guarantor of the retribution principle.

The portrayal of Yahweh as a warrior in the third scene is reminiscent of Israel's early history when God delivered them out of Egypt, led them through the wilderness and fought for them when they entered into the land of Canaan. The author uses cosmic phenomena to describe Yahweh's power: earthquake, volcanic outburst, mudslide, thunderstorm, and tsunami. All these frightful natural forces are at the disposal of Yahweh. This reflection on God's past deeds and power also helps to give assurance that he will come again to deliver his people in the future (3:13-14).

Throughout the book, we see that there is a development in the character of Yahweh. He is first seen as inactive and indifferent in scene one. His handling of human affairs seems inscrutable and contradictory to his nature. But as the story unfolds, he is shown to be patient and has a plan for human history in

---

[28] Stanza 1 shows the aloofness of God. See the discussion in chapter 2.

[29] In stanza 5, Habakkuk accuses God of not acting according to his nature.

[30] If the divine command to write down the vision alludes to Isa 30:8ff, then this may also serve as an admonishment for the Israelites that "In repentance and rest you shall be saved, in quietness and trust shall be your strength" (Isa 30:15).

scene two. And finally, the display of his majestic power and the imagery of Yahweh as a warrior in scene three show that not only does he possess unimaginable power he also cares for his people, and just as he came in the past to deliver his people, he will come again to save them in the future.

*Habakkuk*

The prophet Habakkuk is portrayed as the narrator in the book. In fact the whole book is framed by his words and he is depicted as a spectator to the theophany. If Yahweh is the protagonist of the story, then Habakkuk is his foil who makes Yahweh stand out by contrast. While Habakkuk is bound by time and space and his problems are current and ephemeral, Yahweh is from eternity (מִקֶּדֶם) and his solution may take a long period to accomplish (2:3b). Habakkuk expects to have a "quick fix" to his problems but Yahweh has appointed a time for everything (2:3a). Unlike Yahweh who shows little emotion in his speeches, Habakkuk does not restrain himself from speaking his mind. He is a skillful orator for his speeches are highly emotive and piercing. He begins the book with a bitter lament, in which he accuses the Lord of ignoring his cry and being insensible to violence in the Judean society (1:2-4). Unlike other prophets (for example, Zephaniah[31] who tends to agree with Yahweh's judgment) Habakkuk dares to challenge Yahweh's decision. As orator, he deploys an arsenal of forms. For example, he employs rhetorical questions to give a pungent criticism of the divine choice of agent, and even confronts God and asks if he is going to let the Chaldeans keep "slaying the nations without mercy?" (1:17) The woe oracles (2:6b-20) also display his oratorical skill by using irony to express his bitter feeling for the Chaldeans. Through his speeches, the character of Habakkuk emerges. He is a man of deep religious conviction and a prophet with a fiery temperament. His sense of justice is deeply rooted in Torah, which teaches reward for the righteous and punishment for the wicked. Thus he could not tolerate any injustice, even when it is perceived to be coming from God. He takes his prophetic post seriously and shows his concern for his people by identifying with them (3:14). After the divine response in 2:4-5, he seems to understand that justice is going to be served by means of retribution.[32]

Habakkuk's voice is not silenced even in the midst of theophany. In fact his speeches frame the whole theophany: his plea to God introduces the theophany, and his soliloquy ends it. He is portrayed as the eye-witness for the event (cf. 3:7 "I saw"). The "I-you" section of 3:8-15[33] confirms Habakkuk's involvement, as well as highlights the purpose of Yahweh's action. In Habakkuk's monologue (3:16-19a), we are given a rare glimpse into his response to the the-

---

[31] See House's analysis on the characterization of Zephaniah, *Zephaniah*, 72.

[32] Wendland, "The Righteous Live by Their Faith," 603, observes that he is humbled after Yahweh's second response, for he humbly pleads to God in 3:2.

[33] This section addresses Yahweh directly as "you," and in verse 14, Habakkuk identifies with the Judean refugees and complains against the invaders of scattering them.

ophany. He bares his soul before his audience: he describes openly his emotional state, his fear, his physical reaction, his trust and his resolution to rejoice in the Lord. His declaration of confidence shows his new understanding of God and his unwavering trust in the Lord, who alone is his victory and his strength. With this renewed trust he is ready to face any situation, even to the point where all life's necessities are deprived.

There is a definite development in the characterization of Habakkuk. In scene one of the book, the prophet begins his spiritual journey as a courageous doubter who questions Yahweh's inactivity in the face of wickedness. His fiery temperament is in full display when he learns of God's plan to judge Judah's wrong. He shows his disapproval by reminding God of his holiness and by pointing out the inappropriateness of his choice of agent. He uses two stanzas (5 and 6) in scene one to express his disapproval: stanza 5 directly complains against Yahweh and stanza 6 against the Chaldeans.[34] Then after Yahweh's second response, he seems to have accepted the inevitability of the invasion and begins to reflect on divine justice. The woe oracles help him to see that divine justice usually takes the form of "reap what you sow," and that the wicked would suffer the consequence of their wicked action. This prepares him for the theophany, in which he finally rests all his concerns and resolves to rejoice in the Lord. Through this brief analysis on the characterization of Habakkuk, we see his transformation from a man who questions God to the one who triumphs in God.

By means of the plot and the characterization of both Yahweh and Habakkuk, the author leads the audience through the odyssey of the issue of theodicy, and explains to them the inevitability of the Babylonian invasion but also assures them of the future salvation and that divine justice will eventually prevail. Meanwhile the righteous are admonished to live faithfully and to wait expectantly for the accomplishment of the vision.

### Themes in Habakkuk

Harmon defines theme as "[a] central idea. In nonfiction prose it may be thought of as the general topic of discussion, the subject of the discourse, the thesis. In poetry, fiction, and drama it is the abstract concept that is made concrete through representation in person, action, and image."[35] In biblical narratives and poetries, themes are usually not stated explicitly and are embodied in various literary elements such as characters, actions, symbols, and images.[36] They require intentional thinking and diligent extraction by the reader, so by

---

[34] See discussion in chapter 2.
[35] Harmon, *Handbook to Literature*, 508.
[36] Shimon Bar-Efrat, "Some Observations on the Analysis of Structure in Biblical Narrative," in *Beyond Form Criticism: Essays in Old Testament Literary Criticism*, ed. P.R. House (Winona Lake: Eisenbrauns, 1992), 200.

examining these elements in the book of Habakkuk, we can uncover the theme(s) embedded in it. [37]

## Theodicy

Theodicy is the central issue that Habakkuk struggles with. In fact the whole book evolves as the prophet tries to deal with his theodic crisis. [38] The first scene presents the background and the cause of the crisis, in which the prophet laments his present situation. The prophet's concern for divine justice is clearly revealed in his dialogue with Yahweh and the repeated use of forensic terms such as judgment/justice (מִשְׁפָּט), righteous (צַדִּיק), [39] wicked (רָשָׁע), as well as a variety of terms such as "violence"(חָמָס), "iniquity" (אָוֶן), "mischief" (עָמָל), "destruction" (שֹׁד), "strife" (רִיב), and "contention" (מָדוֹן), which are used to describe the pervasiveness of crimes in his society in order to arouse Yahweh to action (1:2-3). Yahweh is viewed as a righteous judge who is supposed to ensure that justice goes forth in human society. Yet the lived reality is quite the contrary which causes the prophet's theodic cry to God. Yahweh's response in 1:5-11 of raising up the Chaldeans further complicates the issue, and Habakkuk is quick to challenge Yahweh's choice of agent to mete out judgment, for to him, to fight evil with a greater evil is incongruent with the holy nature of God (1:13). Not only does this wicked agent not respect anybody's law except his own (1:7), he does not even honor God but worships his own might as God (1:11, 16). Moreover, Habakkuk implicates God for making humans vulnerable like sea creatures with no ruler to protect them (1:14), [40] and allows the Chaldeans to treat human beings like fish (1:15). Thus scene one presents the theodic crisis, and scenes two and three engage to resolve the issue of theodicy by answering the questions raised in the first scene.

## The righteous shall live by his faithfulness

Closely related to the issue of theodicy is the prophet's concern for the well-being of the righteous. The prophet is not contemplating a philosophical and

---

[37] Tremper Longman III states that since God is at the center of the Old Testament, themes about Yahweh and his relationship with his people are the most important themes in the Old Testament. See his discussion, "The Literature of the Old Testament," in *A Complete Literary Guide to the Bible*, ed. L. Ryken, and T. Longman III (Grand Rapids: Zondervan, 1993), 104-105.

[38] A term coined by Brueggemann, by which he means that there is a theodic settlement within a community which teaches that moral behavior is rewarded and evil behavior is punished. But when the lived reality does not accord well with this settlement, then a theodic crisis arises to challenge it. See W. Brueggemann, "Some Aspects of Theodicy in Old Testament Faith," *Perspectives in Religious Studies* 26 (Fall, 1999): 257.

[39] For a discussion of the concept of righteousness as a forensic term, see Robertson, *Nahum, Habakkuk, and Zephaniah*, 175-76.

[40] This is a direct undoing or violation of God's own creation order.

speculative question of theodicy; he is concerned about an existential question: how are the righteous going to live in the midst of evil, when oppression and violence circumvent them? His concern for the righteous can be seen from his repeated statements that the righteous are oppressed by the wicked (1:4b, 13b).

The divine plan to bring in the Chaldeans makes the situation even worse, for Habakkuk knows that the righteous would probably suffer along with the wicked. So he follows Abraham's example, who challenges God when he learns of divine plan to destroy Sodom and Gomorrah, "Will you sweep away the innocent along with the guilty? . . . Shall not the Judge of all the earth do justice?" (Gen 18:23-25). The fate of the righteous and Yahweh's reputation as the righteous judge are intricately bound together, for according to the retribution principle, Yahweh should ensure the well-being of the righteous.

The answer to this pressing issue is recorded in the second divine response to Habakkuk, "But the righteous in his faithfulness shall live" (2:4b). Not only is this short statement an important assurance to the prophet, it is of crucial significance to both Jews and Christians.[41] Although there is a debate as to the meaning of "in his faithfulness" (בֶּאֱמוּנָתוֹ),[42] the general idea is clear, that the righteous one will live as he remains faithful to his faithful God. In other words, for those who persevere to the end, they will live; yet their perseverance relies on God's grace and faithfulness.[43] Finally, in Habakkuk's confession of confidence (3:16-19), he demonstrates, in concrete imagery, the living out of this assurance.

### Reap what you sow[44]

The prophet employs the technique of irony to present the theology of retribution. This is particularly obvious in the section of woe oracles in 2:6-20 which

---

[41] Jewish Rabbi Nachman ben Isaac (ca. A.D. 350) summed up the 613 Mosaic laws to the one commandment recorded here. The threefold citation of Hab 2:4 in the New Testament (Rom 1:17; Gal 3:11; Heb 10:38) attests to its importance to the Christian faith. The NT writers' interpretation of the Hab 2:4b may have been influenced by Gen 15:6 because of the proximity of the two words "believe" and "rigteousness": when Abraham believed in the Lord's promise and was reckoned by God as his righteousness, "And he believed in the Lord, and He reckoned it to him as righteousness" (וְהֶאֱמִן בַּיהוָה וַיַּחְשְׁבֶהָ לּוֹ צְדָקָה). The Book of James does not quote Hab 2:4 directly, although it explains the relationship between faith and work, and invokes Gen 15:6 to illustrate that faith needs work to be made perfect (Jas 2:14-23).

[42] See the discussion on this term in chapter 2.

[43] The ambiguity of בֶּאֱמוּנָתוֹ allows this interpretation; if one takes the pronominal suffix as God.

[44] Koch, "Is There a Doctrine of Retribution in the Old Testament?" 61, sees this metaphor of planting and harvesting as an indicator of Action-Consequence sequence. However, Miller, *Sin and Judgment*, 123, points out that "the imagery seems to express the notion of correspondence between sin and judgment as much as it does the consequential relationship."

describes the divine judgment[45] of the wicked in a form of "reversal of imagery."[46] Those who instigate injustice and violence in human society for self-gain will experience their well-deserved judgment at the end. This reversal of fortune can also be found in other parts of the book, albeit implicitly. For example, in scene one when the Judeans refuse to obey God's law and pervert justice (מִשְׁפָּט), then they must suffer injustice under Nebuchadnezzar (1:4, 7); and in scene three when the Chaldeans are rejoicing in their slaughtering of the victims, they in turn will be killed by their own weapons (3:14; cf. Ps 37:14-15).

## The sovereignty of God

God's sovereignty is another issue that this book seeks to explore. The sovereignty of God is initially challenged by the prophet when God reveals that he is raising the Chaldeans to be his agent for judgment. Instead of pleading with God to withhold his decision, as Amos does (Amos 7:1-6), Habakkuk questions how a holy God can stand by idly and let the righteous be swallowed by the wicked (1:13). This is almost like an open revolt against God's authority by his own prophet. God's sovereignty is also ignored by the Chaldeans for they do not acknowledge him or worship him, but rather attribute their success to their own might (1:11b, 16).

In Yahweh's second response to Habakkuk, the sovereignty of God is firmly affirmed by the certainty of the coming of the vision and his justice is revealed by the due judgment of the wicked in the woe oracles. His glory is seen in spite of human wickedness (2:14), and he is in full control in his holy abode despite the pandemonium in human society (2:20).

Then in a highly mythical language, the majesty of God is in full display in a theophanic vision (3:3-15). He is first presented as heavenly king coming with an entourage of pestilence (דֶּבֶר) and plague (רֶשֶׁף).[47] The reaction of the natural elements is described in a vivid way to inspire awe and dread (3:3-7). Secondly, Yahweh is portrayed as a warrior coming to deliver his people (3:8-15). With the display of divine majesty and might, as well as with a statement of the divine purpose of theophany (3:13a), the author wipes out any doubt concerning the sovereignty of God—he has a plan and a time set for Israel's and other nations' history, and he certainly has the power to accomplish it.

In sum, after examining the interaction of literary elements: images, symbol, actions, and personalities, four themes of the book emerge, namely, theodicy, the righteous shall live by his faithfulness, retribution theology, and the sovereignty of God.

---

[45] Some may argue that the woe oracles are not divine judgment but fate—"what goes around comes around." But I contend that since God is the guarantor of this action-consequences principle, it is a divine judgment after all.

[46] Janzen, *Mourning Cry*, 35, explains that God's judgment is expressed "in terms which take up the very terminology or imagery of the indictment."

[47] These two agents of judgment are also the names of West-Semitic gods "Deber" and "Resheph." See discussion in chapter 2.

## Questions raised by Habakkuk

As we discussed earlier the main theme of Habakkuk is theodicy. To him, God as a righteous Judge is supposed to uphold justice by punishing the wicked and rewarding the righteous. But when the righteous continue to endure suffering due to the oppression by the wicked and there is no end in sight, he questions theodicy and demands an answer from God. Some scholars, such as Achtemeier, argue that the book is not dealing with theodicy for God's justice is presumed.[48] But it is precisely because of the incongruity of God's action and his nature that prompts Habakkuk to question God. If Habakkuk had not understood Yahweh to be a holy and just God, he would not have such a problem with theodicy.

The first chapter of the book focuses on his theodic cry and the next two chapters engage in resolving the issues raised earlier. The prophet begins his search for an answer with a lament cry "How long?" and asks God why he would not save and why he turns a blind eye to the prevalence of evil. His bold complaint is based on the conviction that there is a divinely ordained order in the universe and that this order is revealed in the Torah.[49] Crenshaw observes that there is a theory of reward and retribution in the ANE, which is derived from the belief that the universe is created in an orderly fashion.[50] Since this principle of reward for the righteous and punishment for the evil, as taught in the Torah (or at least presumed in the dialogues), is violated, the prophet feels the need to confront Yahweh with his neglect of upholding justice, and implies that divine negligence causes the perversion of justice; "Therefore law grows numb and justice never goes forth, for the wicked surround the righteous; therefore judgment goes forth perverted" (1:4).

Some scholars argue that the commotion described in 1:1-4 is caused by the invasion of the Chaldeans, for there is no reason for Habakkuk to get angry if he is the one who asks Yahweh to discipline Judah in the first place. But, as suggested by Thompson, Habakkuk may be questioning the "prophetical doctrine" that God would use a wicked nation as his agent to punish Israel.[51] Moreover, Habakkuk might have only wished Yahweh to intervene by raising a righteous ruler, someone like Josiah, to right the wrong and to reform the Judean society. The changing of the ruling party would have caused the least disturbance to Judah, and to bring Judah back to a righteous path. Habakkuk would rather have Yahweh himself mete out judgment, just as David chose for

---

[48] Achtemeier, *Nahum-Malachi*, 31, thinks that Habakkuk "is not primarily about the justice of God," because "it is taken for granted that God is just (1:13)."

[49] The fact that "the wicked surround the righteous" is given as evidence that "Torah becomes slack" and "justice never prevails," means that there is a core conviction that Torah is supposed to maintain the order in the society.

[50] Crenshaw, "Theodicy," in *ABD* 6:446. See also Schmid's view in idem, "Popular Questioning of the Justice of God in Ancient Israel," *ZAW* 82 (1970): 383.

[51] Thompson, "Prayer, Oracle and Theophany," 35.

his own punishment in 2 Sam 24:10-16. To Habakkuk, disciplining Judah is one thing, but letting the floodgate open by bringing in the Chaldeans to destroy it altogether is quite another, especially when the Judeans are more righteous than the Chaldeans; and there are still righteous people like himself living among them.

The mention of the righteous and the wicked (1:4, 13) indicates that the prophet is not merely concerned about the speculative question of theodicy; instead he is also probing the existential question of how the righteous are going to live in the midst of evil and how they are to deal with the crisis. The mayhem caused by the moral decay of the society is emphasized to arouse the divine intervention.[52] In other words, the prophet is concerned about the survival and the welfare of the righteous. Perhaps Crenshaw is correct to say that the crucial question for humanity is not the reconciliation of God's existence with the presence of evil, but rather the quest for the positive meaning of life in the face of the tentacles of death and suffering.[53]

The divine solution of bringing in the Chaldeans to rectify the issue of Judean evil complicates the situation and worsens the problem. Based on his understanding of God's nature, Habakkuk cannot comprehend how a holy God can use an unrighteous nation to be a judgment for his own people. Not only are the Chaldeans ferocious and brutal like wild beasts such as leopards, evening wolves, and vultures which have no regard for human life (1:8), they do not respect anybody's law except their own (1:7),[54] and they do not honor Yahweh but rely on their own strength as if a god (1:11). And yet Yahweh appoints such a nation as his judgment against Judah (1:12b), and gives them unending success (1:10, 15-17) that they even proceed to undo God's creation by treating humanity as fish and creeping things (1:14-15). This description of the Chaldeans makes Yahweh's choice of agent look even more unjust,[55] for the prosperity of the wicked is a direct challenge to the righteous rule of a just God. Habakkuk's questions in 1:13b show the incongruity between God's holy nature and his action, as well as accuse God of being unjust, "Why do you look on the treacherous ones, and you are silent while the wicked swallows the one more righteous than him?"[56] He even holds God responsible for making humankind "like the fish of the sea"[57] so as to be slaughtered by the Chaldeans. Then he

---

[52] The emphasis on the "destruction and violence" in the society is done by the unusual arrangement of the chiastic pattern of the two surrounding clauses in v. 3 as discussed earlier.

[53] Crenshaw, "Popular Questioning," 382.

[54] I see an irony here: since the Judeans do not obey God's Torah, they are forced to accept the Chaldean's law.

[55] The similar assessments on the Chaldeans by both Yahweh and Habakkuk (1:9-11, 15-17) highlight the ferocity and brutality of Yahweh's agent.

[56] The pivotal positioning of "you remain silent" (תַחֲרִישׁ) implicates Yahweh of tacitly approving the wicked ones to swallow the righteous.

[57] For a discussion on the imagery of "fishes and creeping thing," see chapter 2.

asks if God is going to give the wicked one a free rein to exploit. The imagery of a fisherman who keeps emptying his trawl is meant to move God to action, and the prophet ends his accusation with a rhetorical question, "Shall he therefore keep emptying his net, and continue slaying nations without pity?" (1:17). It is noteworthy to see that these questions appeal to the attributes of the Lord as revealed in his covenantal name, namely, justice and mercy (cf. Exod 34:6-7). As Bruce aptly states, "If God had not revealed himself to be the God of righteousness, establishing judgment and justice as the foundation of his throne, there would not be this problem: it would simply have to be accepted as a fact of life that the weaker should go to the wall (compare Eccles. 4:1). But as it was, God's character had to be vindicated."[58]

## Resolution of the issue of theodicy in Habakkuk

God's answer in 2:2-5 begins to settle Habakkuk's restlessness. This divine response also serves as the turning point of the book, for the questions raised by Habakkuk in scene one find their resolution from this point onward.

### God has appointed a time for judgment (2:3-5)

As a response to the prophet's question of "How long?" and his accusation that God is oblivious to evil, Yahweh tells him to write down the vision for the future. The Lord insists that the vision is set for an appointed time (לַמּוֹעֵד) no matter what people think of it. The prophet is warned that this appointed time may be slow in coming, but it will surely come. The fact that the author emphasizes the certainty of the coming of the vision may indicate that he is well aware of the charge of false prophecy. That may be the reason for him to emphasize that the vision "will not lie" (וְלֹא יְכַזֵּב), and that it "will not delay" ( לֹא יְאַחֵר). Yahweh's command to write down the vision is reminiscent of Isa 30:8, and the description that it "hastens to the end" may indicate that the time for the fulfillment of the vision is approaching soon. Meanwhile the righteous are admonished to wait patiently for the vision to come. They are promised to have life if they faithfully put their trust in the Lord, "But the righteous in his faithfulness will live" (וְצַדִּיק בֶּאֱמוּנָתוֹ יִחְיֶה).[59] This promise addresses the prophet's existential problem and allays his concern for the well-being of the righteous. This phrase also helps to direct human behavior in the present and near future.[60] Yahweh's insistence that the vision will come and his description of the arrogant one (2:4-5) make Habakkuk realize that the coming of the Chaldeans is

---

[58] Bruce, "Habakkuk," 835.

[59] Isa. 30:15 also reminds the Israelites that "In repentance and rest you shall be saved; in quietness and in trust shall be your strength." This would be a good motto for the righteous to conduct their lives during the time of distress.

[60] Weis defines מַשָּׂא as a "prophetic exposition of divine revelation," which informs human action in the present and near future. Yahweh's response here is part of the "מַשָּׂא" that Habakkuk saw. For a discussion on this term, see chapter 2.

inevitable but that they will not endure. Habakkuk then begins to see how God's justice works in the world and proceeds to pronounce judgment on the wicked ones by means of the five woe oracles.

### Woe oracles as divine retribution (2:6-20)

In order to deal with the issue of the prevalence of evil in the world, especially when it is caused by the invaders, woe oracles are pronounced against those who practice crimes and violence, even if they are God's agents of judgment. The fact that five woes are pronounced illustrates the extent of the crimes committed by the invaders.[61] Though the object of the woe oracles is not named in our passage, it is highly likely that Nebuchadnezzar is in view in our context.[62] Its ambiguity may be intentional, because by leaving it in a general term, it makes anyone who commits the same crime subject to the due judgment. Moreover by not mentioning Nebuchadnezzar's name, the writer might be making a point as though he never existed in history.

It has long been recognized that some of these woe oracles resemble the ones pronounced by other prophets against various groups. For example, the mention of "nest" (קֵן) in the second woe reminds us of the pronouncement against Edom by Jeremiah (Jer 49:16) and Obadiah (Obad v. 4), and may even allude to Isaiah's accusation against Assyria (Isa 10:14). The language used for the description of the crime in the second woe, especially the mention of unjust gain for one's house, is reminiscent of Jeremiah's woe against Jehoiakim (Jer 22:13-14). Thus Habakkuk follows the prophetic tradition and uses general terms to give the woe oracles a universal function: whoever practices such crime, whether Judean or foreign nations, will be subject to the same divine judgment.

The section on woe oracles directly addresses Habakkuk's concern about the prevalence of evil and the inactivity of Yahweh in the first chapter. Only then he realizes that divine retribution may take the form of "Action-Consequences-Construct,"[63] and that God is in control of human affairs.[64] The awareness of God's plan prompts him to humble himself to worship God and to cry out the

---

[61] For a detailed discussion on the five woe oracles, see chapter 2.

[62] The description of the crimes committed fits the historical portrayal of Nebuchadnezzar.

[63] A term used by Koch, "Is there a Doctrine of Retribution," 68, by which he means that there is an inherent connection between human action and the consequences that befall the person who performs that action, but he does not think that is due to divine retribution. I think that his definition for retribution is too narrow. Since this inherent connection is built in by God, I prefer to see the "Action-Consequences-Construct" as a form of divine retribution.

[64] Notice that in the third woe, he attributes the burning down of the unjust city to the Lord. Also in the fourth woe, the punishment for the one who makes others drunk is to drink from "the cup in the right hand of the Lord."

doxologies in verses 14 and 20.[65] Not only do these doxologies contrast human foolishness and divine holiness, they also reveal the prophet's change of perspective and attitude: from a frustrated doubter who challenges God to one who humbles himself and calls the world to keep quiet before the Lord. The doxologies are also important in the resolution of Habakkuk's theodicy questions, for they reaffirm that God is in control and his glory will prevail at the end.

Some see that Yahweh is powerless in combating the Chaldeans since they are free to do all kinds of violence and no one can take them to court (1:7-10). That is the reason for Habakkuk to turn to the conventional wisdom of woe oracles which talk about "deed-consequence connection" or "fate." However, since this "deed-consequence connection" is ordained by God, and Yahweh is the one who ensures that this process takes place, the woe oracles are best seen as divine judgment. Moreover, the irony in the woe oracles also demonstrates the correspondence of the sins committed by the perpetrator and the apt judgments by the Lord. Lest anyone still has any doubt concerning the veracity or the efficacy of the woe oracles, the theophany in the third chapter of Habakkuk puts all those concerns to rest.

*Theophany: a manifestation of God's power (3:3-7)*

Contrary to Hiebert's view that the third chapter is not integral to the book of Habakkuk,[66] I see this chapter as pertinent to the resolution of the issue of theodicy raised in the book, for it shows the direct involvement of Yahweh by depicting his theophany. Also since the Babylonian military might and earthly power is the main topic in the opening chapter of the book,[67] it is only appropriate that it would be matched by Yahweh's majesty and cosmic power in the closing chapter.

Habakkuk begins his prayer with a plea to Yahweh to renew his work and to show his mercy. There is a debate on whether the ensuing theophany is a visionary experience of the prophet or his rehearsal of God's deeds in the past. To support the latter view, it is stated that the prophet has heard of Yahweh's work from the past (3:2; cf. also 3:16), so he is rehearsing God's past deeds. But in 3:7, the prophet is portrayed as a witness to the theophany, and he is said to have seen "the tents of Cushan under distress, and the curtains of Midian quivered." It is quite possible that as he meditates on God's past deeds, the vision of

---

[65] Contrary to Roberts, *Nahum*, 123-4, who sees that 2:13a and 14 are the work of a later glossator who misses "the point of the original *hôy*-saying in Hab 2:12 + 13b and of the larger compositional unit in which it is placed", the interjection of doxologies here confirms the prophet's perception of the Lord's involvement in human history.

[66] For my arguments against Hiebert's view, see chapter 1.

[67] Out of the six stanzas identified in chapter 1, at least four of them (Stanzas 2, 3, 4, and 6) are used to describe the Chaldeans. For the division of these stanzas, see chapter 2.

theophany arises in his mind.[68] Some argue that Hab 3:3-15 should be classified as epiphany rather than theophany. But, as Rooker defines it, theophany is "a form of divine revelation wherein God's presence is made visible (or revealed in a dream) and is recognizable to humanity."[69] I concur with Rooker's view that this broader definition of theophany is the safest approach which allows one to include any form of divine revelation. Regardless of one's view on this issue, one thing we know for sure: in the present literary context, the theophany is a direct answer to his plea in 3:2.

The psalm describing the theophany has many archaic features. This prompts some scholars to think that this is an ancient theophanic poem that the writer incorporates into his writing. Janzen opines that the archaic feature here is "highly strategic—it is an archaizing with a view to contemporizing."[70] Not only are the archaic features reminiscent of Israel's early history,[71] they also enhance the mystic nature of the theophany. While the Chaldeans are described as animals pawing the ground, eager to go across the land to invade, God's marching from the South is depicted as the sun rising high above with nothing escaping from its sight.[72] This makes the military might of the Chaldeans look like pawns in the great plan of God. The language of theophany is highly mythical, and the awesome natural forces such as pestilence and disease, volcanic and seismic activities, are used to describe the divine power. This demonstration of God's power is important, for it shows that all the frightful, marvelous natural forces are at the disposal of Yahweh, and the seemingly unstoppable power of evil, such as the military might of the Chaldeans, is not comparable to his power. This would allay the prophet's concern that the wicked have unceasing success as described in stanza 6 of the first scene.

*God as a warrior to fight for his people (3:8-15)*

The mention of rivers and sea in Habakkuk's rhetorical questions concerning Yahweh's purpose of coming (v. 8a) prompts some scholars to postulate that

---

[68] Janzen comments that to remember "is to recall, to call forward into the present, the efficacies which are a constituent part of the self through one's past experience, and which are woven irrefragably into those events and those other parties being recalled." For a detailed discussion on actualization, see his article, "Eschatological Symbol," 408-11.

[69] M.F. Rooker, "Theophany," in *Dictionary of the Old Testament: Pentateuch*, ed. T.D. Alexander and D.W. Baker (Downers Grove: IVP, 2003), 860.

[70] Ibid., 410.

[71] Description of God's coming from the south is a common motif in such psalms as Moses' blessing (Deut 33:2), Deborah's song of victory (Judg 5:4-5), and the song of Moses (Exod 15:15), all of which are considered to be ancient.

[72] Professor Glen Taylor disagrees with the view that the description of Yahweh as the sun in this text must necessarily be merely poetic. If the solar imagery is taken seriously, the reader may be led to contemplate the role of Shemesh as god of justice and giver of the law. For his study on solar Yahwism in Israel, see his book, *Yahweh and the Sun*.

the prophet is borrowing images from the ANE mythology whereby the great god (Marduk/Baal) defeated the primeval chaotic waters personified in a sea god named Yam. While that remains a possibility,[73] it is more likely that the prophet is reflecting on the historical events of his people, namely, the exodus experience and the early conquest of the land.[74] Yahweh's action against the sea and rivers may refer to the splitting of the Reed Sea (Exod 14:21-8) and Jordan River (Josh 3:14-7). Yahweh is depicted as a warrior getting ready for battle, riding on chariot with his weapons drawn (vv. 8b-9). The fact that his chariot is called "your chariots of salvation" (מַרְכְּבֹתֶיךָ יְשׁוּעָה), indicates that Yahweh is coming to fight for his people. Later in verse 13a, it is stated clearly that that indeed is the case.

The cosmic reaction to the Yahweh's coming is also recorded: the rocking of the mountains, the downpour of torrential rain, the flooding of the water, the thundering of the storm, and the standing still of the sun and the moon in their high abode. The last celestial phenomenon seems to recall the incident recorded in Josh 10:12-14 when the Lord made the sun and the moon to stand still for a whole day upon the request of Joshua. The description in this section is intentionally reminiscent of God's past deliverance, for the writer wants to remind his audience that just as God fought for his people in the past, he will come again to deliver his people and defeat his enemy, namely Babylon, thoroughly in the future (vv. 13-15).[75] The portrayal of God as a warrior fighting for his people and the description of the utter destruction of the enemy also answer the prophet's earlier accusation against God that he allows the wicked to swallow up the righteous (1:13).

### Song of triumph: the faithful prevails (3:16-19)

The prophet begins the book with a complaint against God (1:2-4), so it is only appropriate for him to end the book with a resolution in a thanksgiving psalm. In the song of triumph (3:16-19), he describes his physical reaction to the theophany in most vivid terms: his belly churned, his lips quivered, his bones seemed to rot away and his legs weakened and trembled. His great fear is not just caused by the awe of the theophany, but also the approaching of the day of distress when the invading army will finally arrive.[76] Yet with the renewed confidence that God's salvation will come after the disaster, the prophet resolves to wait expectantly for that day to come (v. 16b).

---

[73] It could be a case of both: Habakkuk could be borrowing the language of ANE mythology to describe the exodus event.

[74] See Robertson, *Books of Nahum*, 232 n. 4, who also thinks that it is best to identify this as describing God's saving acts of the Exodus.

[75] For a discussion of how the writer uses the imagery of "house" and "person" to portray the total destruction of Babylon, see chapter 2.

[76] Robertson, *Books of Nahum*, 243, also thinks that it is the devastation that the Israelites have to go through that makes Habakkuk tremble from head to toe.

This recognition of God's power and his justice evokes in Habakkuk a deep sense of contentment and joy that could have only come from his total trust in the Lord. The condition in his world remains unchanged, or is getting worse. The description in verse 17 depicts a total desolation of the land, which could be due to war.[77] However, knowing that God is in control and that his justice will prevail eventually rejuvenates his strength and his trust in the Lord. That is why he can still sing this most profound declaration of confidence, "Yet I, in Yahweh, I will exult. I will rejoice in the God of my salvation. Yahweh, the Lord is my strength, and he will make my feet like the hinds, and upon my high places he will make me tread" (3:18-19a). Not only will Habakkuk wait patiently, but he will exult and rejoice, for he knows that the Lord is his strength and that he will ultimately triumph. He is so sure of his salvation that he is offering his praise and thanksgiving to the Lord now.[78] His resolution also demonstrates an appropriate human response to the Lord's promise that "the righteous will live by his faithfulness" (2:4b).

## Summary and conclusion

In chapter one of the book of Habakkuk, we see that the prophet openly questions God's justice and his dealings with human beings. He goes to the rampart to watch for the advancing Babylonians and to get ready for God's response. After God's revelation in 2:3-5, he realizes that God has a plan and a time to set right all wrongs, and that the righteous are admonished to trust and to wait expectantly for the vision to come to pass. The woe oracles explicitly manifest God's justice by showing the destiny of the wicked, and at the end prompt Habakkuk to call the earth to be silent before the Lord (2:20). He then pleads to God to renew his wonderful salvific deeds as in the past (3:2). God's response comes in the form of a theophany.[79] The theophany shows God's majesty and power, as well as the purpose of his coming: to deliver his people from the oppression of the wicked. This theophany is vital to settle all the issues raised in earlier chapters, for it provides assurance that God has the power and the passion to see his grand plan accomplished. Also when one is privileged enough to be privy to God's glory as manifested in the theophany, the enormous impact on one's faith is unimaginable. Little wonder that Habakkuk can sing such a beautiful triumph song of confidence in 3:17-19. This declaration of confidence

---

[77] Roberts, *Nahum*, 157-8, opines that the crop failure may be due to the absence of God rather than the Babylonian oppression. But this dichotomy may be false in view of the argument of the book.

[78] This is what S.B. Frost called "anticipatory thanksgiving." See his discussion in his article, "Asseveration by Thanksgiving," *VT* 8 (1958): 383.

[79] There is a unique feature of this theophany in Habakkuk, which is not in other theophanies such as Job, Exodus, Genesis, Isaish 6, namely, God does not speak in Habakkuk 3. Habakkuk is portrayed as a reporter, reporting divine action, his purpose of coming, and the consequences of the theophany.

also brings the divine-human relationship to a whole new level. Habakkuk demonstrates that human beings can trust God without any ulterior motive: he trusts God for who he is and not for the material blessings that very often associate with divine presence. Habakkuk also becomes a paradigm of the righteous as described in 2:4, who wait faithfully for his faithful God to accomplish the vision.

## Theodicy in other biblical passages

### Job

Like Habakkuk, the book of Job also wrestles with the issue of theodicy. The book of Job begins with a prologue whereby Job, a blessed man of great wealth with ten children, is described as "blameless and upright; he feared God and shunned evil" (1:1). This assessment of Job's character is made by the narrator, God (1:8, 2:3), and even Job himself (9:15, 20, 21; 31:1-40), lest anyone doubt the integrity of Job. The narrative then shifts to the heavenly divine council where the Satan attends. God's open praise for Job prompts the Satan to question Job's motive for being righteous. The Satan claims that there is no disinterested righteousness with human beings.[80] Then a plan is devised to test Job's faithfulness by stripping away all his belongings, his servants and his children. Despite the sudden calamity, Job remains faithful to God. On the second divine council, God again praises Job for remaining faithful. But Satan is not ready to concede failure just yet and incites God to let him inflict physical pain on Job. God allows him to do so but sets a limit to spare Job's life. Job's wife, unwilling to see him suffer any longer, advises him to abandon his integrity and to curse[81] God and die (2:9). But Job refuses and retains his integrity. His three friends come to comfort him and sit with him quietly for seven days and nights. Thus the prologue provides us with background knowledge of the suffering of a blameless, righteous man; and prepares us for one of the most magnificent literatures dealing with the issue of human suffering. Job's cursing of his birthday in chapter 3 sets the stage for the three cycles of disputation with his friends (4:1-14:22; 15:1-21:34; 22:1-27:23). And after a by-stander, Elihu, gives a long speech (32-37), God finally appears and speaks to Job (38:1-40:1; 40:6-41:34). God's speeches in the whirlwind render Job speechless and he humbles himself before God and renounces all his charges against God and recants the words he

---

[80] Disinterested righteousness means that people do what is right not because of the reward that God bestows on virtuous behavior, but for the sake of righteousness. Crenshaw, *A Whirlpool of Torment: Israelite Traditions of God as an Oppressive Presence*, Overtures to Biblical Theology (Philadelphia: Fortress, 1984), 59, thinks that both the issues of disinterested righteousness and the innocent suffering are the theme of the book, depending on whether one views things from God's viewpoint or from Job's viewpoint.

[81] The Hebrew text actually says "bless" (בָּרֵךְ), which is used euphemistically for "curse" in the opening chapters of Job (1:5, 11, and here 2:9).

has said in ignorance. Then Job is vindicated and restored to double his former wealth in the epilogue (42:7-17).

As many scholars point out, the Job we see in the prologue (chapters 1 and 2) is drastically different from the Job in subsequent chapters where he engages in confrontational disputes with his three friends. Lennart Boström thinks that the two presentations of Job are meant to describe Job as two diametrically opposed ideals, namely, the ideal of submission and silence as described in the prologue (Job 1-2); and the ideal of challenge and non-acceptance as described in the subsequent chapters (3-37).[82] It is the latter model that Habakkuk reflects.

*Questions raised in the book of Job*
The main issue of Job's dispute with his friends is the relationship between retribution and human suffering. The problem is that Job and his friends all attribute human suffering to retribution theology,[83] albeit from different perspectives. From the perspective of the comforters, Job must have sinned, since great disaster befalls him, and God is always just in carrying out retribution. But from Job's point of view, since he knows that he has done nothing to deserve such treatment (and the reader of the prologue knows that it is true), his suffering is a violation of the retribution principle. Therefore God must have been capricious and has not been fair to him, or is incapable of controlling the forces of chaos. That is the cause of his theodic cry and the reason for his longing to take God to court and to have an arbiter give a fair judgment (9:33).

Another question that is closely related to the suffering of Job is the one raised by the Satan, "Does Job fear God for nothing?" (1:9) In other words, can human beings have disinterested righteousness?[84] Like Habakkuk, who in his declaration of confidence shows that the righteous can trust God even without any material blessings (Hab 3:17-19a), Job's reactions to the calamities in the prologue give an affirmative answer to this question. But this does not mean that he does not question divine justice, and his speeches in the subsequent chapters clearly demonstrate his struggle.

Theodicy is obviously a question that Job wrestles with. All along Job maintains his innocence, and while he does not doubt God's power and might,[85] he questions God's justice; "If it is a contest of strength, he is the strong one! If it is a matter of justice, who can summon him?" (9:19). To Job, God is the ultimate source of evil, for he is the one who perverts justice and destroys both the

---

[82] L. Boström, "Patriarchal Models for Piety," in *Shall Not the Judge of All the Earth Do What Is Right? Studies on the Nature of God in Tribute to James L. Crenshaw*, ed. D. Penchansky, and P.L. Redditt (Winona Lake: Eisenbrauns, 2000), 62-71.

[83] In a nutshell, retribution theology teaches that God rewards the righteous and punishes the wicked.

[84] Crenshaw, *Whirlpool of Torment*, 59.

[85] Some think that Job does question God's power to mete out justice to the wicked (cf. 21:7ff). However, it is not a matter of divine power but divine will to carry out justice.

blameless and the wicked alike (9:22), he takes joy in the perishing of the innocent (9:23), and gives the earth to the wicked; "If it is not he, who then is it?" (9:24). To counter his friends' argument that the wicked will get their due judgment, Job fervently points out the cruel reality that the wicked always seem to enjoy prosperity and well-being (21:7-31), and that death is the common lot for all humankind (21:23-26). Job's embittered accusation against God is similar to Habakkuk's complaint when the prophet accuses God of raising up the more wicked one to do the destruction and making human beings vulnerable like creeping creatures (Hab 1:13-14).

Job's greatest pain, I would argue, does not come from the great loss of his earthly possessions: wealth, health, fame, and family; nor does it come from his friends' persistent false accusations, but from a perceived broken relationship with his God. And this broken relationship is due to the apparent divine injustice done to him. He could not understand why God, with whom he had intimate friendship (29:2-25), would take pleasure in oppressing him for no apparent valid reason (9:17; 10:2-7). Only a personal encounter with God could resolve his deepest anguish. That is why he wants to argue his case before him (13:15). His greatest dilemma, however, is that he has no one to turn to except God: his greatest adversary is at the same time his only hope (16:19-20).[86] Hence he petitions for a trial by giving his declaration of innocence (31:1-40).[87] Despite all the calamities and his friends' accusations, he vouches to maintain his integrity and his righteousness (27:5-6). And amazingly, he still believes in retribution theology (24:18-25; 27:13-23).

*How do the divine speeches answer Job's concern?*
A cursory reading on the divine speeches in chapters 38-41 seems to show that God does not answer Job's question at all. He appears to be oblivious to Job's concern of the suffering of the righteous and the prosperity of the wicked. Not only does he not reveal the reason for Job's suffering, the rhetorical questions he poses to Job are so intimidating that some think that God is bullying Job to submission.[88] However, Job's reaction in 42:1-6 seems to indicate that he is satisfied with God's answer,[89] and that he has gained knowledge which he did

---

[86] Westermann comments that Job "clings to God against God," and that Job's perseverance through suffering makes him come close to the figure of the mediator. See his article, "The Role of the Lament in the Theology of the Old Testament," *Int* 28 (1974): 32.

[87] According to Michael Brennan Dick, this type of oath of innocence would compel the plaintiff to present the evidence against the defendant before the judge. Hence Job is using the same ANE court procedure here to force God to present his case against him. See Dick's article, "Legal Metaphor in Job 31," *CBQ* 41 (1979): 37-50.

[88] Crenshaw calls God a "blustering deity." See his essay, "The Shift from Theodicy to Anthropodicy," in *Theodicy in the Old Testament*, ed. J.L. Crenshaw (Philadelphia: Fortress, 1983), 9.

[89] Some may argue that this passage is redactional, but I am only interested in the message that the final form of the text conveys. For a diametrically opposed view on the

not know before; "I have heard of You by the hearing of the ear, but now my eye sees You" (42:5). That invites the reader to search deeper to see how the divine speeches bring such changes in Job.

Some scholars argue that the theophany itself is an answer to Job's request. Earlier Job has demanded to see God and complained about the aloofness of God (13:15-16, 18-24; 16:19-21; 31:35, 37). Now God grants him that wish and appears in a whirlwind to meet him (38:1). However, as Matitiahu Tsevat argues, the design and construction of the book demand a divine answer.[90] Also Job's declaration of innocence in chapter 31 obliges God to give a verdict, either to vindicate him or to convict him.[91]

Yahweh's first speech begins with a rhetorical question, "Who is this that darkens counsel by words without knowledge?" (38:2) and with an imperative to Job, "Gird up your loins[92] like a man, I will question you, and you shall declare to me!" (38:3) Then, with a series of questions God quizzes him on his knowledge of "cosmology, oceanography, meteorology, astronomy, and zoology" (38:4-39:30).[93] The purpose of these questions is not to humiliate him but to lead him out of his own world and to let him see his own proper place within God's magnificent creation.[94] Earlier Job sees himself as the center of God's target and laments that the Almighty singles him out to oppress him (19:8-20; cf. 10:13-17). He perceives that God has turned from being his Creator to be his worst enemy (10:8-12; cf. 13:24, 26-27) and accuses God of "wrongful dispossession," by taking away forcefully all his possession without reason (9:12-18). In her article, Sylvia Huberman Scholnick points out that the rapid-fire questions are designed to discredit his accusations by showing his ignorance of the

---

interpretation of this passage, see J.B. Curtis, "On Job's Response to Yahweh," *JBL* 98 (1979): 498-511. Meanwhile many scholars are not satisfied with Job's "sudden break-down" and try to come up with various explanations, including the suggestion that "Job's repentance is a clever ruse to avoid annihilation after he attained his goal, a moral victory." See the discussion of Jung's view in J.G. Williams, "You Have Not Spoken Truth of Me": Mystery and Irony in Job," *ZAW* 83 (1971): 248. Williams sees God's compliment of Job in 42:7 as divine condemnation of himself and admission of his destructive and capricious act (ibid., 247-50). But this reading runs against the writer's view, for it is Job who repents and recants upon dust and ashes.

[90] M. Tsevat, *The Meaning of the Book of Job and Other Biblical Studies: Essays on the Literature and Religion of the Hebrew Bible* (New York: Ktav, 1980), 11. Cf. also R.A.F. MacKenzie, "The Purpose of the Yahweh Speeches in the Book of Job," *Biblica* 40 (1959): 437-38.

[91] Dick argues that "Job 31 functions as the legal appeal of a defendant for a formal judicial hearing." See his article, "Legal Metaphor in Job 31," 49.

[92] S. Huberman Scholnick, "The Meaning of *Mišpat* in the Book of Job," *JBL* 104 (1982): 527, states that to "gird the loins" has a forensic force, which means that God is accepting Job's challenge to a litigation settlement of the issue.

[93] R.B. Zuck, *Job* (Chicago: Moody Press, 1978), 165.

[94] F.I. Anderson, *Job: An Introduction and Commentary*. TOTC (Downers Grove: IVP, 1976), 269.

created world, whereas God uses his knowledge of creation to establish his sovereignty over the universe so as to address Job's charges against him: since God is the rightful owner of everything in the universe, Job cannot accuse him of wrongful deprivation.[95] Also, by describing his role as King rather than Judge, God defines for Job the true nature of divine justice as sovereignty:[96] that Job's suffering is not a result of retribution but rather the divine prerogative to administer his governance over a complex kingdom.[97] She explains that just as a human king has the regal power to draft men and women to be his servants and maids and to appropriate properties for his own use (1 Sam 8:9-17), God as divine King also has the executive authority to remove Job's family and property in order to test his subject.[98] Thus Job misunderstands his suffering as a result of divine judicial decision, when God is only exercising his sovereign authority. Also, by asking Job to gird himself like a man, God gives him a chance to speak for himself and treats him as equal. Job is obviously overwhelmed by the grandeur and wonder of the creation, so when God asks him to respond, he can only say; "See, I am of small account; what shall I answer you? I lay my hand on my mouth" (40:4). Some scholars, such as Athalya Brenner and John Briggs Curtis, interpret Job's silence as disapproval rather than awe.[99] But this contradicts what the text says, for Job admits his own "smallness" (קַלֹּתִי) and restraints himself from speaking. However, most scholars realize that Job has not abandoned his charges against God at this point yet, so a second divine speech is necessary.

In order for God to persuade Job to drop all charges against him and to let him see his own self-righteous attitude, God challenges Job to gird himself up for a second round in the contest (40:7). He asks Job pointedly, "Will you really annul my judgment? Will you condemn me that you may be justified?" (40:8)[100] Earlier in his disputation with his friends, in order to exonerate himself, Job has vehemently accused God of thwarting justice (9:21-24), and depicted him to be, to use Tryggve Mettinger's words, "the omnipotent tyrant, the cosmic thug."[101] Thus God challenges Job to use his own power to bring down the proud and to destroy the wicked (40:11-13). In other words, God questions

---

[95] S. Huberman Scholnick, "Poetry in the Courtroom: Job 38-41," in *Directions in Biblical Hebrew Poetry*, JSOTSup 40, ed. E.R. Follis (Sheffield: SAP, 1987): 185-92.

[96] Scholnick, "Meaning of *Mišpat*," 521-29, explains that there are two meanings of the word מִשְׁפָּט in Job: a "forensic" meaning and a meaning of "sovereign authority."

[97] Scholnick, "Poetry in the Courtroom," 192-4.

[98] Scholnick, "Meaning of *Mišpat*," 522-3.

[99] A. Brenner, "God's Answer to Job." *VT* 31 (1981): 133. See also J.B. Curtis for his speculative re-created speech of Job in his article, "On Job's Response to Yahweh," 507.

[100] Translation from NASB.

[101] T.N.D. Mettinger, "The God of Job: Avenger, Tyrant, or Victor?" in *The Voice from the Whirlwind: Interpreting The Book of Job*, ed. L.G. Perdue, and W.C. Gilpin (Nashville: Abingdon, 1992), 44.

Job if he has the power and ability to execute justice on earth: if he cannot even handle his fellow humankind, how can he challenge God? Brenner interprets this as a partial "admittance of divine failure."[102] This can hardly be correct. For in verse 9, God asks Job, "Have you an arm like God, and can you thunder with a voice like his?" This implies that while Job does not have the power to perform all these duties, God certainly can. Just as previous rhetorical questions contrast the divine sovereignty and wisdom with Job's ignorance of divine judgment, so here God exposes Job's feebleness and questions his ability to challenge divine justice.

Then Yahweh introduces two primordial monsters, Behemoth and Leviathan, and questions Job's ability to subdue them.[103] The identification of Behemoth and Leviathan ranges from earthly animals, which are identified to be hippopotamus and crocodile respectively, to mythical monsters.[104] Mettinger, along with many scholars, asserts that both the Behemoth and Leviathan represent the chaotic power that is the enemy of God.[105] However, while Leviathan has been referred to as cosmic chaos in 3:8, and that the description in 41:10-13 [Eng 41:18-21] seems to fit a mythical being, there is no evidence that both Behemoth and Leviathan are portrayed as the enemy of God here. Rather, they are magnificent creatures, with fearful and extraordinary power, which are created and controlled by God. J.V. Kinnier Wilson opines that these two animals are used to challenge Job to take up the mantle of a Creator-god and a Hero-god in order to let Job realize his own incapability so as to humble him.[106] While I do not agree completely with his opinion, his article does give some good insight. I concur with him that 40:8-14 serve as introduction to the following pas-

---

[102] Brenner, "God's Answer to Job," 133.

[103] Contrary to Curtis, "On Job's Response to Yahweh," 498, who thinks that the passages on Behemoth and Leviathan (40:15-41:34) are secondary and dismisses them as out of place but only serve to delay Job's response, these two animals play a role in bringing forth Job's final confession.

[104] Anderson, *Job*, 288, interprets them as the earthly animals; while M.H. Pope, *Job: A New Translation with Introduction and Commentary*, AB 15 (New York: Doubleday, 1973), 320-22 and 329-32, sees them as the mythological and supernatural characters.

[105] Mettinger, "The God of Job," 46. See also J.C.L. Gibson, "On Evil in the Book of Job," in *Ascribe to the Lord: Biblical and Other Studies in Memory of Peter C. Craigie*, ed. L. Eslinger and G. Taylor, JSOTSS 67 (Sheffield: JSOT Press, 1988), 408. Other less popular interpretations of Behemoth and Leviathan include: Brenner, "God's Answer to Job," 134, who speculates these monsters represent the darker side of God; and J.G. Gammie who sees them as didactic means to caricature Job and to teach him how to survive the tides of suffering. See his article, "Behemoth and Leviathan: On the Didactic and Theological Significance of Job 40:15-41:26," in *Israelite Wisdom: Theological and Literary Essays in Honor of Samuel Terrien*, ed. J.G. Gammie, W.A. Brueggemann, W.L. Humphreys, J.M. Ward (New York: Union Theological Seminary, 1978), 217-26.

[106] J.V. Kinnier Wilson, "A Return to the Problems of Behemoth and Leviathan," *VT* 25 (1975): 5-14.

sages concerning these two monsters, and that God invites Job, not to become God as Wilson thinks,[107] but to view from God's perspective—to be in the front row seat of the divine creation theater. In the scene of Behemoth, it is a scene of serenity and tranquility: although it is an awesome beast with mighty power, it feeds on grass and lives in harmony with other animals, and is not alarmed by the apparent dangers. However, the scene with Leviathan gives a totally different picture: it is portrayed as a fierce, powerful, mythical monster that no one would even dare come close to, let alone subdue. Yet God challenges Job to have a match with this monster. The divine point is that if no one is fierce enough to even rouse the Leviathan,[108] who then is able to stand against God? (41:2 [Eng 41:10]) God intends to show Job that the Lord is the Creator and owner of all; including both the passive Behemoth and the combatant Leviathan, and that both animals act according to their divine given instinct and perform within their given boundary. Then as a direct challenge to Job, he says, "Who has given to me that I shall repay [him]? [Whatever] is under the whole heaven is mine" (41:3 [Eng 41:11]).[109] God's purpose is to let Job recognize his own creatureliness and to see his presumption so as to persuade him to drop his case against God.

Even if we take the two monstrous animals to represent evil power that opposes God, by questioning Job's ability to subdue and control Behemoth and Leviathan, God shows Job that he is indeed the Creator God who controls all powers in the universe, and that no force, not even the chaotic evil force, is strong enough to withstand him or to thwart his will and purpose.[110] Hence Job is invited to submit himself to God and to trust in the wisdom and justice of God.

Some scholars, such as Tsevat and Edwin M. Good, conclude that the divine speeches actually deny the existence of retribution.[111] Tsevat goes so far as to say, "No retribution is provided for in the blueprint of the world, nor does it exist anywhere in it. None is planned for the nonhuman world and none for the human world. Divine justice is not an element of reality."[112] But as E.W. Nicholson comments, the problem with this view is that Job has already rejected the doctrine of retribution in his debate with his friends, and it is highly unlikely that the divine speeches simply endorse Job's view, especially the speeches

---

[107] Ibid., 5.

[108] This may also be the divine response to Job's cursing of his birthday when he asks those who are "prepared to rouse Leviathan" to curse the day (3:8).

[109] Translation from NASB.

[110] Hartley, *Book of Job*, 534.

[111] Tsevat, "The Meaning of Job," 28-35; E.M. Good, "The Problem of Evil in the Book of Job," in *The Voice from the Whirlwind: Interpreting The Book of Job*, ed. L.G. Perdue, and W.C. Gilpin (Nashville: Abingdon, 1992), 67-68.

[112] Tsevat, "The Meaning of Job," 31.

that reproach Job as well.[113] Also as stated by Scholnick, the author of Job seeks to expand the understanding of divine justice: that divine justice goes beyond the juridical system to include a system of divine sovereignty.[114] Thus Job's suffering is not due to retribution, but is the result of a divine executive decision to test his subject's loyalty. While the book of Job serves to correct the rigid and overly simplistic application of the doctrine of retribution in attributing all human suffering to sin and punishment, it does not reject the doctrine *per se*, and it is certainly wrong to conclude that divine justice is not "an element of reality" but only a "dream."[115] If there is no divine justice and no retribution, then there would not be any issue of theodicy and there is no point of lamenting to God, since everything just happens by chance. The divine rhetorical questions in 40:8-13 concerning the humbling of the proud and the crushing of the wicked confirm the existence of divine retribution. Furthermore, the restoration of Job in the epilogue serves not only as a vindication for Job but also as an affirmation of the doctrine. Indeed, divine grace and justice converge in Job's restoration.

While God's speeches do not directly answer Job's question concerning the suffering of the righteous, the rhetorical questions in the divine speeches give a chance for Job to see his ignorance and his own presumptuous self-righteous attitude. They also help to lift his eyes from his own miserable situation to see the grandeur and wonder of God's creation, and invite him to put his trust in the Creator God who has created the universe in perfect wisdom and harmony, and who continues to sustain the world with care and providence. Walther Eichrodt suggested that the divine speeches include a "mysterious inner bond between the creator and the creation, on account of which people feel themselves addressed and seized in the depths of their being by God's rule, even when they do not understand it."[116] Though Job's suffering is great and inexplicable, and is overwhelming and excruciating, there is still a glimpse of hope because God is in control, for just as the raging sea has a boundary, likewise, all human suffering and evil force would have a limit.[117] The theophany provides him with the necessary strength and providence to carry on, as well as brings the divine-human relationship to a new level. Hence God's righteous ones are urged to

---

[113] E.W. Nicholson, "The Limits of Theodicy as a Theme of the Book of Job," in *Wisdom in Ancient Israel*, ed. J. Day, R.P. Gordon, and H.G.M. Williamson (Cambridge: Cambridge University Press, 1995), 79.

[114] Scholnick, "Meaning of *Mišpat*," 521.

[115] Tsevat, "The Meaning of Job," 31.

[116] W. Eichrodt, "Faith in Providence and Theodicy in the Old Testament," in *Theodicy in the Old Testament*, ed. J.L. Crenshaw (Philadelphia: Fortress, 1983), 35.

[117] Nicholson, who follows J.D. Levenson to view that God did not eliminate all his adversaries of chaos in his primeval victory, nonetheless affirms that "the power of chaos, though not eliminated, is confined, and that God has given his pledge to his creation, renders evil less absolute than it would otherwise be." See his discussion in the article, "The Limits of Theodicy," 81-82.

thrust themselves to their Creator in time of suffering and take refuge and comfort in his presence.

*Similarity between Habakkuk and Job*

Both Habakkuk and Job are honest and courageous doubters who dare to question God.[118] In fact, Job challenges God to go to court, and is convinced that if he is given a fair trial, he will be acquitted while God will be found guilty of injustice (9:21-24; 23:4-17). But he doubts if he could ever get a fair trial and accuses God of perverting justice by indiscriminately destroying both the blameless and the wicked (9:22), by blindfolding the judges (9:24), and by wronging him (19:6). There is a similarity in the language used by both Job and Habakkuk in their complaints that when they cry "violence" (חָמָס) there is no answer/saving, and when they "call for help" (שָׁוַע) there is no justice/listening (Job 19:7; Hab 1:2). This shows that both of them are suffering some undeserved, violent loss and yet God does not seem to care.[119] Also both of them are ready to argue and debate with God; "I would lay my case before him and fill my mouth with arguments (תּוֹכָחוֹת). I would learn what he would answer me, and understand what he would say to me" (Job 23:4-5; cf. Hab 2:1). The words that they utter out of their anguished souls are so blunt that they are close to blasphemy; nonetheless they are honest and they retain their integrity by remaining truthful to their belief. It is this honesty that makes them refuse to reduce pain and suffering to guilt and failure, and urges them to challenge God with their "theodic protest."[120]

Both Job and Habakkuk resolve their issues after the theophany. Robert S. Fyall is certainly right when he observes that in all great Old Testament theophanic passages, the true "seeing" is the revelation and messages that associate with the theophany.[121] The theophany and the revelation allow Job and Habakkuk to gain a much deeper knowledge of the divine attributes and of God's dealings with the human world. This knowledge changes their perspective and allows them to see that God as Creator governs and sustains his creation no matter how chaotic and miserable the situation might be from the human point of view. This new perspective also enables them to view God not only as a

---

[118] G.W. Coats explains that the faith of Israel allows for "struggle with God to work out the meaning of loyal obedience," and that obedience to God is not an "obedience of automaton." See his helpful discussion in his essay, "The King's Loyal Opposition: Obedience and Authority in Exodus 32-34," in *Canon and Authority*, ed. G.W. Coats, and B.O. Long (Philadelphia: Fortress, 1977), 92.

[119] Scholnick points out that חָמָס also has the meaning of "gained by illegal means," and Job is using this term to charge God with "unlawful seizure of his property." See her article, "The Meaning of *Mišpat*," 525.

[120] A term coined by Walter Brueggemann, by which he means the protest against Yahweh for not carrying out the divine justice according to the covenantal promise. See his article, "Some Aspects of Theodicy in Old Testament Faith," 263-64.

[121] R.S. Fyall, *Now My Eyes Have Seen You: Images of Creation and Evil in the Book of Job*, NSBT 12 (Downers Grove: IVP, 2002), 178-79.

righteous judge but also as a sovereign of the universe. There is a difference between the two theophanies: while the theophany in Habakkuk is based on Yahweh's act of deliverance in Israel's history (albeit with cosmic imagery), the one in Job is grounded in creation. This may be due to the fact that Habakkuk deals with the national catastrophe and tries to make sense of Yahweh's role in the historical events,[122] while Job belongs to the wisdom literature and engages in finding a solution for the enigma of human suffering.[123] Both accounts of deliverance and creation are manifestations of divine power and are intended to impress upon the viewers the sovereignty of God over the universe. Another major difference is that Job is dialogical while Habakkuk is descriptive. This may be due to the fact that Habakkuk has had the dialogue with God earlier (Hab 1-2), and that the prophet is portrayed as an eye-witness to the theophany (cf. 3:7). Moreover, the theophanies serve to address their accusation of the aloofness of God so as to affirm his care for his creation, as well as his concern for his servants' pleas.

Finally, as I read them, both Habakkuk and Job are satisfied with Yahweh's response and respond with humility to reconcile with him. They declare their reconciliation with God publicly: Habakkuk in the form of praise and thanksgiving (Hab: 3:17-19), while Job retracts his case[124] against God and recants[125] upon dust and ashes (Job 42:5-6).

*Psalm 73*

Prosperity of the wicked is the main concern of Psalm 73. The problem is so acute to the psalmist that he almost slips. Thus this psalm is a testimony of his spiritual journey. As for the genre of Psalm 73, some scholars see it as a wisdom psalm,[126] because of its content and affinity with the wisdom psalms 37

---

[122] Westermann classified Hab 3:3-15 as an oracle of salvation which depicts God's intervention in the third person. See *Praise and Lament*, 63.

[123] This is a unique feature of Wisdom tradition whereby theophany is always grounded in creation rather than history.

[124] The verb מאס "reject, despise" lacks an object, which prompts many to translate it reflexively "I despise myself." However, Curtis, "On Job's Response to Yahweh," 505, sees God as the unstated object of the verb, and translate it as, "Therefore I feel loathing contempt and revulsion [towards you, O God]." But this runs against the tenet of what follows in 42:7, for if Job has said that, God could not have praised Job and rejected his three friends. A more reasonable suggestion is by N. Habel, *Job* (Philadelphia: Westminster, 1985), 582-83, who suggests that the object may have been מִשְׁפָּט, "justice, cause, case," as in 31:13.

[125] The Niphal root of נחם has the meaning of "repent, change one's mind." Thus Job changes his mind and withdraws his case against God.

[126] W.A. VanGemeren, "Psalms," in *The Expositor's Bible Commentary*, ed. Frank E. Gaebelein (Grand Rapids: Zondervan, 1991), 5: 475. In his recent article, J.K. Kuntz adds Ps 73 to his list of "wisdom psalms." See his article, "Reclaiming Biblical Wisdom Psalms: A Response to Crenshaw," *CBR* 1 (2003): 151.

and 49.[127] However some scholars classify Ps 73 as a thanksgiving psalm by its form and literary style.[128] They argue that Ps 73 begins and ends with a reason to praise God, which makes this psalm more akin to a thanksgiving psalm. W. Brueggemann and P.D. Miller suggest that this is a royal psalm because of the affinity of the vocabulary to other royal psalms, and the positioning of this psalm at the beginning of the third book of the psalter.[129] But the obvious question with this interpretation is why the royal speaker does not do anything about the wicked since he has the regal power to do so. Other suggestions for the genre of this psalm include: an individual psalm of lament, and a psalm of confidence.[130] Due to the subject matter and the reflective mood of the psalm, I think it is best described as a wisdom psalm.

The structure of this psalm can be arranged in a concentric pattern, with the turning point at verse 17.

A      Belief and Complaint (vv. 1-3)
         Thesis: "**Surely** God is <u>good</u>..." (v. 1)
         Complaint: reality contradicts theology (vv. 2-3)
         **B**      Description of the Wicked (vv. 4-12)
            Their health and prosperity (vv. 4-7)
            Their arrogant and powerful words (vv. 8-12)
            **C**      Lament of the Godly (vv. 13-16)
               "**Surely** in vain have I kept my heart pure..." (vv. 13-14)
               Inner struggle (vv. 15-16)
               **D**      Change of perspective: Reflection in God's
                    sanctuary (v. 17)
            **C'**      Realization of God's Justice (vv. 18-20)
                "**Surely** you place them on slippery ground..." (v. 18)
               The destiny of the wicked (vv. 19-20)
         **B'**      Confession and Confidence (vv. 21-26)
            Confession (vv. 21-22)
            Declaration of confidence (vv. 23-26)
**A'**      Conclusion and Hope (vv. 27-28)
         "As for me, nearness to God is <u>good</u> "

---

[127] R.E. Murphy states that the content of wisdom psalms usually reflects the wisdom themes in the Old Testament such as the contrast between the wicked and the righteous, the two ways, retribution, and the fear of the Lord. See his essay, "A Consideration of the Classification, 'Wisdom Psalms,'" in *Congress Volume: Bonn, 1967*, VTSup 9 (Leiden: Brill, 1963), 160.

[128] Bentzen, *Introduction to the Old Testament*, 1:161; Mowinckel, "Psalms and Wisdom," 208; Murphy, "A Consideration of the Classification," 164; Kuntz, "The Canonical Wisdom Psalms of Ancient Israel," 207. However in his more recent article, "Reclaiming Biblical Wisdom Psalms," 151, Kuntz has reconsidered his position, and classifies Ps 73 as a "wisdom psalm." E.A. Martens, "Psalm 73: A Corrective to a Modern Misunderstanding," *Direction* 12 (1983): 19.

[129] W. Brueggemann and P.D. Miller, "Psalm 73 as a Canonical Marker," *JSOT* 72 (1996): 45-56.

[130] See the discussion in M.E. Tate, *Psalms 51-100*, WBC (Nashville: Nelson, 1990), 231.

The particle אַךְ "surely" is strategically placed at the beginning of vv. 1, 13, 18 to indicate the three contrastive phases of the psalm, and it serves to propel the movement of the psalm. The psalmist uses the initial "surely" to affirm the goodness of God in v. 1. From then on the psalm moves downward until he hits the trough when the second "surely" appears, lamenting that he keeps his heart pure in vain (v. 13). Then he ascends to a new height when he reaffirms God's justice in the third "surely." Other key words that stitch the psalm together include "heart,"[131] which occurs six times in vv. 1, 7, 13, 21, and twice in v. 26; as well as the mention of "heaven" and "earth" (vv. 9, 25). Moreover, the psalmist employs the imagery of body parts to characterize the wicked: sleek body, bulging eyes, arrogant mouth, and oppressive tongue (vv. 4-9); as well as for self-description: embittered heart, pierced kidneys, right hand, failing flesh (vv. 21-26). Finally, the use of the word טוֹב "good" in the first and last verse functions as an *inclusio* to the psalm.

## Content of Psalm 73

The psalmist begins the psalm with a thesis statement, "Surely God is good to Israel, to the pure in heart" (v. 1). But this thesis is immediately challenged by the reality that he experiences—the prosperity of the wicked. This crash of theology and reality almost causes him to lose his foothold. The traditional teaching of retribution does not appear to be working, for the wicked ones seem to enjoy all the best that life can offer—health and wealth (vv. 4-12). This may mean that God does not care, or worse still that God does not have any knowledge, as the wicked ones claim, "How could God know? Is there knowledge with the Most High?" (v. 11). If that is the case, it is pointless to keep the heart pure and the hands clean, especially when all one gets for being righteous is constant pain and endless suffering (vv. 13-14). But to abandon his belief of maintaining a pure heart and to throw in his lot with the wicked is not an easy option for the psalmist, for he is concerned about the spiritual well-being of God's people (v. 15, lit. "generation of your children"). If he lets his true feelings be known, he may have caused some devastating effect to the faith community.[132] That is the reason he keeps his doubt to himself and struggles to understand and resolve the issue privately. His private deliberation on the issue has not been an easy journey until he enters into the sanctuary of God; then he gains a different perspective as he reflects on the fate of the wicked (vv. 16-17). He then realizes that God's justice will eventually prevail and that the wicked will suffer a sudden and complete destruction (vv. 18-20). This new insight makes him feel ashamed of his secret envy for the prosperity of the wicked and

---

[131] For the significance of "heart" in this psalm, see M. Buber, "The Heart Determines: Psalm 73," in *Theodicy in the Old Testament*, ed. J.L. Crenshaw (Philadelphia: Fortress, 1983), 109-18.

[132] This may indicate that the psalmist is one of the leaders in the Temple. If we take the superscription "A psalm of Asaph" at face value, then this is a psalm by one of David's choirmasters, a leading position of the Levitical priests.

his former attitude towards God as he confesses that he was like a "brute beast" (בְּהֵמוֹת, lit. "Behemoth") before God. He reaffirms his relationship with God who never leaves him even when he is in the valley of doubt (vv. 23-26), and concludes that it is good to be near God (v. 28).[133]

*Questions raised in Psalm 73*
Prosperity of the wicked is the issue that the psalmist struggles with. The reason for such a struggle is the conflict between the reality of life and the traditional theology of retribution which has nurtured him. And to make the matter worse, compared to the easy life of the wicked, he seems to be under constant infliction and trouble. Thus he envies the arrogant, and questions if there is divine justice in the world.

*How does the psalmist resolve his issue?*
After rigorous pondering and searching for answer, the psalmist finally resolves his struggle when he enters into the sanctuary. We are not told exactly what causes him to change his mind or how he finds solace. Craig C. Broyles suggests that it may have been the entrance liturgy when one has to declare innocence before entering the gate to the Temple that prompts him to re-think the precarious position of the wicked before God.[134] Tate proposes that he may have had a visionary experience in the Temple like the one experienced by Isaiah.[135] It seems to me that as he focuses on God in worship, he meditates on God's majesty, on God's being and His wonderful deeds in the past. He is able to see from the perspective of the end and cast backward to the present. He then understands that although the wicked may seem to enjoy prosperity now, they are actually treading on thin ice,[136] and that their destruction will be sudden and complete. Hence the psalmist rediscovers the certainty of divine justice.

This new insight on the fate of the wicked also prompts him to reconsider his own relationship with God. He suddenly recognizes his own stupidity of jeopardizing the precious relationship he has with God by secretly envying the fleeting success of the wicked. He confesses his own foolishness by describing himself as "senseless and ignorant," and calling himself a "Behemoth" (vv. 21-22), the primordial beast who represents chaotic and evil power. This deep sense of remorse is necessary before he can rediscover and enjoy anew his intimate relationship with God.[137] Then the psalmist enters into the final phase of

---

[133] J.C. McCann Jr. helpfully points out that the "good" in the thesis statement (v. 1) is defined as "prosperity, ease, and increased wealth" as portrayed in vv. 4-12, but at the end, the psalmist redefines "good" as "nearness to God." See his essay, "Psalm 73: A Microcosm of Old Testament Theology," in *The Listening Heart: Essays in Wisdom and the Psalms in Honor of Roland E. Murphy, O. Carm,* ed. K.G. Hoglund, E.F. Huwiler, J.T. Glass, and R.W. Lee, JSOTSup 58 (Sheffield: JSOT, 1987), 251.

[134] C.C. Broyles, *Psalms,* NIBC (Peabody: Hendrickson, 1999), 300-301.

[135] Tate, *Psalms,* 238.

[136] חָלָק means "smooth surface or "slippery ground."

[137] VanGemeren, "Psalms," 5:482.

"new orientation," to use Brueggemann's term.[138] He then realizes what matters most in his life is the presence of God who never loosens his grip on him, "Yet I am always with you; you hold me by my right hand" (v. 23). God's guidance is not just temporary but eternal, "You guide me with your counsel, and afterward you will take me to glory" (v. 24). There is a debate on the meaning of the second colon of this verse. Some take it as an allusion to life after death, but others see it as metaphorical language. My view is that the use of the verb "take" (לקח) may allude to God's taking of Enoch in Gen 5:24.[139] Also the mention of "heaven" in v. 25, as well as the failure of "flesh" and "heart" in v. 26 may suggest afterlife. David C. Mitchell suggests that the concept of some form of resurrection from death is a familiar belief in ANE world.[140] Little wonder that the psalmist desires nothing besides God in heaven and on earth, and reclaims God to be the strength of his heart and his portion forever (vv. 25-26). Hence the psalmist concludes that those who are far from God will perish while it is good for him to be near God (vv. 27-28).

*Similarity between Habakkuk and Psalm 73*
The similarity between Ps 73 and Habakkuk lies in the subject matter and the psalmist's struggle to resolve his issue. The subject matter is the prosperity of the wicked and the perceived failed divine justice. The incongruity between the retribution theology and the lived reality causes deep inner struggle for the psalmist. As Habakkuk endures watching the wicked having endless success, the psalmist envies the wicked enjoying their arrogance and prosperity. Both of them are frustrated by God's apparent obliviousness to the prosperity of the wicked. But unlike Habakkuk, the psalmist does not challenge God directly; he struggles internally, entertaining the thought of abandoning his insistence of purity so as to throw in his lot with the wicked. After a period of internal and external torment the psalmist eventually resolves his struggle when he finds solace in the sanctuary.

Like Habakkuk, who takes pleasure in Yahweh even without any material sustenance (Hab 3:18), the psalmist finds out that the most important thing in life is the presence of God and though his situation remains unchanged, he realizes that nothing is better than to have communion with God, so he also ends his psalm with a declaration of trust and confidence in the Lord, "Whom have I in heaven but you? And earth has nothing I desire besides you. My flesh and my heart may fail, but God is the strength of my heart and my portion forever" (vv. 25-26). Both Habakkuk and the psalmist of Ps 73 have the assurance that

---

[138] W. Brueggemann arranges the psalms into three general groups, the psalms of orientation, disorientation, and new orientation. See his discussion in *The Message of the Psalms: A Theological Commentary* (Minneapolis: Augsburg, 1984), 19-23.

[139] See Crenshaw, *Whirlpool of Torment*, 107.

[140] D.C. Mitchell, "'God Will Redeem My Soul from Sheol': The Psalms of the Sons of Korah," *JSOT* 30 (2006): 365-84. He also notes that redemption from Sheol is a dominant theme of Korahite tradition.

their future is in the hand of their God, and they both claim God to be their strength (Hab 3:19; Ps 73:26).

## Psalm 77

Like Psalm 73, the superscription of Psalm 77 attributes it to be a psalm of Asaph. Many scholars find it difficult to assign Psalm 77 to a particular genre. It shifts from an individual lament psalm to a community hymn of praise on God's historic deeds in the past.[141] The structure of this psalm can be divided into seven stanzas with a concentric pattern. The second half of the psalm either answers, or contrasts with, the first half of the psalm, with the turning point at stanza IV: I and I' forms a contrast when the individual cry for help (vv. 2-3) ends up with confidence in God's guidance of his people (v. 21). In II, the hymn of the night where the aloofness of God is lamented, is contrasted with II', the hymn of the theophany when the power of God is celebrated. The rhetorical questions in III are answered by the recounting of God's holy acts in delivering his people in III'. The turning point of the psalm is at IV when the psalmist remembers the mighty deeds of God in the past.

| I | Cry for help (vv. 2-3 [Eng. 1-2]) |
|---|---|
| II | Remembrance of God in hymns of the night (vv. 4-7 [Eng. 3-6]) |
| III | Rhetorical questions on God's character (vv. 8-10 [Eng. 7-9]) |
| IV | Remembrance of God's mighty deeds (vv. 11-13 [Eng. 10-12]) |
| III' | God's holy acts of deliverance (vv. 14-16 [Eng. 13-15]) |
| II' | Hymn of theophany (vv. 17-20 [Eng. 16-19]) |
| I' | Confidence of God's guidance of his people (v. 21 [Eng. 21]) |

Although some scholars see this psalm as a redaction of several fragments,[142] there are evidences that argue for the unity of the psalm. Key words such as "voice/sound" (קוֹל), "hand" (יָד), "remember" (זכר), "ponder/muse" (שׂיח) link the whole psalm together.[143] The concentric pattern of the psalm shows that the second half of the psalm responds to the concern raised in the first half.

### Content of Psalm 77
Waiting for divine response to one's prayer can be a frustrating and daunting experience at times (especially when one is under a distress situation, whereof every moment can be painful) and doubt about claims that God cares for his faithful ones easily arises. In Psalm 77, the psalmist laments and muses to himself that his prayer in time of distress is not answered (vv. 2-3 [Eng. 1-2]). He thinks of God and the good old years of the past, but that only makes the pre-

---

[141] H.G. Jefferson, "Psalm LXXVII," *VT* 13 (1963): 87, identifies it to be a mixed type with the first part (vv. 2-10) as a lament and the second part (vv. 11-21) as a hymn. S. Terrien, *The Psalms: Strophic Structure and Theological Commentary* (Grand Rapids: Eerdmans, 2003), 553, mentions that this type of composition that shifts from lament into hymn of praise is characteristic of the psalms of Asaph.

[142] VanGemeren, "Psalms," 5:498.

[143] For a more detailed discussion, see Tate, *Psalms*, 272-73.

sent situation of apparent divine absence even more unbearable (vv. 4-7 [Eng. 3-6]), "Let me remember God and I moan. Let me muse/meditate and my spirit faints. You have held my eyelid [open]. I am so disturbed that I cannot speak" (vv. 4-5 [Eng. 3-4]).

This prompts him to reconsider the creedal statement of Exod 34:6 about God's nature, "Yahweh, Yahweh, a God compassionate and gracious, slow to anger, and abundant in steadfast love and truth."[144] His rhetorical questions in vv. 8-10 [Eng. 7-9] are direct reflections of that statement, "Will Yahweh reject forever? Will he not be favorable again? Has his steadfast love ceased forever? Has his promise come to an end for all times? Has God forgotten to be gracious? Has he in anger shut up his compassion?" Key words such as "compassion" (רחם), "gracious" (חנן), "steadfast love" (חסד), and even "anger" (אף) link the two passages together.

When the psalmist focuses on God's character, a new hope dawns on him and he now recalls God's deeds in a new light (vv. 11-13 [Eng. 10-12]). Many scholars see verse 11 [Eng. 10] as the turning point of the psalm, although they cannot agree on its translation. The ambiguity lies in the understanding of two words in this verse: חַלּוֹתִי and שְׁנוֹת.[145] The following are some of the various translations:

Then I thought, "To this I will appeal (חַלּוֹתִי): the years (שְׁנוֹת) of the right hand of the Most High." (NIV)

Then I said, "It is my grief (חַלּוֹתִי) that the right hand of the Most High has changed (שְׁנוֹת)." (NASB)

And I said, "It is my fault (חַלּוֹתִי) that the right hand of the Most High has changed (שְׁנוֹת)." (JPS)

Yet, I say, "Can it become weak (חַלּוֹתִי)? Is the right hand of the Most High changed (שְׁנוֹת)?" (Gunkel)[146]

The above translations either fail to capture the idea of the psalmist's change of mood from despair to hope (e.g., NASB), or are not clear on how they obtain their translations (e.g., NIV and JPS). J.A. Emerton proposes to emend the word חַלּוֹתִי to תְּחַלָּתִי "my hope," and he translates this verse: And I said, "That is my hope: the years of the right hand of the Most High."[147] Reading it this way, the psalmist turns from despair to hope as he meditates upon the wonderful saving deeds of Yahweh in the past, which rejuvenate his confidence in

---

[144] Marvin Tate follows J.S. Kselman's lead and sees that the rhetorical questions raised in vv. 8-10 are framed according to Exod 34:6. See Tate, *Psalm*, 272-73.

[145] For a thorough discussion of the various translations on the two words, see J.A. Emerton, "The Text of Psalm LXXVII 11," *VT* 44 (1994): 183-94.

[146] Tate, *Psalms*, 270 notes 11.a.

[147] Emerton, "The Text of Psalm LXXVII 11," 193.

God's help for the future (vv. 14-16 [Eng. 13-15]). Janzen mentions that to re-call God's deed in the past is to call forward the efficacies and energies of Yahweh's past work.[148]

The theophanic hymn (vv. 17-20 [Eng. 16-19]), which further describes the mighty power of God and the cosmic reaction to the divine presence, is framed by verses 16 and 21 [Eng. 15 and 20] that depict Yahweh as a redeemer and a shepherd.[149] Thus the psalm ends with a high note that the purpose of the the-ophany is for the salvation of God's people, and implies that God would do the same for his people in the future.

*Questions raised in Psalm 77*
The issue that bothers the psalmist of Ps 77 is the aloofness of God at the time of his distress. Lindström explains that in the psalter, evil is existential and vic-tim-orientated, which usually raises the theodic question of the divine role in suffering: "how does God engage with evil? What does God do to overcome it?"[150] He further notes that the tendency of lament psalms is not to blame the victim but to complain about the divine absence which causes the suffering.[151] This seems to be the case in Ps 77 when the psalmist laments that God has ig-nored his cry for help to the extent that he suffers insomnia. Moreover, Yah-weh, as a covenantal God of Israel, has obliged himself to hear the cry of his people and to do something about their suffering. But when God ignores their cry, theodic protest is launched against God. The psalmist's questions on Yah-weh's nature (vv. 8-10 [Eng. 7-9]) serve as a protest against God that he is not acting according to his declared nature, as well as a soul-searching experience that enables him to make an ultimate decision to cling to God.

*How does the psalmist resolve his issue?*
Psalm 77 records the spiritual journey of the psalmist as he waits for the divine answer to his prayer. We are not told of the actual situation that prompts this psalm. However, we know that it is a time of trouble and that the psalmist ear-nestly prays for his deliverance, "In the day of my trouble I sought the Lord, my hand was stretched out at night, my soul refused to be comforted" (v. 3 [Eng. 2]). We are also informed of his insomnia because of this spiritual torture and his attempts to focus on God by meditation during those sleepless nights (vv. 5-7 [Eng. 4-6]). All these efforts seem to be futile and after a lengthy peri-od of time,[152] out of his desperation, he asks a series of rhetorical questions based on the creedal statement of Exod 34:6.

---

[148] Janzen, "Eschatolgical Symbol," 410-11.

[149] Jefferson, "Psalm 77," 87, observes that v. 16 makes a good parallelism to v. 21.

[150] F. Lindström, "Theodicy in the Psalms," 256.

[151] Ibid., 256-57.

[152] The use of words such as "forever" (עוֹלָמִים), "everlasting" (נֶצַח), "for all generation" (לְדֹר וָדֹר) in his questions shows that he has been waiting for a long time for the di-vine response.

These bold and poignant questions (vv.8-10 [Eng. 7-9]) require the psalmist to carefully consider his options and to make up his mind. If his answer is positive, then he might as well give up his trust on God because there is no hope of salvation. But if his answer is negative, then he should persevere in his faith, for God will keep his promise and he will show his favor and steadfast love again. This is a critical moment, a moment of decision which would have ultimate importance. Deliberation for an answer helps to clear the psalmist's doubt, for now he focuses on God's character and not his present situation. Hence he is able to give thanks to God for his past deliverance of his people (vv. 14-16 [Eng. 13-15]).[153]

The theophany, which is framed by vv. 16 and 21, describes God's power and his majesty, as well as his inscrutable way, "your way was in the sea, and your paths in many waters, and your footprints cannot be known" (v. 20 [Eng. 19]). Despite his great act of deliverance, which is witnessed by all of his people, God's way remains hidden and his timing may not be fathomed by the human mind. However the best course of action for the people of God is to wait for him for he is their shepherd and redeemer. Hence the theophany functions as the climax of God's salvation to his people in the second part of this psalm.

*Similarity between Habakkuk and Psalm 77*
The composite nature of Psalm 77 is somewhat similar to Habakkuk which also consists of various genres. Like Habakkuk, Psalm 77 also begins with a personal lament and ends with a theophanic hymn. However, in the lament section, Habakkuk directly challenges God while the psalmist of Psalm 77 only muses to himself.

In her article, Jefferson states that 45% of the words used in Ps 77:17-20 also appear in Hab 3:10-12.[154] This similarity of wording is due to the same subject matter that both writers are dealing with. They are both writing about the theophany, and the descriptive quality is very similar in both passages. Words such as: "they saw you" (רָאוּךָ), "waters" (מַיִם), "the deep" (תְּהוֹם), "down pour of waters" (זֶרֶם מַיִם), "sound" (קוֹל), "lightning" (בְּרָק), "your arrows flashed" (חֲצָצֶיךָ יִתְהַלָּכוּ), are present in both passages to highlight the sound and sight of the majestic scene of theophany.

The major concern of Psalm 77 is the apparent divine abandonment in the time of trouble. Similar to Habakkuk's initial complaint, the psalmist's anxiety grows as his prayer is not answered for a prolonged period of time. His attempts to seek God seem to bring more discouragement and disquiet. His remembrance of God only makes the present situation even more intolerable; "Let me remember God and I moan; let me meditate and my spirit faints" (v.

---

[153] Contra Tate's assessment, *Psalms*, 275, that these verses are the continuation of the previous painful reflection and that these verses are meant to challenge God regarding his failure to deliver Israel. But these verses are more akin to a thanksgiving hymn than a complaint.

[154] Jefferson, "Psalm 77," 89.

4). Tate explains that "the very thought of God, who is the hope of deliverance, has become the source of pain and spiritual distress."[155] The cohortative form of the words "remember" (אֶזְכְּרָה) and "meditate" (אָשִׂיחָה) occur three times, twice in the lament section of vv. 4 and 7, and only once in v. 12 and v. 13 respectively. This shows his desperate effort of trying to remain confident in a God who seems so detached, and to curb his doubt.

Finally his daring rhetorical questions on the creedal statement about God lead him to gain a new perspective through meditating on God's past great deeds. The recalling of the theophany also gives him new hope on God's future deliverance for his people. Like Habakkuk, the psalmist also has an existential concern of how to survive the torturous situation in the face of unanswered prayer. And just as Habakkuk finds solace after the theophany, the psalmist also finds comfort and new hope upon meditating on the theophanic experience at the Exodus.

*Jeremiah*

Jeremiah is probably the prophet of whom we have the most complete profile among all the prophets in the Old Testament. The confessions of Jeremiah,[156] which record his personal laments to God and the responses,[157] provide us with a window to his sufferings and his struggles with God, within himself, and with others.[158] Sheldon Blank suggests that the reason for Jeremiah to record his prayers is to make himself a paradigm.[159] He cites God's command to Jeremiah to remain single in 16:1-2 as an example of prophet as paradigm.[160] The private word of God to Jeremiah's private life is developed to have a broad implication for the people (16:3-4). Thus Jeremiah serves as an analogy and a paradigm for his people and that is the reason for him to make public his confessions. Terence E. Fretheim, however, thinks that the confessions serve as God's procla-

---

[155] Tate, *Psalms*, 274.

[156] Most scholars identify several prayers of Jeremiah in chapters 11-20 as his confessions, though there are minor variants as to specific passages. I follow Crenshaw's lead, *Whirlpool of Torment*, 31, and identify the following six passages as his confessions: 11:18-12:6; 15:10-21; 17:14-18; 18:18-23; 20:7-12 (13); 20:14-18. The last passage is not a prayer to God but Jeremiah's curse on his own birthday.

[157] S. Blank, "The Confessions of Jeremiah and the Meaning of Prayer," *HUCA* 21 (1948): 331, defined "confession" as prayer plus the answer to prayer.

[158] I am aware of some scholars' view that there may be layers of traditions behind Jeremiah's confessions. However, I opt for a synchronic reading of his confessions rather than engaging in recovering each historical layer. For a discussion on such layers in Jer 15:10-21, see E. Gerstenberger, "Jeremiah's Complaints: Observations on Jer 15 10-21," *JBL* 82 (1963): 393-408. For an opposing view, see S. Blank, "The Prophet as Paradigm," in *Essays in Old Testament Ethics*, ed. J.L. Crenshaw and J. T. Willis (New York: KTAV, 1974), 120-22. Cf. also J. Bright, "A Prophet's Lament and Its Answer: Jeremiah 15:10-21," *Int* 28 (1974): 59-74.

[159] Blank, "The Prophet as Paradigm," 113.

[160] Ibid., 122-23.

mation to the people, for Jeremiah is the embodiment of God's word and his lament mirrors the divine lament before the people.[161]

Two studies, released about the same time, propose different functions for Jeremiah's confessions. A.R. Diamond thinks that Jeremiah's confessions, in their present context, are to "serve a distinctly apologetic purpose of constructing a theodicy of Yahweh's judgment upon Judah."[162] The fact that Jeremiah, the messenger of God, is being persecuted and rejected provides an explanation for God's judgment on Judah's wickedness. Meanwhile Kathleen M. O'Connor suggests that the main public function of Jeremiah's confessions is to authenticate his claim as the true prophet of Yahweh by his supporters.[163]

*Content of Jeremiah's confessions*
Von Rad was certainly correct when he said that Jeremiah's suffering, disillusionment and despair originates from his prophetic call.[164] His pronouncement of God's words brings to him nothing but sorrow and pain: strife and contention (15:10), isolation and rejection (15:17), taunts (17:15), derision and insults (20:7-8), and even plots against his life from his own family (11:18-19), from the people for whom he intercedes (18:18-20), and from his own close friends (20:10b). The reason for the ill-treatment is that his message of judgment collides with the popular belief that God would never let Jerusalem fall into foreign hands. Thus he is being treated as a false prophet and ostracized as a naysayer. The pain of being persecuted and cast out by the whole population proves too much for Jeremiah to bear, such that he even considers giving up his prophetic role (20:9a). But, to his dismay, abandoning his call is not an option either, because the word of God is like a burning fire within him (20:9b). The oppressions from outside and the struggles from within are so great as to make Jeremiah hurl, out of his desperation, bold accusations at God, calling him a "deceptive brook" (15:18), the one who "seduces" him and "overpowers" him (20:7), and even to question divine justice (12:1).

Paradoxically, Jeremiah finds God his staunchest ally. God is the one who informs him of the plot against him by his own people in Anathoth (11:18; 12:6), and promises that he is going to punish them for their crime (11:21-23). God is also the judge whom he appeals to and pleads his case (11:20; 12:1-4; 15:15; 17:14-18; 18:19-23; 20:12). Moreover, the Lord is portrayed as a warrior fighting for his cause (20:11). And although God's words are the main source

---

[161] T.E. Fretheim, *The Suffering of God: An Old Testament Perspective* (Philadelphia: Fortress, 1984), 158.

[162] A.R. Diamond, *The Confessions of Jeremiah in Context: Scenes of Prophetic Drama*, JSOTSup 45 (Sheffield: JSOT, 1987), 189.

[163] Kathleen M. O'Connor, *The Confessions of Jeremiah: Their Interpretation and Role in Chapters 1-25*, SBL Dissertation Series 94 (Atlanta: Scholars Press, 1988), 95-96.

[164] G. Von Rad, "The Confessions of Jeremiah," in *Theodicy in the Old Testament*, ed. J.L. Crenshaw (Philadelphia: Fortress, 1983), 97.

of his suffering, they are his joy and his heart's delight and he gladly eats them.[165] He is also happy to bear the Lord's name (15:16).

In his confessions, Jeremiah states his case before God in law-court language, and he appears as defendant.[166] The Lord responds to his prayers on several occasions: to pronounce judgment on his opponents (11:21-23; 15:13-14), to promise deliverance (15:11, 21), to admonish him (12:5), to rebuke him so as to call for his repentance and to restore him (15:19-20).[167]

Some of his confessions (17:14-18; 18:18-23; and 20:7-13) do not have a divine response, although in the last one cited above Jeremiah answers himself by asserting that the Lord is with him like a mighty warrior; then it ends with a praise to the Lord (20:11, 13). The last confession in 20:14-18 differs from all the previous ones in form and content: it is not a prayer to God and does not call for vengeance on his enemies, but rather it is a curse on his birthday and on the innocent well-wishing friend who brought the news of his birth to his father. The cursing of his birthday is to show the depth of his suffering and depression. Von Rad insightfully explained that Jeremiah, as God's messenger going down to destruction along with his people, becomes a "pointer" towards God, and that "his confessions testify to the severity of God's wrath."[168]

*Questions raised in Jeremiah's confessions*
The problem facing Jeremiah is his prophetic office. The message he is given to proclaim is in direct conflict with the popular Zion theology of the inviolability of Jerusalem. Hence not only is his message rejected, he is also persecuted, ostracized, cursed, isolated; even his life is endangered. He could not understand why a faithful messenger as he would have to suffer such grievances. In his laments, he complains against those who mistreat him and asks God to vindicate him. His complaints become so bitter that he turns his anger against God and accuses God directly.

He questions God's justice by laying charges against God of making the wicked prosperous, "Yet I would speak with you about your justice: Why does the way of the wicked prosper? Why do all the faithless live at ease?" (12:1)

---

[165] The image of eating the Lord's word finds parallel in Ezekiel 3:1-3 when the prophet is commanded to eat the scroll of God's word. This may be a concrete image to remind the people that "man does not live on bread alone but on every word that comes from the mouth of the Lord" (Deut 8:3).

[166] Blank, "Jeremiah and the Meaning of Prayer," 332-33. Balentine, however, opines that in his lament, Jeremiah takes the role of a prosecutor and summons God as defendant. See Balentine, *Prayer in the Hebrew Bible*, 153.

[167] Von Rad's observation, "The Confession of Jeremiah," 90, that "there is no statement declaring that Jeremiah has sinned by his words, nor is there any denunciation of them," contradicts the fact that Yahweh calls Jeremiah to return/repent (שׁוּב) and admonishes him not to speak worthless (זלל) words. See also Bright, "A Prophet's Lament and Its Answer," 72.

[168] Von Rad, "The Confession of Jeremiah," 98.

Like the psalmist of Psalm 73, Job and Habakkuk, Jeremiah joins the chorus of honest doubters who challenge theodicy.

In the depth of his anguish, Jeremiah also questions God's faithfulness, "Why is my pain unending and my wound grievous and incurable? Will you be to me like a deceptive brook, like a spring that fails?" (15:18) Earlier, Jeremiah contrasts Yahweh, the living water, to the leaking cisterns dug by the people (2:13), but in his darkest hour when no help seems to be in sight, he questions whether Yahweh is a deceptive brook that cannot be trusted.[169]

*How does Jeremiah resolve his issues?*

Unlike the previous passages from the other books of the Old Testament that we have discussed, the confessions of Jeremiah, as they stand, do not end on a positive note, if we take the final form of the confessions in their places seriously.[170] In fact, his final confession—the cursing of his birthday in 20:14-18 is so bitter and out of tune with the previous verse (20:13) that its placement here is usually considered redactional and not much attention is paid to its shift of mood.[171] However the fact that Jeremiah remains God's faithful prophet despite all his grievances and complaints shows that he must have resolved some of his issues, albeit temporarily along the way, so that he would have the strength to continue.[172]

Upon examination of his confessions, we find God does respond to several of his concerns. In 11:21-23 God promises to punish the people of Anathoth for their plot against Jeremiah. In response to Jeremiah's charge of divine injustice in 12:1-4, God answers him with ambiguous and seemingly unrelated rhetorical questions; "If you have raced with foot-runners and they have wearied you, how will you compete with horses? And if in a safe land you fall down, how will you fare in the thickets of the Jordan?" (12:5) This is hardly an answer at all! It is as if God is saying to him, "If you think this is tough, you haven't seen anything yet! Get ready for it." Then God informs him of the plot against his life by his own family (12:6). Instead of responding to his question regarding divine justice, God redirects his attention to another question—his survival in the midst of adversity.[173] God's revelation of the plot against his life by his own family may serve as a reminder for him to rely only on divine providence to stand firm and be obedient.

---

[169] Diamond comments that by calling Yahweh a "deceptive brook," Jeremiah in effect reduces Yahweh to the status of idols. See Diamond, *Confessions of Jeremiah*, 75.

[170] One should be reminded that we do not know when or under what circumstances Jeremiah utters these confessions. Any attempt to relate any confession to Jeremiah's life situation is tentative at best.

[171] P.C. Craigie, P.H. Kelley, and J.F. Drinkard Jr., *Jeremiah 1-25*, WBC, vol 26 (Dallas: Word, 1991), 277.

[172] So Bright, "A Prophet's Lament and Its Answer," 74.

[173] Von Rad, "The Confession of Jeremiah," 91.

God rebukes Jeremiah when he calls him a "deceptive brook, a spring that fails" (15:18). This rebuttal is necessary, not only to stop Jeremiah from plunging any further into his own trap of self-pity, but also to remind him of his status as God's spokesman. If Jeremiah is to continue in his office as God's prophet, then a complete trust on God is required, for trust is a vital element in their relationship. Then God reiterates his promise which is given to Jeremiah when he first calls him; "It is they who will turn to you, not you who will turn to them. And I will make you to this people a fortified wall of bronze; they will fight against you but they shall not prevail over you, for I am with you to save you and deliver you," says the Lord. "I will deliver you out of the hand of the wicked and redeem you from the grasp of the ruthless" (15:19b-21, cf. 1:17-19).

These divine responses are essential for his survival. They give him strength to face adversity and encourage him to take refuge in God. Though his condition remains precarious, and at times he is at the verge of buckling, the Lord's presence becomes his strength so that he prevails over his persecutors, and he would be able to sing praise to the Lord (20:11, 13).

*Similarity between Habakkuk and Jeremiah's confessions*

Both Habakkuk and Jeremiah are God's prophets who bare their souls before God. They do not hesitate to speak their true feelings towards God, even if their language sounds audacious and blasphemous. Habakkuk questions God's justice and his holiness while Jeremiah calls him a deceptive brook and accuses God of seducing him.

While Habakkuk implicitly accuses Yahweh of letting the wicked be prosperous by not interfering and standing idly by, Jeremiah brings Yahweh to court and explicitly accuses him of planting the wicked and making them prosperous (Jer 12:1-2). Despite their frustration and doubt, both prophets see God as the righteous judge and plead their cases before him, trying to move him into action.

Moreover, they both employ the conventional lament form to present their cases. Some of the terms they used are very similar, albeit in different contexts. While Jeremiah complains that he has to pronounce the message of "violence and destruction" (חָמָס וָשֹׁד) which results in his ostracism (Jer 20:8), Habakkuk protests that "destruction and violence" (וְשֹׁד וְחָמָס) are before him (Hab 1:3).[174] Jeremiah laments that although he has neither lent nor borrowed (15:10), he is regarded as a man of "strife" (רִיב) and "contention" (מָדוֹן); meanwhile Habakkuk, using the same words, grumbles that "strife" exists and "contention" arises (Hab 1:3). Both prophets complain that they have to see trouble (עָמָל), although in Jeremiah's case, it is his personal suffering (Jer 20:18), while Habakkuk has the mischief of the society in sight (Hab 1:3).

---

[174] According to Seidel's Law, reversal of the word order is a sign of quotation.

## Conclusion

From the above passages, we see that throughout the generations, people struggle to reconcile the issue of theodicy in the midst of human suffering. The situation that they have to face differs but they all have one theme in common: the
issue of the suffering of the righteous. This issue is a direct challenge to theodicy, for being the righteous Judge of all the earth, God is supposed to uphold
justice by rewarding or saving the righteous and punishing the wicked. However, when the experience in life differs from the teaching, people try to find answers and meanings to their suffering. They are not looking for a philosophical
or speculative answer, but a practical and existential solution.

They seek to maintain their faith in a benevolent and just God while their
lived reality seems to suggest that there is no divine justice in the world. In order to do that, they employ different strategies. They lament to God, appealing
to his compassion in order to arouse him to action. Sometimes their laments
even turn to bold accusations against God, reminding him of his obligation to
his faithful ones. Balentine suggests that this type of honest and bold praying is
not only inevitable but necessary in order to avoid falling into deep despair
while waiting for relief.[175] They meditate on God's words and his past deeds,
trying to draw strength from previous testimonies on divine character. This
reactualization of Yahweh's past deliverance revivifies his work and gives the
much needed energy for them to prevail over their present dire situation and to
face the unknown future with hope.[176] Their strategies seem to work, for when
one is in the depth of spiritual crisis, the best way is to face it honestly. The
process of lamenting and complaining gives the sufferer a proper channel to
vent out frustration, pain, and hurt, and to let the healing process begin.[177]

The one thing that bothers the writers of our passages most is the apparent
divine injustice: God is either perceived to be oblivious to human suffering
through negligence and indifference (in the cases of Habakkuk, the psalmists of
Psalms 73 and 77), or actively inflicting pain on the victims without cause (in
the cases of Job and Jeremiah). Thus they bring the issue to God and demand
an answer from him. Through theophany and divine revelation, they are able to
gain a deeper understanding of God and to attain to a whole new level of divine-human relationship. Not only do the new relationship and understanding
rejuvenate the strength of those afflicted and enable them to triumph over their
dreadful situations, they also allow them to see anew God as a righteous sovereign of the universe, whose justice would prevail at the end.

---

[175] Balentine, *Prayer in the Hebrew Bible*, 188.
[176] Janzen, "Eschatological Symbol," 410-11.
[177] Brueggemann, "Some Aspects of Theodicy," 265.

# CHAPTER 4

# Habakkuk in Prophetic Literature

Many scholars would agree that Habakkuk is unique among the prophetic literature in its message and its presentation. In this chapter I will seek to find out
the relationship of Habakkuk to other prophetic literature. In order to do that, it
is helpful to see how Habakkuk differs from other prophetic literature in handling the issue of theodicy. Hence I will first examine the issue of theodicy in
other prophetic literature; then I will discuss the uniqueness of Habakkuk. Also
I will investigate to see how the issue of theodicy in the book of Habakkuk fits
into its placement in the overall arrangement of the Twelve.

## Theodicy in other prophetic literature

Searching for meaning in the face of anomalies, especially during calamity and
when good deeds are not rewarded and bad deeds are not punished, inevitably
gives rise to the question of theodicy.[1] Crenshaw suggests that there are three
answers given to the apparent injustice of God in the ancient Near East: (1)
human beings are innately evil, therefore they deserve what they get; (2) the
gods are unjust for they are not upholding justice by allowing the innocent to
suffer; and (3) limitation of human knowledge, since the gods are hidden.[2] All
these responses may be found in some forms in Israelite attempts to grapple
with the problem of theodicy.

In this section, I will examine the Israelite struggle to deal with the issue of
theodicy in the prophetic literature. I will investigate the prophetic disputation
with the *vox populi*[3] as expressed in the prophetic books, and the prophetic attempts to correct the misconception of the people. I will also discuss the relationship between prophecy and covenant to understand why the prophets' view
is so fundamentally different from the view of the people. Then I will look into
some of the prophetic laments to see if any of the prophets share the same sentiment and the inquisitive spirit as the populace.

---

[1]  See the discussion in Crenshaw, "Popular Questioning," 380-82.
[2]  J.L. Crenshaw, *Prophetic Conflict*, 38. See also Balentine's helpful summary of perspectives on theodicy in the Hebrew Bible in his book, *Prayer in the Hebrew Bible*,
190.
[3]  For a detailed discussion on *vox populi*, see Crenshaw, *Prophetic Conflict*, 21-36.

## *Prophetic disputation with* Vox Populi

When facing calamity, the most popular sentiment displayed by the people is to blame God and to accuse him of injustice. Most of the classical prophets engage in justifying God by disputing with the *vox populi* which questions God's justice.[4] One of the examples of this kind of disputation is found in Ezekiel 18 when the prophet tries to dispel the people's proverbial saying of "the parents have eaten sour grapes, and their children's teeth are set on edge" (Ezek 18:2b). This proverbial saying reflects the despondence of the exiles that they are the innocent victims of the previous generation's sins, and their resignation to their sealed fate.[5] Ezekiel counteracts their saying by stressing the accountability of each individual (vv. 5-18),[6] but finds them dismissing his answer by questioning him; "Why should not the son suffer for the iniquity of the father?" (v. 19a) They would rather attribute their suffering to their ancestors' sins than admit their own guilt. Furthermore when Ezekiel exhorts them to repent and offers them divine forgiveness (vv. 21-24), they reject him by accusing the Lord of being unfair; "Yet you say, 'The way of the Lord is unfair.' Hear now, O House of Israel: Is my way unfair? Is it not your ways that are unfair?" (v. 25, 29) The people's response shows that not only do they not admit their guilt, they do not share the prophet's view of God.[7] Ezekiel then reiterates divine justice and urges them to repent and live, for God does not take pleasure in their death (vv. 26-32). The purpose of the prophet's disputation with the people is to correct their view and to tell them that instead of blaming God or others for their misfortune, they should examine themselves with honesty and turn from their way so as to receive a new heart and spirit, and live.

The dispute over God's justice continues even in the post-exilic period when Malachi argues with the people; "You have wearied the Lord with your words. Yet you say, 'How have we wearied him?' By saying, 'All who do evil are good in the sight of the Lord, and he delights in them,' or by asking, 'Where is the God of justice?'" (Mal 2:17) The prophet's quotation of the people's complaint not only shows that the people doubt divine justice because of the prosperity of the wicked, they also use it as an excuse to deal treacherously with

---

[4]  Ibid., 30-1.

[5]  Daniel I. Block, *The Book of Ezekiel Chapters 1-24*, NICOT (Grand Rapids, Eerdmans, 1997), 558-61, explains that the doctrine of transgenerational accountability is widespread in the ancient Near East; and that the problem facing Ezekiel is not the punishment of the children for the fathers' sins but rather the popular belief in the immutable fatalism which leads to the loss of hope and faith in God.

[6]  Ezekiel 18 was widely held by many as the introduction of the doctrine of individual responsibility, but recent scholars have largely abandoned this view. See discussion in Block, *Book of Ezekiel Chapters 1-24*, 556-57. Katherine Doob Safenfeld also mentions that the introduction of individual responsibility is for the sake of the restoration of the community. See her article, "Ezekiel 18:25-32," *Int* 32 (July 1978): 296.

[7]  Block, *Book of Ezekiel Chapters 1-24*, 585.

each other.[8] Malachi responds to the people's charge of divine injustice by announcing that the Lord is sending his messenger to prepare his way and that he will come suddenly to purify his temple by refining the Levites and judging the evildoers, namely, the sorcerers, adulterers, perjurers, and those who defraud the laborers as well as the oppressors of the weak (3:1-5).

The disputation intensifies as the prophet accuses the people of robbing God by withholding tithes and offerings. The people justify their rejection to serve the Lord by saying; "It is vain to serve God. What do we profit by keeping his command or by going about as mourners before the Lord of Hosts? Now we count the arrogant happy; evildoers not only prosper, but when they put God to the test they escape" (Mal 3:14-15). The people's complaint reveals an underlying problem: their disappointment over the unfulfilled promises when the expected prosperity of the restored Jerusalem never materialized. It also shows that they view religious piety as a means to obtain material blessings from the Lord. But when the expected blessings do not materialize, they refuse to serve God. Also they implicitly accuse God of not carrying out justice and letting the evildoers "get away with murder." Recognizing that there may be some honest doubters among the people and that the prosperity of the wicked may be too damaging to their continued trust in the Lord, Malachi encourages them to remain loyal to the Lord regardless of the situation by telling them that a "scroll of remembrance" is written before the Lord and that the righteous and the wicked will have two very different destinies in the Day of Judgment (3:16-21 [Eng. 4:3]).[9]

The people's religious pragmatism is not new, for during Jeremiah's forced exile in Egypt, he has had a hard time convincing the Israelite refugees to abandon their idolatrous practices. Jeremiah begins his admonition by reminding the exiles of their ancestors' idolatrous sins that brought disastrous consequences to

---

[8]   E. Ray Clendenen divides the Book of Malachi into three main sections corresponding to the three main themes of the book: 1:2-2:9; 2:10-3:6; and 3:7-4:6. Such division links the people's complaint about divine justice to their unfaithful acts in 2:10-16, and their question on theodicy can be taken to mean that they are justifying their own treacherous acts since God either delights in the evildoers or he does not care to mete out justice. See his essay, "C.J.H. Wright's 'Ethical Triangle' and the Threefold Structure of Malachi" in *Annual Meeting of the Evangelical Theological Society 2003* (Nashville: Broadman & Holman Publishers, 2003), 10.

[9]   Some scholars view this as an attempt to avoid the question of failed prophecy by mentioning such a scroll so as to push the matter to a future eschaton whereby divine justice will finally take place. See the discussion in J.L. Crenshaw, "Theodicy in the Book of the Twelve," 185-86. Nogalski, however, argues that the "book of remembrance" is not the same as the "book of life" which records the name of the righteous whom the Lord will remember in the judgment day. But rather it is a book which reminds the God fearers of God's grace, patience, and justice so that they will be able to distinguish between the righteous and the wicked in order to live accordingly. See J.D. Nogalski, "Recurring Themes in the Book of the Twelve: Creating Points of Contact for a Theological Reading," *Int* 61 (2007): 134-45.

Judah; then he warns them not to provoke God's anger again by worshipping other gods, so as to avoid bringing destruction upon themselves (Jer 44:1-14). His message, however, is flatly rejected, because they do not share his view of history:

> As for the word that you have spoken to us in the name of the Lord, we are not going to listen to you. Instead we will do everything that we have vowed, make offerings to the queen of heaven and pour out libations to her, just as we and our ancestors, our kings and our officials used to do in the towns of Judah and in the streets of Jerusalem. We used to have plenty of food, and prospered, and saw no misfortune. But from the time we stopped making offerings to the queen of heaven and pouring out libations to her, we have lacked everything and have perished by the sword and by famine (Jer 44:16-18).

To them, during the reign of Manasseh when the worship of Asherah and all the host of heaven was at its height (2 Kgs 21:3),[10] Judah seemed to enjoy relative peace and prosperity.[11] But ever since Josiah succeeded in halting the idolatrous practice during his reign, Judah's fortunes seemed to take a worse turn. Moreover, Josiah's untimely violent death and the subsequent national events must have led many Judeans to believe that his religious reform was a "retrograde step" that led to the downfall of the country.[12] Furthermore, his death would undoubtedly raise question on divine justice and must have been a real blow to the retribution principle which advocates reward for good deeds.[13] Jeremiah's disputation with the exiles shows the fundamental difference between their interpretations of the historical event of 586 BCE: the prophet sees it as Yahweh's righteous judgment on the sins of the people while the people attribute it to their cessation of the idol worship during Josiah's reform. The people's rejection of the Lord reveals their disappointment in the Lord caused by the destruction of Jerusalem. According to them, the fall of Jerusalem either means

---

[10] David N. Freedman mentions that one of the titles for Asherah is "the queen of heaven." See his article, "The Biblical Idea of History," *Int* 21 (1967): 34. But this identification of "the queen of heaven" is hotly contested. Other proposals are: the Assyrian-Babylonian goddess Ishtar, the Canaanite goddess Astarte (Ashtoreth), or the Egyptian goddess Anat. Regardless of her exact identity, "the queen of heaven" seems to be a fertility goddess. See J.A. Thompson, *The Book of Jeremiah*, NICOT (Grand Rapids: Eerdmans, 1980), 679.

[11] For a discussion on the debate between Jeremiah and the people on the interpretation of historical events, see Freedman, "The Biblical Idea of History," 33-35.

[12] Thompson, *Jeremiah*, 674.

[13] For the disillusionment caused by Josiah's death and the surprising lack of comments about this tragic event in the Old Testament, see the discussion in S.B. Frost, "The Death of Josiah: A Conspiracy of Silence," *JBL* 87 (1968): 369-82. The biblical writer tries to mitigate the theodic question by attributing Judah's misfortune to the sins of Manasseh, "Still the Lord did not turn from the fierceness of his great wrath, by which his anger was kindled against Judah, because of all the provocations with which Manasseh had provoked him" (2 Kings 23:26).

that Yahweh is not capable of protecting his own city or that he does not care and does not carry out his obligation as Israel's covenant God. Either way, they justify their idolatrous practices and refuse to listen to the prophet's warning. Jeremiah then gives them a sign that the Lord is going to punish them in Egypt. The sign is that Pharaoh Hophra, the Egyptian king, will be killed by his enemies (Jer 44:29-30).[14]

*Prophetic attempts to correct the misconceptions of the people*

The *vox populi* reflects the people's bitter disappointment as their confidence in Yahweh is shattered by the catastrophic event of the exile in 586 BCE. The reason for their disenchantment is their over confidence that Yahweh will keep his covenant and protect Israel regardless of their morality, despite the constant and persistent warnings from the prophets. The people's ignorance, that the covenant with Yahweh demands ethical standards in their daily life, results in the corruption among their leaders and decay in the society. Micah describes the popular belief in his days; "Its rulers give judgment for a bribe, its priests teach for a price, its prophets give oracles for money; yet they lean upon the Lord and say, 'Surely the Lord is with us! No harm shall come upon us'" (Micah 3:11).[15] The people's mind is so callous that they have a false sense of security, and forget that their national well-being depends on their observation of the moral obligations that are required by the covenant. Micah then tells them what God requires of them is "to do justice, and to love kindness, and to walk humbly with [their] God" (6:8b).

Amos attempts to correct their misconception by telling them that their election does not exempt them from God's judgment, but the opposite is true, "You only have I known of all the families of the earth; therefore I will punish you for all your iniquities" (Amos 3:2; cf. 9:10). Amos' warning results in what Crenshaw calls "doxologies of judgment" in Amos 4:13; 5:8-9; and 9:5-6. These doxologies, which explicitly mention the Lord's name, function as judgments in order to exonerate God's punishment on Israel as just and righteous; and to give a universal aspect to his justice.[16]

Jeremiah also tries in vain to shake the Judeans out of their deceptive reliance on their traditional religious institution, namely, the temple; "Amend your ways and your doings, and I will let you dwell in this place. Do not trust in these deceptive words: 'This is the temple of the Lord, the temple of the Lord, the temple of the Lord'" (Jer 7:3b-4). He even accuses them of turning the temple into a "den of robbers" (7:10). To Jeremiah, even the "law of the Lord"

---

[14] The sign was fulfilled when Hophra was killed by his general Amasis. See Thompson, *Jeremiah*, 682.

[15] For more examples of prophetic confrontation with the people, see Crenshaw, *Prophetic Conflict*, 24-26.

[16] J.L. Crenshaw, "Theodicy and Prophetic Literature," in *Theodicy in the World of the Bible*, ed. A. Raato and J.C. de Moor (Leiden: Brill, 2003), 252-53.

(תּוֹרַת יהוה), which the people boast about, is nothing but a "lie" (שֶׁקֶר) made by the "false pen of the scribes" (8:8), and is not to be trusted.

### Prophecy and covenant

The people's rejection of the prophetic messages is due to their delusion that they have the covenant with Yahweh; and that the prophets are merely trying to impose unnecessary laws on them. However, Clements mentions that from the earliest stage, Israel's covenant with Yahweh has consisted of a foundation of law expressed in decalogic form to establish a standard of conduct among the people.[17] Thus the prophets are not the inventors of the law, but rather they aim to remind Israel of her covenantal obligation as a people of Yahweh.[18]

Most of the time, the prophets borrow the ancient near eastern legal procedure and use the "*rîb* oracles"[19] or the so-called "prophetic lawsuit" to accuse the people of breaking the covenant and to proclaim the divine judgment. These "*rîb* oracles" aim to justify Yahweh's action against his people by laying out the Lord's charges against Israel in law-court language. The prophetic insistence that the people have sinned against Yahweh by breaking his covenant presupposes that the people know the divine demand proclaimed in the covenant law.[20] The prophets' main concern is the well-being of the covenantal relationship between Yahweh and Israel; and they emphasize that the only way to maintain that relationship is for Israel to obey the covenant law.[21] Hence when they see that the relationship is threatened by Israel's sins, they pronounce the "*rîb* oracles" to forewarn the people of Yahweh's judgment.

The structure of the lawsuit has five constituent parts:[22] (1) an introduction describing the scene of judgment, which usually involves summoning the heav-

---

[17] R.E. Clements, *Prophecy and Covenant*, Studies in Biblical Theology 43 (London: SCM Press, 1965), 23. Also, G.E. Mendenhall, ""Ancient Oriental and Biblical Law," *BA* 17 (May 1954): 28, believed that the Decalogue was the foundation of the Sinai covenant, by which laws and stipulations were derived.

[18] Clements also comments that the prophets are not teachers of a new doctrine of God or of a new morality. Rather they are God's messengers reminding the people of their covenantal tradition which is not "devoid of theological insights and moral value." See Clements, *Prophecy and Covenant*, 16.

[19] For a detailed discussion on the use and the meaning of the word רִיב in the Old Testament, see J. Limburg, "The Root רִיב and the Prophetic Lawsuit Speeches," *JBL* 88 (1969): 291-304. He also concludes that in all but one prophetic lawsuit oracle (Isa 3:13-15), the word רִיב is used to announce Yahweh's "complaint" or "accusation" against his people. "*Rîb* oracles" is also known as "covenant lawsuit," for the theme is built around Israel's covenant with Yahweh.

[20] Clements, *Prophecy and Covenant*, 16.

[21] Ibid., 25.

[22] For a detailed discussion on the form of the prophetic covenant lawsuits and their possible origins, see H.B. Huffmon, "The Covenant Lawsuit in the Prophets," *JBL* 78 (1959): 285-95. See also L.C. Allen's discussion on Micah 6:1-8 as a covenant lawsuit in his commentary, *The Books of Joel, Obadiah, Jonah, and Micah*, NICOT

en and earth, and other natural elements such as hills and mountains, as witnesses to hear Yahweh's accusation against Israel for breaking his covenant; (2) accusation by the plaintiff stating Yahweh's case against his people; (3) refutation of defendant's possible arguments; (4) pronouncement of guilt; (5) sentence or warning. Westermann identified the following passages as the "prophetic lawsuits": Isa 1:18-20; 3:13-15; 5:1-7; Mic 6:1-5; Hos 2:4-17; 4:1-3, 4-6; 5:3-15; Jer 2:5ff; 25:31; Mal 3:5.[23] Michael De Roche, on the other hand, argues that the term "prophetic lawsuit" is a misnomer since "lawsuit" means that it requires a third party as a binding arbiter. But in the case between Yahweh and Israel, Yahweh is both the plaintiff and the judge while Israel is the defendant. As such, in the above passages, only Isa 5:1-7 can be rightfully called a "lawsuit" for it involves a plaintiff (Yahweh), a defendant (vineyard),[24] and a judge (Judah); while the rest of the passages are the *rîb*-oracles since they all involve only two parties (Yahweh and his people).[25] However, it is not unusual for the king to be both a plaintiff and a judge in a royal court. For example, in 1 Sam 22:11-16, Saul summons Ahimelech to his court and accuses him of conspiring against him by providing help to David. The trial results in the massacre of Nob (1 Sam 22:18-19). In 1 Kgs 2:42-45, King Solomon summons Shimei to accuse him of violating the previous parole condition and subsequently pronounce his death sentence. In both of these incidents, the king is both the plaintiff and the judge.

Regardless of whether the *rîb*-oracles can be termed "prophetic lawsuits," they express Yahweh's contention with Israel: he accuses them of breaking his covenant by ignoring justice and doing violence (e.g. Isa 1:21-23; 5:7; Hos 4:1-3), by causing all kinds of social ills (e.g. Amos 4:1; Mic 6:2-13; 7:3-6), and by turning away from him to follow other gods (e.g. Jer 2:10-11; cf. Hos 2:4-8). The prophets even go so far as to say that not even one righteous person remains in the land; "Run to and fro through the streets of Jerusalem, look around and take note! Search its squares and see if you can find one person who acts justly and seeks truth—so that I may pardon Jerusalem." (Jer 5:1; cf. Mic 7:2) The divine request to seek for a righteous person recalls Abraham's plea for Sodom and Gomorrah when God agrees to forgive the doomed cities for the sake of ten righteous persons in Gen 18:23-32.[26] Here the standard is lowered

---

(Grand Rapids: Eerdmans, 1976), 363-64; and M. O'Rourke Boyle's discussion on Amos 3:1-4:13 in her article, "The Covenant Lawsuit of the Prophet Amos: III 1-IV 13" *VT* 21 (1971): 338-62.

[23] Westermann, *Basic Forms of Prophetic Speech*, 199-200.

[24] The vineyard turns out to be Israel.

[25] M. De Roche, "Yahweh's *Rîb* against Israel: A Reassessment of the So-called 'Prophetic Lawsuit' in the Preexilic Prophets," *JBL* 102 (1983): 563-74.

[26] Crenshaw comments that the Yahwist, who is responsible for Gen 18:17-33, "recognizes that there is more injustice in the death of a few innocent people than in the sparing of a guilty multitude." See the discussion in his article, "Popular Questioning," 385.

that only one righteous person is enough to ward off divine judgment. Yet to Jeremiah's dismay, not even one such individual can be found (5:2-5). Thus the prophets justify Yahweh's judgment on Israel by condemning their sins.

The people's reaction to the prophetic messages and their treatment of the prophets also implicate them and justify Yahweh's judgment on Israel and Judah. Hetty Lalleman-de Winkel concludes that the rejections of the prophetic words by the kings in both Amos' and Jeremiah's days render the prophetic intercessions ineffective and the divine judgment irreversible.[27] In the case of Amos, he is confronted by Amaziah, the priest of Bethel, which resulted in his expulsion from the Northern Kingdom of Israel (Amos 7:10-12). This then brings forth the prophetic pronouncement of the exile of Israel (7:16-17). In the case of Jeremiah, his message brings him great personal sufferings as expressed in his confessions (Jer. 11:18-12:6; 15:10-21; 17:14-18; 18:18-23; 20:7-12 (13); 20:14-18). His persecution and rejection by the people serve as an apologetic means to justify Yahweh's judgment on Judah.[28] Thus the prophets defend theodicy by condemning Israel of breaking the covenant and rejecting God's message delivered by the prophets.

Crenshaw opines that the prophetic emphasis on a covenantal and "holy war" tradition, together with the ancient Near East worldview of a moral world governed by the retribution principle may have given rise to the question of theodicy; and that the principle of grace fits poorly into such a worldview.[29] However the covenant between Yahweh and Israel entails reciprocal responsibilities between both parties.[30] Yahweh elects Israel to be his people by delivering them from servitude and by granting them his covenant. Israel, as people of Yahweh, has to live out the ethical demands imposed on them as expressed in the covenant law. The purpose of the law is to ensure the continuance of the covenantal relationship between Yahweh and his people. Thus the law is a gift of grace for it gives Israel a moral and ethical standard to regulate her life as the people of Yahweh, and to protect the covenant from destruction.[31] Israel's obedience to the law is not a precondition of the covenant, but is an expression of her loyalty to Yahweh.[32] Israel has no right to accuse Yahweh of injustice when

---

[27] H. Lalleman-de Winkel, *Jeremiah in Prophetic Tradition: An Examination of the Book of Jeremiah in the Light of Israel's Prophetic Traditions* (Leuven: Peeters, 2000), 237-38.

[28] Diamond, *Confession of Jeremiah*, 189.

[29] Crenshaw, *Prophetic Conflict*, 36.

[30] Clements, *Prophecy and Covenant*, 69, comments that "the existence of a covenant implied of necessity the existence of a series of obligations into which the covenant members were contracted."

[31] Ibid., 77.

[32] Ibid., 74.

she is the one who breaks the covenant and, as a result, experiences the cove-nantal curses.[33]

Although law is a gift of grace, it does contain the judgment of God against the offenders. Judgment for the transgressors of law is necessary to protect the integrity of the law and to manifest divine justice. Hence while grace and jus-tice may seem to be two bipolar terms, they are two sides of the same coin; and reflect the dual attributes of Yahweh as proclaimed in his name in Exod 34:6-7; "The Lord, the Lord, a God merciful and gracious, slow to anger, and abound-ing in steadfast love and faithfulness, keeping steadfast love for thousands, for-giving iniquity, transgression and sin, yet by no means clearing the guilty, by visiting the iniquity of the parents upon the children and the children's children, to the third and fourth generation." In fact, Raymond C. Van Leeuwen argues that the final redactor of Hosea-Micah uses this passage as a base text in devel-oping an overarching theodicy vis-à-vis the incidents of 722 and 586 B.C.[34] Moreover, it is this covenantal name of God, which reflects the two polarities of divine character,[35] namely grace and justice, that Israel constantly appeals to in her laments in time of distress.

### Prophetic complaint against Yahweh

The populace's complaint about God's justice is usually dismissed as due to their lack of the knowledge of the Lord or due to their rebellious nature. How-ever when the protest comes from God's own called ones—the prophets—then the issue of theodicy becomes too acrid to ignore.

When we examine the prophetic complaints against Yahweh, we will find that they share the inquisitive sentiment of the populace and raise questions concerning God's justice such as the one raised by Jeremiah. Sometimes they question God's action such as the complaint raised by Isaiah about "the harden-ing of the heart," or even challenge the justness of God's compassion[36] as raised by Jonah.

### Jeremiah

The most glaring example of prophetic complaint about theodicy is from Jere-miah when he complains to God about the prosperity of the wicked, "You will be in the right, O Lord, when I lay charges against you; but let me put my case to you. Why does the way of the guilty prosper? Why do all who are treacher-

---

[33] Clements states that it was not Yahweh, but Israel, who broke the covenant by diso-beying the law, that caused Yahweh to terminate the covenant. See his discussion in ibid., 76.

[34] Van Leeuwen, "Scribal Wisdom and Theodicy," 31-49.

[35] D.A. Carson insists that the diverse polarities in the nature of God as revealed in the Bible must be maintained in order to have a sound doctrine of God. See his discus-sion in *How Long, O Lord? Reflections on Suffering and Evil* (Grand Rapids: Baker, 1990), 225-27.

[36] T.E. Fretheim, "Jonah and Theodicy," *ZAW* 90 (1978): 227.

ous thrive?" (Jer 12:1). The frustration comes from the prophet's attempt to reconcile the belief in divine justice and his own lived reality. However, the prophet's question is not an academic exercise or philosophical speculation; rather, it is a concern for his own survival. His question arises from the fact that those who plot to kill him seem to flourish while he, God's faithful servant, has to endure dire danger. That is the reason for his declaration of his own innocence (12:3) right after the description of the wicked. The imagery of the wicked being planted securely and bearing fruit in Jer 12:2 is a direct reversal of what is declared in Ps 1:3-4.[37] Thus Jeremiah implicitly accuses God of injustice by granting prosperity to the wicked rather than to the righteous.

As a usual practice, the Lord seldom answers questions on theodicy raised by human beings. For example, when Job asks the Lord why he has caused him to suffer for no apparent reasons, not only does God not answer him directly but he also challenges Job's right to question his justice (Job 40:8). Likewise, when Habakkuk questions his character (Hab 1:13), the Lord ignores his question but commands him to write down his vision. From God's perspective, divine justice is a matter of divine sovereignty, and should not be subject to human scrutiny.[38] It is one of those mysteries that God does not choose to reveal. In the case of Jeremiah, God does not answer his question on theodicy, but addresses his underlying concern and cautions him not to trust in human support (12:6). When Jeremiah gets frustrated because of the endless suffering he has to endure for God's sake and accuses Yahweh of deceiving him, the Lord admonishes him to repent and to rely solely on divine providence and deliverance (15:20-21). Hence God is more interested in helping his people to stand firm in the face of adversity rather than to answer their questions on theodicy.

Jeremiah's complaint against theodicy is of a personal nature. It arises out of his mistreatment by all the people around him even though he has done nothing to deserve it. He calls himself "a man of strife and contention to the whole land," though he has never lent nor borrowed (15:10). He knows that it is the message that he proclaims in God's name that brings him all the grievances and the ill treatments (15:15b).[39] That is why he is enraged at God when there is no end in sight for his pain and suffering; "Why is my pain unceasing, my wound incurable, refusing to be healed? Truly, you are to me like a deceitful brook, like waters that fail" (15:18). His complaint reveals his bitterness at God when he is forced to deliver an unpopular message which leads to his persecution. Not only is he angry at God, he is also perturbed at the people's blatant rejec-

---

[37] See the discussion in Thompson, *Jeremiah*, 353-54.

[38] Some may say that there is no answer for theodicy. Nicholson, "The Limits of Theodicy," 82, comments that "all theodicies ultimately fail or at best have limited plausibility."

[39] Brueggemann mentions that as bearer of the word of God, one may anticipate rejection in the world. In Jeremiah's case, it is not just the rejection by the people, but his vulnerability is met by "*toughness* and *ruthlessness*" from God. (Italics his.) See in his article, "The Book of Jeremiah: Portrait of the Prophet," *Int* 37 (1983): 133-45.

tion of his message (18:18). He is particularly dismayed by the people's ingratitude and their evil plans to harm him that he calls upon God to vindicate him by bringing calamity upon them (18:19-23). It is noteworthy that Jeremiah never questions theodicy with regard to Yahweh's judgment on Judah, for he knows that it is the people's rejection of his message that brings divine judgment upon themselves (18:11-17). His problem with theodicy is a personal one, for he sees himself to be a righteous person as described in Ps 1:1-2, and he does not understand why God would let his own faithful servant suffer so much.

Despite his frustration and even disappointment at God as expressed in his confessions (Jer 15:18; 20:7-8), he never turns his back against God and goes to serve other gods like his fellow exiles in Egypt do (44:16-18). He laments and complains to God alone; and he relies on God to vindicate him (20:12). Balentine comments that despite facing the silence of God, Jeremiah continues to pray and his prayer becomes even more intense and urgent as the despair increases. [40] As a matter of fact, the honesty and openness expressed in his confessions demonstrate his intimate relationship with his God. It is this relationship which helps to sustain him through all adversity, and he remains God's faithful servant and ministers among the exiles even when he is forced to go to Egypt with them.

### Isaiah

Isaiah does not question God's justice explicitly but blames God for hardening the people's hearts and withholding his compassion; "Why, O Lord, do you make us stray from your ways and harden our heart so that we do not fear you?" (Isa 63:17a). His lament shows that God is responsible for "hardening the heart"[41] of the Israelites. He knows that even the people's repentance depends on God's compassion to reverse his previous judgment of hardening their hearts. That is the reason for the prophet to appeal to God's mercy and his faithfulness and pleads on behalf of the people for God to return and reestablish his relationship with them.

### Jonah

In Jonah, it is the divine compassion on the Assyrians, the notorious enemy of Israel, that angers the prophet. Jonah does not question God's compassion *per se*, for he knows full well God's compassionate nature. This is reflected in his prayer to God, "O Lord, is not this what I said while I was still in my own country? That is why I fled to Tarshish at the beginning, for I knew that you are a gracious God and merciful, slow to anger and abounding in steadfast love, and ready to relent from punishing" (Jonah 4:2). Jonah knows from Israel's experience that God is willing to pardon people and to relent from sending

---

[40] Balentine, *Prayer in the Hebrew Bible*, 162.
[41] The "hardening of heart" recalls the message Isaiah receives in his commissioning theophany when Yahweh tells him to "make dull the heart of this people" (Isa 6:10).

judgment when they repent from their sins.[42] That is why he runs away to Tarshish in an attempt to flee from the Lord so as to avoid his mission of going to Nineveh (1:1-3). Jonah's action shows that he does not want Nineveh to repent, for he questions the justness of proffering divine mercy to such an evil nation as Assyria, under whose hand Israel has suffered tremendous loss.[43] To Jonah, God's compassion on Assyria, a nation whose wickedness reaches before God himself (1:1), indicates divine caprice and injustice.[44] In response to Jonah's resentment, God twice questions Jonah's right to be angry, "Is it right for you to be angry?" (4:4, 9).[45] He uses the growing up and withering of a vine as an object lesson to teach Jonah that he has no right to question God's justice and sovereignty; "You are concerned about the bush, for which you did not labor and which you did not grow; it came into being in a night and perished in a night. And should I not be concerned about Nineveh, that great city, in which there are more than a hundred and twenty thousand persons who do not know their right hand from their left, and also many animals?" (4:10-11) God's argument is twofold.[46] Firstly, since the vine does not belong to Jonah, its growing up is purely a gift from God. Therefore Jonah has no right to be angry when it is taken away by God. Secondly, the plant is only short-lived and insignificant, "came into being in a night and perished in a night," yet Jonah is concerned about its existence; then how can he blame God for concerning about the well-being of the city of Nineveh when so many lives are at stake? Moreover, Jonah's story also reveals that Yahweh, as a universal sovereign, cares for the other nations just as much as he cares for Israel.[47]

### Summary of theodicy in other prophetic literature

In sum, from the perspective of the *vox populi*, God's justice is always questioned in time of crisis; in other words, the people always accuse God of being unjust to them. Their disenchantment is due to the false security that God would always protect them regardless of their moral stance; so when calamity befalls them, instead of admitting their own guilt, they blame God for not keeping the covenant and letting Israel suffer loss. Also they get discouraged when the promised blessings fail to materialize and they question God's justice and faithfulness, and even turn away from him. The prophets, on the other hand, almost always blame the people's sins for bringing harm upon themselves, and

---

[42] Fretheim explains that Israel's very life depends on God's repentance of sending calamity, so it is not the changeableness of God that bothers Jonah. See Fretheim, "Jonah and Theodicy," 228.

[43] Ibid., 227.

[44] Ibid., 234.

[45] Fretheim insightfully mentions that while the divine questions in 4:4 and 4:9 are set in parallel, their content is quite different: 4:4 concerns God's deliverance of Nineveh and 4:9 concerns divine destruction of the vine. See ibid., 233.

[46] For a detailed discussion, see ibid., 234-5.

[47] I will discuss more implications of Jonah's story later.

justify God's judgment as just and righteous. They try to encourage the people to persevere through thick and thin by waiting expectantly for the coming of the eschaton. Sometimes, though rare, we hear the anxious cry from the prophets who share some of the popular sentiments. Habakkuk is among those who dare to question God's character and challenge divine justice.

## Habakkuk's uniqueness in prophetic tradition

Habakkuk is unique among the prophetic literature in both its content and its presentation of the message. While most of the other prophetic books engage in warning Israelites of their breaking of the covenant with Yahweh, and prophesying the coming of the foreign invasion as the just divine judgment, Habakkuk challenges God's justice for his appointment of the brutal Babylon as a judgment on Judah. According to Habakkuk, this is incongruous with Yahweh's nature, and a gross miscarriage of divine justice since Judah is a more righteous nation than Babylon (Hab 1:13). To him, God, as a righteous judge, is supposed to calculate degrees of righteousness, and favor the less unrighteous. But in reality this is not the case; hence he challenges theodicy on behalf of the people by complaining against God. This open challenge against divine justice reflects the popular sentiment and would certainly attract attention and gain approval from his audience. It is this bold challenge, on behalf of the people, against God that makes Habakkuk unique among the prophetic literature.[48]

Some prophets, for example, Amos and Jeremiah, intercede and plead for the people when they feel that the Lord's judgment is too severe for the nation to bear; "O Lord God, forgive! I beg you! How can Jacob stand? He is so small!" (Amos 7:2, 5) Meanwhile Jeremiah pleads for the people to the extent that the Lord forbids him to do so; "Do not pray for the welfare of this people" (Jer 14:11), and tells him that even if Moses and Samuel were there, they could not change his mind of sending calamity to Judah (Jer 15:1). But while they may engage in beseeching God relentlessly on behalf of the nation, none of them dares to challenge God directly and explicitly as Habakkuk does.

The book of Habakkuk is also unique in its presentation of the message. Although it consists of various genres (namely, lament, woe oracles, and victory psalm), it is framed by a lament.[49] While other prophetic books also contain lament form, none of them use it as a framework for the whole book. The reason for the use of lament in Habakkuk is due to its subject matter, the issue of theodicy, since lament is the most appropriate genre to complain to God. Because of the book's affinity to the lament psalms in the Psalter, some may even

---

[48] Though Jeremiah also challenges against God, his challenge is of a personal nature, and he never questions God's justice of punishing Judah. Meanwhile Jonah questions God's justice of proffering mercy to a wicked nation such as Assyria, despite their repentance.

[49] For a discussion of how the book of Habakkuk fits into the structure of a communal lament, see chapter 2.

see Habakkuk more as a psalmist than a prophet. However, the two superscriptions designating him "Habakkuk the prophet,"[50] together with the Lord's command for him to write down the vision in 2:2-5, and the subsequent woe oracles, as well as his theophanic experience, affirm him as a prophet.

One of the most distinctive features of prophetic speeches is that the prophets claim to speak the word of God. Hence they authenticate their words by using the messenger formula such as "Thus says the Lord" (כֹּה אָמַר יהוה).[51] The prophets see themselves as the servants of the Lord commissioned to convey the message of their Master to the world, just as the heralds relating the royal message to the people in the ancient world. The messenger formula is usually associated with the announcement of judgment as part of the prophetic judgment speech against the people, or sometimes oracles of hope.[52] But in Habakkuk no such formula appears in the book.[53] In fact, in contrast to most of the other classical prophets who always indict their contemporaries, Habakkuk issues no explicit warning to Israel against their sin and he does not even urge them to repent and return from their way.[54] This peculiarity may be due to the fact that the book concerns the prophet's complaint to God against the divine action of sending the Chaldeans as judgment to Judah. It mainly records the prophet's dialogues with Yahweh and his theophanic experience. Thus it is not surprising that no such messenger formula appears. Furthermore, the pronouncement of woe oracles on Babylon is put in the mouth of the oppressed nations to attain the ironic effect, and is not presented as direct oracles from God.

In sum, Habakkuk is unique among the prophetic literature in that the prophet boldly challenges theodicy on behalf of the people. Unlike other prophets, who mainly act as the mouthpiece of the Lord to warn and condemn the people, and to urge the people to return to God, Habakkuk stands on the side of the people and acts as their representative to challenge the divine decision to use

---

[50] Although superscriptions may be a later editorial addition, they reflect that tradition recognizes Habakkuk as a prophet very early on.

[51] Other phrases that are used to bolster their authority include: the reception formula, "The word of the Lord came to" (הָיָה דְבַר־יהוה אֶל); and the oracle formula, "Declares the Lord" (lit. "uttered of the Lord" נְאֻם יהוה). But none of these formulae appear in Habakkuk.

[52] Westermann, *Basic Forms of Prophetic Speech*, 131, gives a basic structure of the prophetic judgment speech which consists of the following elements: (1) Summons to hear, (2) Accusation, (3) Introduction to the announcement by the messenger formula (with "therefore"), (4) Announcement of judgment, either punishment or salvation. See also examples of prophetic judgment speech against Israel in pages 174-75 of his book.

[53] The only place where the commissioning of the messenger appears in this book occurs when God commands Habakkuk to write down the vision in 2:2. But it is presented as the divine speech.

[54] Other prophets who are commissioned to prophesy against foreign nations and do not engage in indicting Israel are: Obadiah, Jonah, and Nahum.

Babylon as a judgment against Judah. He employs the form of a lament to raise his concern and to complain to God, for this is the most appropriate genre. There is no familiar messenger formula in Habakkuk for the book focuses on the dialogue between Habakkuk and the Lord, and is not directed towards the Israelites. The woe oracles, which according to Westermann are a variant form of the prophetic judgment speech,[55] are put in the mouth of the oppressed nations to achieve irony, and thus there is no need for the messenger formula.

## Habakkuk in the Book of the Twelve

In this section I will investigate the relationship between the theme of theodicy in Habakkuk and its placement in the Book of the Twelve. I will first examine to see if there are literary clues to suggest that the book of the twelve Minor Prophets can indeed be read as a composite whole. Then I will briefly describe the positioning of the twelve books. Finally I will discuss the placement of Habakkuk in the Twelve.

### *The unity of the Twelve*

While no one denies that the Book of the Twelve is a collection of twelve individual prophetic books which bear the names of the prophets purported to have written them,[56] scholars have long noticed that there are editorial activities in the Book of the Twelve, which inform the reader to read the twelve Minor Prophets as a literary whole.[57] Literary techniques such as repetition of phrases, catchwords, motifs, and themes are employed to link them into a composite unity.[58] Some of the notable examples happen at the seams between individual

---

[55] Westermann, *Basic Forms of Prophetic Speech*, 199-200. G.W. Ramsey, "Speech-Forms in Hebrew Law and Prophetic Oracles," *JBL* 96 (1977): 55, also sees the woe oracle as a form of prophetic judgment speech.

[56] Ehud Ben Zvi avers that the Twelve were being written in one scroll since antiquity, but questions its unity and sees little evidence that it is intended to be read as a whole. He argues that the most significant internal evidence is the titles of the twelve prophetic books which set them apart as individual books, just like Isaiah or Jeremiah or Ezekiel. See his essay, "Twelve Prophetic Books or 'The Twelve': A Few Preliminary Consideration," in *Forming Prophetic Literature: Essays on Isaiah and the Twelve in Honor of John D.W. Watts*, ed. J.W. Watts, and P.R. House, JSOTSup 235 (Sheffield: Sheffield Academic Press, 1996), 125-56.

[57] Most contemporary scholars read the Book of the Twelve as a literary unit. For some of the scholarly works in this area, see J.W. Watts and P.R. House, eds, *Forming Prophetic Literature: Essays on Isaiah and the Twelve in Honor of John D.W. Watts*, JSOTSup 235 (Sheffield: Sheffield Academic Press, 1996); J.D. Nogalski and M.A. Sweeney, eds, *Reading and Hearing the Book of the Twelve*, SBL Symposium Series (Atlanta: SBL, 2000); P.L. Redditt and A. Schart, eds, *Thematic Threads in the Book of the Twelve* (Berlin: Walter de Gruyter, 2003). For a canonical view of the Twelve, see Seitz, *Prophecy and Hermeneutics*, 195-219.

[58] Nogalski observes that there are at least five types of intertextuality in the Book of the Twelve: quotations, allusions, catchwords, motifs, and framing devices. See the

books. For example, Joel 4:16 [Eng 3:16]; "The Lord will roar from Zion, and from Jerusalem he will give his voice," is repeated at Amos 1:2, the book that follows Joel. Another deliberate link between Joel and Amos is the portrayal of the fertility of the land in the day when God's people are restored in Joel 4:18 [Eng 3:18] and Amos 9:13. At the end of Amos (9:11), "Edom" is mentioned, which is then picked up by Obadiah. Both Jonah (4:2) and Micah (7:18) end with partial quotations from Exod 34:6-7, while Nahum begins with God's character as portrayed in the Exod 34 passage (Nah 1:2-3; cf. Exod 34:6-7, 14). In Habakkuk 2:20, the earth is called to keep silent (הַס) before the Lord; this command is given also in Zephaniah 1:7 and Zechariah 2:17 [Eng 2:13].

Other literary links include the agricultural motifs such as the fertility and famine of the land and the locust imagery that run through the Book of the Twelve. Themes such as judgment and restoration of God's people, the Day of the Lord, and theodicy[59] also serve as threads that stitch them together.[60] All these literary evidences urge one to read the Twelve as a complex, yet unified whole. Hence it is pertinent to see how Habakkuk fits into the scheme of the larger corpus of the Twelve.

### The positioning of the twelve Minor Prophets

Most scholars would agree that the arrangement of the Twelve[61] is not just by their chronological order,[62] but that other factors such as the length of the text, catchwords and comparable material at the seams of the books also play a role.[63] House comments that the positioning of the twelve books is to highlight the main points of the prophetic message, which are: the sin of Israel and the nations (Hosea-Micah), the punishment of the sin (Nahum-Zephaniah), and the

---

detailed discussion in his essay, "Intertextuality in the Twelve," in *Forming Prophetic Literature: Essays on Isaiah and the Twelve in Honor of John D.W. Watts*, ed. J.W. Watts, and P.R. House, JSOTSup 235 (Sheffield: SAP, 1996), 102-24.

[59] Van Leeuwen notices that the scribal redactors use Exod 34:6-7 as a base text to elaborate a theodicy in the first six books of the Twelve. See his essay, "Scribal Wisdom and Theodicy," 33.

[60] Nogalski identifies four themes that provide a lens for reading the book of the Twelve as a composite unity: the Day of the Lord, the fertility of the land, the fate of God's people, theodicy problem. For a detailed discussion, see his article, "Recurring Themes in the Book of the Twelve," 125-36.

[61] Ben Zvi, "Twelve Prophetic Books," 134, notes that there are four different sequences of the twelve books in addition to the Masoretic order, and that the diverse orderings of the twelve books undermines the hypothesis that the Twelve is supposed to be read as a single book.

[62] The chronological ordering in the Twelve is only a very rough approximation. Chronologically, most scholars favor the primacy of Amos. For a detailed discussion, see House *The Unity of the Twelve*, 64-67.

[63] D.L. Petersen, "A Book of the Twelve?" in *Reading and Hearing the Book of the Twelve*, ed. J.D. Nogalski and M.A. Sweeney (Atlanta: Society of Biblical Literature, 2000), 6.

restoration of both from that sin (Haggai-Malachi).[64] He further observes that the plot of the Twelve forms a U-shaped comic framework: the fortune of Israel and other nations begins with Hosea and spirals downward until it hits the lowest point at Habakkuk, and starts to inch upward to Malachi.[65] House's scheme is not without criticism: Aaron Schart calls it "too imprecise," for all three elements—sin, punishment, and restoration—are present in all individual books.[66] Ben Zvi accuses him of minimizing the hope marker in the individual books such as Hosea, Joel, Amos and Micah in order to promote the overall plot of the Book of the Twelve.[67] Despite these criticisms, House's proposal of a U-shaped comic plot for the Book of the Twelve seems to fit the historical context: the fate of Israel and Judah spiraled down from the mid-eighth century (Hosea-Micah) to the darkest period of universal mayhem during the late-seventh to early-sixth century BCE, especially after the death of Josiah in 609 BCE (Nahum-Zephaniah);[68] then the restoration came during the Persian period (Haggai-Malachi).

A brief description of the positioning of the Twelve is in order. The choice of Hosea as the introduction of the Twelve, I believe, is to depict the covenant between Yahweh and his people within a familial setting: the marriage bond between a husband and wife, the relationship between parents and their children.[69] This is the closest circle for a person. Yahweh portrays himself as a husband betrayed by his unfaithful wife (Israel) to illustrate the hurt he endures, and to make the indictment against Israel of breaking the covenant by worshipping idols that much more poignant (Hos 2:2, 5).[70] Thus this sets the tone for

---

[64] House *The Unity of the Twelve*, 68. See the chart for the structure of the Twelve on page 72.

[65] Ibid., 123-24.

[66] A. Schart, "Reconstructing the Redaction History of the Twelve Prophets: Problems and Models," in *Reading and Hearing the Book of the Twelve*, ed. J.D. Nogalski and M.A. Sweeney (Atlanta: SBL, 2000), 39.

[67] Ben Zvi, "Twelve Prophetic Books," 128.

[68] A. Joseph Everson suggests that both the location of Habakkuk in the Book of the Twelve and the theme of the Day of the Lord indicate that Habakkuk was remembered in conjunction with the tragic death of Josiah in 609 BCE. See his essay, "The Canonical Location of Habakkuk," in *Thematic Threads in the Book of the Twelve*, ed. P.L. Redditt, and A. Schart (New York: Walter de Gruyter, 2003), 165-74.

[69] John D.W. Watts sees that Hosea 1-3 and Malachi function as a frame for the Book of the Twelve because they both use domestic relations to tell "the theme of the love of God for Israel." See his essay "A Frame for the Book of the Twelve: Hosea 1-3 and Malachi," in *Reading and Hearing the Book of the Twelve*, ed. J.D. Nogalski and M.A. Sweeney (Atlanta: SBL, 2000), 210. Gerlinde Baumann also recognizes the marriage metaphor that begins the Book of the Twelve in Hosea 1-3. See her essay, "Connected by Marriage, Adultery and Violence: The Prophetic Marriage Metaphor in the Book of the Twelve and in the Major Prophets," in *Society of Biblical Literature 1999 Seminar Papers*, SBL Seminar Papers Series 38 (Atlanta: Society of Biblical Literature, 1999), 553.

[70] For more specific charges against Israel, see Hos 4:1-14.

the rest of the Twelve. Joel warns Israel of the divine judgment and calls for repentance. He ends the book with the judgment of the nations and the roaring of the Lord from Zion. Amos is regarded as the first prophetic book within the Twelve chronologically, but is placed after Joel canonically.[71] The reason for this may due to the fact that in Joel, there is still a chance for repentance (Joel 2:12-27), while in Amos, Israel seems to have forfeited the opportunity and hence judgment is inevitable (Amos 7:7-9; 8:3ff). Thus the editor of Amos resumes the catchwords of the roaring of the Lord from the previous book and picks up the theme of the sin of the nations and Israel, and ends with the restoration of Israel and Edom (9:11-15). The mention of Edom then anticipates Obadiah.

Obadiah continues the plot with an accusation against Edom of her aloofness and lack of compassion toward Judah (vv. 11-14). Jonah then shows the aloofness of Israel (in the person of Jonah) and his lack of compassion towards a foreign nation (Assyria). There are several implications one can draw from the story of Jonah. Firstly, God desires sinners to repent—even a wicked nation like Assyria is given a chance to repent; how much more so he would wish Israel to heed his voice and repent. Secondly, while Assyria is given only forty days to repent and the Assyrians grasp that opportunity to avert their doom, Israel, from the time of Amos to her exile, is given forty years to repent before calamity comes, yet the people ignore the prophetic warning that resulted in their exile in 722 BCE.[72] Thirdly, as suggested by Julia M. O'Brien, reading Jonah retrospectively would show that the fall of Nineveh is not due to Yahweh's lack of compassion for other nations.[73] Nineveh's ultimate downfall is due to her own wickedness. Jonah's recital of Yahweh's attributes in 4:2 anticipates both Micah and Nahum. Micah focuses on the sin of Israel and Judah and their judgment, but also gives them hope for the future restoration based on Yahweh's attributes as proclaimed in Exod 34:6-7 (Mic 7:18-20).[74]

Nahum begins with the Exodus 34 passage and prophesies Yahweh's punishment on Nineveh, the destroyer of Israel, by the hand of Babylon. Habakkuk

---

[71] Sweeney thinks that the MT places the two programmatic books (Hosea and Joel) at the beginning of the Twelve: Hosea deals with the disrupted relationship between Israel and the Lord and calls for Israel's repentance; while Joel outlines the threat posed against Israel by a foreign nation and envisions the defeat of the enemy and the restoration of Jerusalem in the Day of the Lord. See his essay, "Sequence and Interpretation in the Book of the Twelve," in *Reading and Hearing the Book of the Twelve*, ed. J.D. Nogalski and M.A. Sweeney (Atlanta: SBL, 2000), 59.

[72] Van Leeuwen, "Scribal Wisdom and Theodicy," 45.

[73] J.M. O'Brien,"Nahum-Habakkuk-Zephaniah: Reading the 'Former Prophets' in the Persian Period," *Int* 61 (2007): 174.

[74] Exod 34:6-7 is used in a very different context to emphasize different aspects of Yahweh's attributes: in Micah, Yahweh's mercy is the basis for Israel's hope for future restoration; but in Nahum, Yahweh's justice is the reason for Nineveh's downfall.

speaks of the inevitability of the Babylonian invasion but also assures the people of Yahweh's destruction of Babylon. Both Nahum and Habakkuk deal with Israel's and Judah's arch-enemies, Assyria and Babylon respectively, so it is only logical that both contain a theophanic hymn celebrating Yahweh as divine warrior fighting on behalf of Israel—Nahum begins with it (Nah 1:3b-6) and Habakkuk ends with it (Hab 3:3-15).[75] These two books also serve to vindicate God's righteousness by punishing the wicked nations, Assyria and Babylon, who are God's instruments to judge Israel and Judah but who have overstepped their mandate (cf. Zech 1:15).[76] Zephaniah describes the awesome Day of the Lord when the universal judgment takes place to purge the sin of all nations, and ends with a future restoration of Jerusalem with worshippers from all nations.

The three post-exilic prophets are at the restoration phase of the comic framework. Haggai mainly concerns the rebuilding and restoration of the temple. Zechariah focuses on Yahweh's intervention for Jerusalem by turning his wrath against the nations and by restoring Jerusalem as God's holy city where God reigns. Malachi, the book end of the Twelve, summarizes major themes found in the Book of the Twelve:[77] the emphasis on love and marriage faithfulness reminds the reader of Hosea (Mal 2:11-16); the admonition of priests echoes Joel and Zechariah (Mal 2:1-9); the stressing of the Day of the Lord as a day of punishment links the book with previous books, particularly Amos and Zephaniah (Mal 4:1f); finally, Malachi's conclusion ties together the Haggai-Zechariah-Malachi corpus by claiming that all facets of restoration will indeed take place, and that Messiah will help the restoration.

### The placement of Habakkuk in the Twelve

This brief survey of the book of the Twelve shows that the twelve individual books can indeed be read as a composite whole, and that their over-all plot fits a U-shaped comedy framework. Reading it this way, Habakkuk is at the lowest point of the Twelve when the Judean society is at a state that is beyond repair and the divine judgment through Babylonian invasion seems inevitable. When facing calamity, questions about theodicy usually surface. Thus it is only appropriate that theodicy is the theme of Habakkuk; and it may also explain why the prophet uses the language of lament to express himself. For in situations when one is in great distress and desperation, lament is the most appropriate language one can use to cry out to the Lord, complain to him, and expect him to give a response. Westermann helpfully pointed out that the cry of distress (and

---

[75] For a discussion on the different rhetorical functions of the divine warrior hymn in Nahum and Habakkuk, see O'Brien,"Nahum-Habakkuk-Zephaniah," 177.

[76] O'Brien also recognizes that both Habakkuk and Nahum seek to answer the theodicy question: how could a wicked nation be an instrument of a righteous God to punish Israel? See ibid., 177.

[77] I follow House's conclusion in this section. See House, *Unity of the Twelve*, 108.

hence the lament) plays an important part in the event of Exodus which leads to the deliverance of the Israelites.[78] This foundational event in Israel's history gives the assurance for God's people that Yahweh hears their lament.[79]

In Habakkuk, the prophet identifies with the oppressed ones in the Judean society during their darkest hour and laments to God, appealing to his compassion, and expecting him to deliver. Like other laments in the psalter, which usually do not identify the enemies, in Habakkuk's initial lament (Hab 1:2-4), the wicked remain anonymous. This anonymity allows the lamenters to express their feelings freely without fear of reprisal by their adversaries, especially if the enemies are from their own community. But to his surprise and dismay, instead of a salvation oracle, Habakkuk gets the most terrifying news—the coming invasion of the Babylonians. Thus this sets the stage for his journey of resolving the issue of theodicy, and grabs the attention of his audience as they follow his dialogues with Yahweh. When he finally resolves the issue of theodicy, Habakkuk demonstrates to his audience how a righteous person is supposed to live in the midst of adversity—to wait expectantly for God's salvation, and to persevere no matter how chaotic the situation is.

In sum, while it is important to read the individual prophetic message as a separate unit,[80] the editorial activities in the Book of the Twelve encourage the reader to read these individual books as a composite whole. As Sweeney aptly points out, this new paradigm of treating the Twelve as a literary whole is not to supplant the older paradigm of reading them individually, but to introduce another dimension which is pertinent to the interpretation of the Twelve.[81] The literary evidences, which include repetition of catchwords, motifs, themes, allusions, are too obvious to ignore. Moreover, the positioning of the Twelve shows that the sequence is a thoughtful and deliberate editorial arrangement that involves chronological and thematic considerations.[82]

If we allow House's proposal of the U-shaped comedy framework as the overall scheme of the Twelve to stand, then Habakkuk is found to position at its lowest point. The placement of Habakkuk at this point is due to the national catastrophe that befalls Judah, which then raises the theodicy question. This placement also explains why the book of Habakkuk is set in a lament frame-

---

[78] For the significance of lament in the Old Testament, see C. Westermann, "The Role of the Lament in the Theology of the Old Testament," *Int* 28 (1974): 20-38.

[79] Brueggemann thinks that lament concerns a redistribution of power: the lesser petitionary party is given a voice and that his speech is taken seriously and heard by the greater party (God). For a detailed discussion, see his article, "The Costly Loss of Lament," *JSOT* 36 (1986): 59.

[80] Ben Zvi argues that one would reach different conclusions for each individual book if the twelve prophetic books are read individually. For his critiques on House and Nogalski, see his essay, "Twelve Prophetic Books," 128-29.

[81] Sweeney, "Sequence and Interpretation," 50.

[82] For a discussion on the differences in arrangement of the Twelve in LXX and MT, see ibid., 56-64.

work—for it is the most appropriate genre to express pain and doubt caused by the extreme atrocity during the darkest hour in Israel's history.

# CHAPTER 5

# Summary and Conclusion

The main concern of this book was to explain the resolution of the issue of theodicy in the book of Habakkuk. I sought to find out how the author presented his message and how he resolved his issue. In this chapter I will first give a brief summary and conclusion of the previous chapters. Then I will discuss Habakkuk's presentation of his message and his resolution of the issue.

## Summary

In chapter 1, I began my research by surveying the previous scholarship on the study of the book of Habakkuk. I concluded that the identification of the "wicked" and the "righteous" in 1:4 and 13 referred to different groups: in 1:4, the "wicked" were the ones within the Judean society, probably the leaders and the powerful ones, and the "righteous" were the oppressed ones in Judah; meanwhile in 1:13, the "wicked" referred to the nation of Babylon and the "righteous" was the nation of Judah. I also agreed with the majority view that the reign of King Jehoiakim (609-598 BCE) was the most likely period for the ministry of prophet Habakkuk.

As for the literary issues regarding the unity of the book, while I did not deny possible editorial activities, it was almost impossible to assign individual verses to a certain period. Hence I employed a holistic approach to read the book as a literary whole in order to gain a better understanding of the meaning of the text. I believed that by engaging in a close reading of the book, paying attention to its literary devices and its use of various literary conventions, I would be able to see how each part of the book works together to resolve the issue of theodicy raised by the prophet.

In chapter 2, I engaged in a close reading of the book of Habakkuk. I demarcated the book into three inter-related scenes, using the literary elements as a guide. I further divided each scene into stanzas and strophes. Scene 1 contains six stanzas, recording the dialogues between Habakkuk and Yahweh, with Yahweh's speech in the middle three stanzas (2-4). Scene 2 consists of seven stanzas, beginning with Habakkuk's action to delay the response so as to highlight Yahweh's revelation at its climax (stanza 2), and the ensuing five woe oracles put in the mouth of the oppressed nations (stanzas 3-7). Scene 3 has its own superscription and subscription to set its limit, and contains nine stanzas. The first stanza and the last two stanzas record Habakkuk's petition (stanza 1) and his reaction (stanzas 8-9), which encompass the theophanic corpus (stanzas 2-7). Thus the implied author highlighted Yahweh's speeches and actions by using a concentric pattern in each scene.

Following my translation of the book, I did a close analysis of the text, stanza by stanza, strophe by strophe, in the comment section. I concluded that the book consists of at least three major genres: lament, woe oracles, and a prayer that contains elements found in a song of victory. The overall framework of the book is a lament, with Habakkuk's initial petition for help (1:2) and his confession of trust (3:17-19a) forming an *inclusio*. The eclectic use of genres reads as the prophet's effort of finding the most appropriate forms to present his message and to express his feelings.

In chapter 3, I focused on the issue of theodicy in Habakkuk. Based on the close reading in chapter 2, I first traced the plot of the book to find out how the author presented his case by means of dialogues and monologues. Then I examined the characterization of the three major players in the book, namely, the Chaldeans, Yahweh, and Habakkuk, to understand their role and contribution to the storyline of the book. By means of these analyses, I was able to come up with four themes embedded in the book, which are theodicy, the righteous shall live by his faithfulness, reap what you sow, and the sovereignty of God. Then I found out Habakkuk raised all his questions concerning theodicy in scene one, and proceeded to answer them in scenes two and three. Yahweh's answer in scene two served as the turning point of the plot, and the ensuing woe oracles aimed to vindicate the divine justice, for God is the defender of the retribution principle. The theophany in scene three played a vital role in solving the issue of theodicy, for it showed the active role of God in Israel's history. Also, not only did it display God's incomparable mighty power, it also demonstrated God's care and concern for his people, and that he would come to deliver them again in the future.

I then turned to examine other biblical passages that dealt with theodicy, to see how the writers of those passages resolved it. I limited my investigation to Job, particularly the divine speeches in Job 38-41; Psalms 73 and 77; as well as Jeremiah's confessions in Jer 11:18-12:6; 15:10-21; 17:14-18; 18:18-23; 20:7-12 (13); 20:14-18. After analyzing these passages, I discovered that they shared some common grounds: firstly, the theodicy question arose from the suffering of the righteous, since it was a violation of a retribution principle which was often viewed as ordained by God. Secondly, they all used lament as their means to appeal to God's compassion and to arouse him to action. Balentine rightly remarks that "[a]t the level of genre, lament has its origin in the existential experience of suffering." [1] In other words, as a natural reaction to suffering, lament is the most appropriate genre, for it gives expressions to an array of emo-

---

[1]   Balentine, *Prayer in the Hebrew Bible*, 168.

tions generated by deep hurt. Thirdly, their resolution came either after a direct theophany or a meditation on God's character and his deeds in the past. Hence I concluded that in ancient Israel, the question of theodicy was not a philosophical but an existential issue: the survival of the righteous in the midst of evil. That was the reason for them to appeal to God who, as a righteous Judge, was their only hope for vindication and triumph over evil. The theophanic experience and meditation on God's past actions gave them assurance of God's care and power, and thus enabled them to stand firm and claim victory over calamity.

Since Habakkuk belonged to the prophetic corpus, it was considered important to see how theodicy was handled in other prophetic literature. Emphasis was placed on how Habakkuk differed from the rest of the group. In chapter 4, I first looked into the issue of theodicy in other prophetic literature by observing the prophetic disputations with the *vox populi* as recorded in various prophetic passages. I concluded that, on the one hand, popular sentiment of the people was to blame God whenever there was a national crisis. On the other hand, the prophets always put the blame on the sin of the people, and justified God's punishment as just and righteous. Occasionally there were some prophets who might share the same sentiment of the people and lament against God. Habakkuk stood with those who dared to challenge God.

As mentioned, I focused on the uniqueness of Habakkuk among the prophetic literature. I concluded that Habakkuk was unique among the prophetic literature in both content and form; while most of the other prophets prophesized the coming of the foreign invasion as God's just punishment of Israel's sin, Habakkuk challenged the divine justice in using a wicked nation to judge Judah. Instead of acting as God's mouthpiece, Habakkuk stood on the side of the people and challenged God's decision. In form, Habakkuk was the only prophetic book that used lament as its overall framework. It also lacked the messenger formula that appeared frequently in other prophetic literature. The reason for this may have been that Habakkuk dealt with his complaint, on behalf of the people, against God, and thus was not meant to address the people directly.

Finally in chapter 4, I explored the placement of Habakkuk in the book of the Twelve and its relationship with the other Minor Prophets. I agreed with those who claim that there were editorial activities in the book of the Twelve to encourage the reader to read it as a composite whole. I also concurred with House's view that the plot of the Twelve formed a U-shaped comedy, with Habakkuk situated at the trough of the book of the Twelve. Reading it this way, it became clear why lament was used as a framework for Habakkuk: it reflected Israel's desperate cry to Yahweh during her darkest hour so as to arouse God to action.

## Habakkuk's presentation of the issue of theodicy

As mentioned earlier, lament as a genre is the most appropriate form to express suffering and pain, for it is a natural response to hurt. Hence a brief discussion of the historical situation of Habakkuk is necessary in order to understand what prompted the author to employ lament as a framework.

I suggested that Habakkuk's ministry was during the reign of Jehoiakim (609-598 BCE). It was a time when Israel's hope of restoration was crushed following the humiliating defeat at Megiddo when Josiah's attempt to stop the Egyptian Pharaoh Neco from assisting the doomed Assyrians resulted in Josiah's death (2 Kgs 23:29-30). Though Neco failed to save Assyria from the Babylonians, on his way back, he deposed Jehoahaz, Josiah's son who succeeded him as king of Judah, and placed Jehoiakim, Jehoahaz's brother, on the throne as an Egyptian vassal. Jehoiakim proved to be an unworthy successor of his father. He showed no concern for the misery of his people: in addition to taxing them heavily in order to pay for the heavy tribute imposed on Judah by Neco (2 Kgs 23:33-35) and later by Babylon, he lavished funds on himself by building a new and magnificent palace, and worse still, he used forced labor to do it, an act condemned sternly by Jeremiah; "Woe to him who builds his house by unrighteousness, and his upper rooms by injustice; who makes his neighbors work for nothing, and does not give them their wages; who says, 'I will build myself a spacious house with large upper rooms,' and who cuts out windows for it, paneling with cedar, and painting it with vermilion....But your eyes and your heart are only on your dishonest gain, for shedding innocent blood, and for practicing oppression and violence" (Jer 22:13-14, 17).[2] As for the religious reform started by Josiah, Jehoiakim abolished it and let the pagan practices creep back in. He threatened and persecuted the prophets who spoke out against him. Jeremiah's life was threatened and had to go to hiding, while another prophet, Uriah, son of Shemaiah from Kiriath Jearim was captured and put to death (Jer 26:20-23). Furthermore, Jehoiakim turned a deaf ear to the Lord's warning through Jeremiah; he showed no fear or respect for the Lord by cutting up and burning the scrolls that contained Jeremiah's warnings (Jer 36:1-26).

This brief historical description of Jehoiakim's reign fits the depiction of Judean society in Habakkuk's initial complaint in 1:2-4 perfectly:[3] the prophet used words such as, "violence," "iniquity," "trouble," and phrases such as, "destruction and violence," "strife and contention," to describe the mayhem in the

---

[2] This woe oracle pronounced by Jeremiah on Jehoiakim was similar to the second woe pronounced by Habakkuk on the Babylonians in Hab 2:9. This showed that Jehoiakim's crime was known to Habakkuk.

[3] Although "the wicked" remain anonymous in 1:2-4, the mention of "law grows numb," indicates that they are likely members of Judean community. The reason for the anonymity of the wicked may have been to avoid possible reprisal against the lamenter by the wicked, especially if the wicked are the powerful ones in the community.

society. He also complained that "law grows numb,"[4] "justice never goes forth," for "the wicked surrounded the righteous," and "judgment goes forth perverted." Under such a tyrannical rule, when prophetic warnings were not only rejected but silenced, God's words were blatantly repulsed, social justice was not carried out, murder and persecution of the prophets were ordered and supported by the state, and lament to God was the only venue that was left for the righteous. Hence Habakkuk lamented to God, accusing him of inactivity in the face of evil, complaining that he allowed the situation to go on too long, and demanding a response from God.

God's surprise answer—that he was about to bring in the Chaldeans as judgment—provoked further complaint from Habakkuk, for to him, the coming of the Chaldeans could only bring more grievances to the people who had already suffered greatly. Thus Habakkuk stood in the tradition of Abraham and Moses, and would not accept the divine decision without a struggle. Hence he used divine attributes to call into question divine actions to show the incongruities between the two (1:12-14). He further complained against the Chaldeans (1:15-17), hoping that it would arouse the compassion of God.

In the midst of great national crisis, Habakkuk stood on the side of the oppressed people and employed the traditional lament cries of "How long?" and "Why?" The book conveys that his cries obviously reached God, for God responded to him. Moreover, by standing on the side of the people, Habakkuk would no doubt gain a wide audience, for he acted as their spokesman before God. Thus I concluded that lament was the most appropriate language for Habakkuk to present his case since lament is an expression of the reality of suffering,[5] and his lament represented Israel's desperate cry for divine intervention during the national crisis.

### Habakkuk's resolution of the issue of theodicy

Yahweh's answer in 2:2-5 served as the turning point of the book. From this point onward, the book was in the resolution phase. Instead of addressing Habakkuk's question on theodicy directly,[6] Yahweh commanded Habakkuk to write down the vision and assured him that the vision would soon be fulfilled.

---

[4] Balentine, *Prayer in the Hebrew Bible*, 184, suggests that the paralysis of the law is not due to the "mishandling or abuse by others but from an inherent failure or weakness in the Torah itself." In other words, Habakkuk is complaining that God allows the social injustice and the chaotic situation to go on and that Torah's promise of reward for faithfulness is a failure. However, the clause "the wicked surrounded the righteous," which is preceded and followed by the mention of the failure of "justice," seems to indicate that the paralysis of Torah is due to the abuse by the powerful ones in the community rather than "an inherent weakness" in the Torah.

[5] Balentine, *Prayer in the Hebrew Bible*, 150.

[6] As a usual practice, Yahweh does not address the question of theodicy directly, and the theodic cry "Why?" seems to linger on. Perhaps this is seen as part of the mystery of God that he does not choose to reveal so as to test the faithfulness of his people.

He also assured him that the righteous would live by his faithfulness. Yahweh's response helped Habakkuk to understand the inevitability of the coming of the Chaldeans, as well as addressed his question of "How long?" and his concern for the well-being of the righteous. But at the same time, Habakkuk also knew that divine justice would not allow the arrogant ones to go unpunished and to boast forever. Hence he reflected on the destiny of the wicked and used the woe oracles to pronounce their due judgment.

Though the woe oracles were put into the mouth of the oppressed nations in order to create irony, they were based on the retribution principle guaranteed by God. Thus the woe oracles functioned to vindicate divine justice, for they ensured that the perpetrators of the crime would reap their well-deserved judgment in the form of "reversal of imagery." Five woe oracles were pronounced to indicate the wide range of crimes committed by the Chaldeans and their consequences. The insertion of doxologies in 2:14 and 2:20 not only served to contrast the vanity and foolishness of human endeavor on the one hand, and the surety of God's glory and his presence on the other hand, it also showed that God was very much involved in human history and that he would ensure that his justice prevailed in the end.

Some question Habakkuk's uniqueness in the prophetic tradition since the prophet at the end affirmed the prophetic retribution doctrine: that God rewards the righteous and punishes the wicked. This would lead one to wonder whether Habakkuk, after all, agreed with the prophetic doctrine that the divine punishment by sending the foreign nations was a just act. However, while Habakkuk affirmed the retribution doctrine, he did not address the question of the rightness of the sending of the Chaldeans. Instead, he simply accepted the Babylonian invasion as inevitable. His concern seemed to focus on the perseverance of the righteous amidst the coming atrocity. Habakkuk's unique contribution was on his resolution to trust the Lord regardless of his situation, and demonstrated to his audience the righteous living in the midst of evil.

The theophany in scene 3 was vital to settle the theodicy issue. Balentine correctly observes that this chapter "provides the final dramatic resolution of Habakkuk's quest for meaningful existence in the midst of suffering," and that Habakkuk has become "paradigmatic for the wider congregation."[7]

At this juncture in Israel's history, when the invasion of the Babylonians was inevitable, and their military might seemed unstoppable, Yahweh's theophany served as a timely response to the prophet's plea to "renew [his] deeds and to make them known" in the midst of devastation. J.H. Hunter mentions that there are two constant elements in theophanic texts: the coming of Yahweh and the effect of this coming on earth.[8] He also notes that the theophanic traditions may be appropriated by biblical writers to serve different purposes in different

---

[7] Balentine, *Prayer in the Hebrew Bible*, 188.
[8] J.H. Hunter, "The Literary Composition of Theophany Passages in the Hebrew Psalms," *JNSL* 15 (1989): 97.

texts.[9] In Habakkuk, the theophany served two purposes. First, the coming of Yahweh and the cosmic reaction described in 3:3-7 aimed at portraying the majestic power of Yahweh in mythical language; the effect of which was to instill awe and wonder in the mind of the audience. This also made the power of the Chaldeans pale in comparison: for while they were described as animals pawing the ground (1:7-8), Yahweh's coming was like the rising sun and nothing could escape his light (3:3-4). Second, the imagery of Yahweh as a warrior in 3:8-15 reshaped the Israelite historical events, such as exodus and early conquest, to demonstrate Yahweh's concern for his people and the purpose of his coming, which was to deliver them from their adversaries. This was important for it settled Habakkuk's earlier accusation that Yahweh did not care and did not save. The descriptions of divine weapons and warfare served to counter the previous description of the Babylonian military might (1:9-11, 15), and to show that while they might gloat over their victims, they themselves would soon be the object of divine judgment (3:13-14). Thus the theophany showed that Yahweh had the power and passion to deliver his people; meanwhile, the righteous must wait patiently for the day to come.

Finally Habakkuk's reaction in 3:16-19 showed the impact of the theophany on him personally. Privileged to be privy to the glory of God as manifested in the theophany, Habakkuk became unswervingly confident in God. Habakkuk's resolution gave a concrete example of the living out of a righteous person in the face of great calamity: to trust and to wait patiently for the Lord, to rejoice in the Lord and to draw strength from him, even when all life's necessities were deprived. This required great determination and resolution to persevere through extreme atrocity. Thus Habakkuk embodied the divine message that "the righteous in his faithfulness will live" (2:4), and became a paradigm for all the suffering righteous to follow.

---

[9]   Ibid., 105.

# BIBLIOGRAPHY

Abrams, M.H. *A Glossary of Literary Terms*, 7th ed. Boston: Heinle and Heinle, 1999.

Achtemeier, Elizabeth. *Nahum-Malachi*. Interpretation. Atlanta: John Knox, 1986.

—. *Preaching from the Old Testament*. Louisville: Westminster/John Knox, 1989.

Albright, W.F. "The Psalm of Habakkuk." In *Studies in Old Testament Prophecy*. Edited by H.H. Rowley, 1-18. Edinburgh: T & T Clark, 1950.

Alter, Robert. *The Art of Biblical Narrative*. New York: Basic Books, 1981.

—. *The Art of Biblical Poetry*. New York: Basic Books, 1985.

—. "The Characteristics of Ancient Hebrew Poetry." In *The Literary Guide to the Bible*. Edited by Robert Alter, and Frank Kermode, 611-24. Cambridge: The Belknap Press of Harvard University Press, 1987.

—. "Introduction, The Old Testament." In *The Literary Guide to the Bible*. Edited by Robert Alter, and Frank Kermode, 11-35. Cambridge: The Belknap Press of Harvard University Press, 1987.

—. *The World of Biblical Literature*. New York: Basic Books, 1992.

Anderson, B.W. "The New Frontier of Rhetorical Criticism: A Tribute to James Muilenburg." In *Rhetorical Criticism: Essays in Honor of James Muilenburg*. Edited by J.J. Jackson and M. Kessler, ix-xviii. Pittsburgh Theological Monograph Series 1. Pittsburgh: Pickwick Press, 1974.

Andersen, Francis I. *Habakkuk: A New Translation with Introduction and Commentary*. The Anchor Bible 25. New York: Doubleday, 2001.

—. *Job: An Introduction and Commentary*. Tyndale Old Testament Commentary. Downers Grove: InterVarsity Press, 1976.

—. "Linguistic Coherence in Prophetic Discourse." In *Fortunate the Eyes that See: Essays in Honor of David Noel Freedman in Celebration of His Seventieth Birthday*. Edited by Astrid B. Beck, Andrew H. Bartelt, Paul R. Raabe, and Chris A. Franke, 137-56. Grand Rapids: Eerdmans, 1995.

Anderson, Robert T. "Was Isaiah a Scribe?" *Journal of Biblical Literature* 79 (1960): 57-58.

Archer, Gleason L. *The Book of Job: God's Answer to the Problem of Undeserved Suffering*. Grand Rapids: Baker, 1982.

Armerding, Carl E. "Habakkuk." In *The Expositor's Bible Commentary*. Edited by Frank E. Gaebelein, 7:493-534. Grand Rapids: Zondervan, 1985.

—. "Images for Today: Word from the Prophets." In *Studies in Old Testament Theology*. Edited by Robert L. Hubbard, Jr., Robert K. Johnston, and Robert P. Meye, 167-86. Dallas: Word, 1992.

174

Avishur, Yitzhak. *Studies in Hebrew and Ugaritic Psalms*. Jerusalem: The Magnes Press, 1994.

Bailey, Waylon, and Kenneth L. Barker. *Micah, Nahum, Habakkuk, Zephaniah*. The New American Commentary. Vol 20. Nashville: Broadmen & Holman Publishers, 1998.

Baker, David W. "Cushan." In *The Anchor Bible Dictionary*. Edited by D.N. Freedman, 1:1219-20. New York: Doubleday, 1992.

—. *Nahum, Habakkuk, and Zephaniah*. The Tyndale Old Testament Commentaries. Downers Grove: InterVarsity Press, 1988.

Balentine, Samuel E. "For No Reason." *Interpretation* 57 (2003): 349-69.

—. "Prayers for Justice in the Old Testament: Theodicy and Theology." *Catholic Biblical Quarterly* 51 (1989): 597-616.

—. *Prayer in the Hebrew Bible: The Drama of Divine-Human Dialogue*. Overtures to Biblical Theology. Minneapolis: Fortress, 1993.

—. "Who Will Be Job's Redeemer?" *Perspectives in Religious Studies* 26 (1999): 269-89.

Balzer, H.R. "Eschatological Elements as Permanent Qualities in the Relationship Between God and Nation in the Minor Prophets." *Old Testament Essays* 4 (1991): 408-14.

Barber, Cyril J. *Habakkuk and Zephaniah*. Everyman's Bible Commentary. Chicago: Moody Press, 1985.

Bar-Efrat, Shimon. "Some Observations on the Analysis of Structure in Biblical Narrative." In *Beyond Form Criticism: Essays in Old Testament Literary Criticism*. Edited by Paul R. House, 186-205. Winona Lake: Eisenbrauns, 1992.

—. *Narrative Art in the Bible*. Journal for the Study of the Old Testament Supplement Series 70. Sheffield: Almond Press, 1989.

Barr, James. *The Scope and Authority of the Bible*. Philadelphia: Westminster, 1980.

—. "Theophany and Anthropomorphism in the Old Testament." In Supplements to *Vetus Testamentum* 7 (1960), 31-38. Leiden: Brill, 1960.

Barré, Michael L. "Habakkuk 3:2: Translation in Context." *The Catholic Biblical Quarterly* 50 (1988): 184-97.

—. "Yahweh Gears Up for Battle: Habakkuk 3,9a." *Biblica* 87 (2006): 75-84.

Barton, John. "History and Rhetoric in the Prophets." In *The Bible as Rhetoric: Studies in Biblical Persuasion and Credibility*. Edited by Martin Warner, 51-64. New York: Routledge, 1990.

—. "Natural Law and Poetic Justice in the Old Testament." *Journal of Theological Studies* 30 (1979): 1-14.

—. *Reading the Old Testament: Method in Biblical Study*. Philadelphia: Westminster, 1984.

—. "Redaction Criticism (Old Testament)." In *The Anchor Bible Dictionary*. Edited by D.N. Freedman, 5:644-47. New York: Doubleday, 1992.

Basser, Herbert W. "Pesher Hadavar: The Truth of the Matter." *Revue de Qumran* 13 (1988): 389-405.

Baumann, Gerlinde. "Connected by Marriage, Adultery and Violence: The Prophetic Marriage Metaphor in the Book of the Twelve and in the Major Prophets." In *Society of Biblical Literature 1999 Seminar Papers*, 552-69. Society of Biblical Literature Seminar Papers Series 38. Atlanta: Society of Biblical Literature, 1999.

Beentjes, Pancratius C. "Inverted Quotations in the Bible: A Neglected Stylistic Pattern." *Biblica* 63 (1982): 506-23.

Bellinger, W.H. Jr. *Psalmody and Prophecy*. Journal for the Study of the Old Testament Supplement Series 27. Sheffield: JSOT Press, 1984.

Ben Zvi, Ehud. "The Prophetic Book: A Key Form of Prophetic Literature," In *The Changing Face of Form Criticism for the Twenty-First Century*. Edited by Marvin A. Sweeney, and Ehud Ben Zvi, 276-97. Grand Rapids: Eerdmans, 2003.

—. "Twelve Prophetic Books or 'The Twelve': A Few Preliminary Consideration." In *Forming Prophetic Literature: Essays on Isaiah and the Twelve in Honor of John D.W. Watts*. Edited by James W. Watts, and Paul R. House, 125-56. Journal for the Study of the Old Testament Supplement Series 235. Sheffield: Sheffield Academic Press, 1996.

Bentzen, Aage. *Introduction to the Old Testament*. Copenhagen: Gad, 1958.

Berlin, Adele. "Characterization in Biblical Narrative: David's Wives." In *Beyond Form Criticism: Essays in Old Testament Literary Criticism*. Edited by Paul R. House, 219-33. Winona Lake: Eisenbrauns, 1992.

—. *Poetics and Interpretation of Biblical Narrative*. Sheffield: Almond, 1983. Reprint, Winona Lake: Eisenbrauns, 1994.

Blank, Sheldon. "The Confessions of Jeremiah and the Meaning of Prayer." *Hebrew Union College Annual* 21 (1949): 331-54.

—. "The Prophet as Paradigm." In *Essays in Old Testament Ethics*. Edited by James L. Crenshaw and John T. Willis, 111-30. New York: KTAV, 1974.

Block, Daniel I. *The Book of Ezekiel Chapters 1-24*. The New International Commentary on The Old Testament. Grand Rapids: Eerdmans, 1997.

Boadt, Lawrence. "The Use of 'Panels' in the Structure of Psalms 73-78." *The Catholic Biblical Quarterly* 66 (2004): 533-50.

Boström, Lennart. "Patriarchal Models for Piety." In *Shall Not the Judge of All the Earth Do What Is Right? Studies on the Nature of God in Tribute to James L. Crenshaw*. Edited by David Penchansky, and Paul L. Redditt, 57-72. Winona Lake: Eisenbrauns, 2000.

Botterweck, G. Johannes, Helmer Ringgren, and Heinz-Josef Fabry, eds. *Theological Dictionary of the Old Testament*. Translated by John T. Willis, Douglas W. Stott, David E. Green. 15 vols. Grand Rapids: Eerdmans, 1974-2003.

Bratcher, D. *The Theological Message of Habakkuk*. Ann Arbor: University Microfilm International, 1985.

Brenner, Athalya. "God's Answer to Job." *Vetus Testamentum* 31 (1981): 129-37.

Bright, John. *A History of Israel*, 4th ed. Louisville: Westminster John Knox Press, 2000.

—. "Jeremiah's Complaints—Liturgy or Expressions of Personal Distress?" In *Proclamation and Presence: Old Testament Essays in Honour of Gwynne Henton Davies*. Edited by John I. Durham, and J.R. Porter, 189-214. London: SCM Press, 1970. New Corrected Edition, Macon: Mercer University Press, 1983.

—. "A Prophet's Lament and Its Answer: Jeremiah 15:10-21." *Interpretation* 28 (1974): 59-74.

Brooke, George. "Qumran Pesher: Towards the Redefinition of a Genre." *Revue de Qumran* 10 (1981): 483-503.

Brotzman, Ellis R. *Old Testament Textual Criticism: A Practical Introduction.* Grand Rapids: Baker Books, 1994.

Brouwer, Arie R. "Facing Death and Growing in Grace." *Perspectives* 8 (Dec., 1993): 8-23.

Brownlee, William H. "Biblical Interpretation among the Sectaries of the Dead Sea Scrolls." *Biblical Archaeologist* 14 (1951): 54-76.

—. "The Habakkuk Midrash and the Targum of Jonathan." *Journal of Jewish Studies* 7 (1956): 169-86.

—. *The Midrash Pesher of Habakkuk*. Missoula: Scholars Press, 1979.

—. "The Placarded Revelation of Habakkuk." *Journal of Biblical Literature* 82 (1963): 319-25.

—. *The Text of Habakkuk in the Ancient Commentary from Qumran*. Philadelphia: Society of Biblical Literature and Exegesis, 1959.

Broyles, Craig C. *Psalms*. New International Biblical Commentary. Peabody: Hendrickson, 1999.

Bruce, F.F. "Habakkuk." In *The Minor Prophets: An Exegetical and Expository Commentary*. Vol. 2, *Obadiah, Jonah, Micah, Nahum, and Habakkuk*. Edited by Thomas Edward McComiskey, 831-96. Grand Rapids: Baker, 1993.

Bruckner, James. *The NIV Application Commentary: Jonah, Nahum, Habakkuk, Zephaniah*. Grand Rapids: Zondervan, 2004.

Brueggemann, Walter. "The Book of Jeremiah: Portrait of the Prophet." *Interpretation* 37 (1983): 130-45.

—. "The Costly Loss of Lament." *Journal for the Study of the Old Testament* 36 (1986): 57-71.

—. "From Hurt to Joy, From Death to Life." *Interpretation* 28 (1974): 3-19.

—. *The Message of the Psalms: A Theological Commentary*. Minneapolis: Augsburg, 1984.

—. "Psalm 77—The 'Turn' from Self to God." *Journal for Preachers* 6 (1983): 8-14.

—. "Some Aspects of Theodicy in Old Testament Faith." *Perspectives in Religious Studies* 26 (Fall, 1999): 253-68.

—. "Theodicy in a Social Dimension." *Journal for the Study of the Old Testament* 33 (1985): 3-25.

—, and Patrick D. Miller. "Psalm73 as a Canonical Marker." *Journal for the Study of the Old Testament* 72 (1996): 45-56.

Buber, Martin. "The Heart Determines: Psalm 73." In *Theodicy in the Old Testament*. Edited by James L. Crenshaw, 109-18. Philadelphia: Fortress, 1983.

Bullock, C. Hassell, *An Introduction to the Old Testament Prophetic Books*. Chicago: Moody Press, 1986.

Burrell, David B. *Deconstructing Theodicy: Why Job Has Nothing to Say to the Puzzle of Suffering*. Grand Rapids: Brazos Press, 2008.

Calkins, Raymond. *The Modern Message of the Minor Prophets*. New York: Harper & Brothers, 1947.

Cannon, W.W. "The Integrity of Habakkuk cc.1.2" *Zeitschrift für die alttestamentliche Wissenschaft* 43 (1925): 62-90.

Carroll, Robert P. "Ancient Israelite Prophecy and Dissonance Theory." *Numen* 24 (1977): 135-51.

—. "Eschatological Delay in the Prophetic Tradition?" *Zeitschrift für die alttestamentliche Wissenschaft* 94 (1982): 47-58.

—. "Habakkuk." In *A Dictionary of Biblical Interpretation*. Edited by R.J. Coggins and J.L. Houlden, 268-69. London: SCM, 1990.

—. "Intertextuality and the Book of Jeremiah: Animadversions on Text and Theory." In *The New Literary Criticism and the Hebrew Bible*. Edited by J. Cheryl Exum, and David J.A. Clines, 55-78. Sheffield: Sheffield Academic Press, 1993. Reprint, Valley Forge: Trinity Press, 1994.

—. *When Prophecy Failed: Cognitive Dissonance in the Prophetic Traditions of the Old Testament*. London: SCM, 1979.

Carson, D.A. *How Long, O Lord? Reflections on Suffering and Evil*. Grand Rapids: Baker, 1990.

Cassuto, Umberto. "Chapter III of Habakkuk and the Ras Shamra Texts." In *Biblical and Oriental Studies II: Bible and Ancient Oriental Texts*. Translated and edited by Israel Abrahams, 3-15. Jerusalem: Magnes, 1975.

Cavallin, H.C.C. " 'The Righteous Shall Live by Faith': A Decisive Argument for the Traditional Interpretation." *Studia Theologica* 32 (1978): 33-43.

Childs, Brevard S. "The Canonical Shape of the Prophetic Literature." In *Interpreting the Prophets*. Edited by James Luther Mays and Paul J. Achtemeier, 41-49. Philadelphia: Fortress, 1987.

—. "The Exegetical Significance of Canon for the Study of the Old Testament." In *Congress Volume: Göttingen, 1977*, 66-80. Supplements to *Vetus Testamentum* 29. Leiden: Brill, 1978.

—. *Introduction to the Old Testament as Scripture*. Philadelphia: Fortress, 1979.

—. "Psalm Titles and Midrashic Exegesis." *Journal of Semitic Studies* 16 (1971): 137-50.

Clark, David J., and Howard A. Hatton. *A Translator's Handbook on the Book of Nahum, Habakkuk, and Zephaniah*. Helps for Translators. New York: United Bible Societies, 1989.

Cleaver-Bartholomew, David. "An Alternative Approach to Hab 1,2-2,20." *Scandinavian Journal of the Old Testament* 17 (2003): 206-225.

Clements, Roland E. "The Form and Character of Prophetic Woe Oracles." *Semitics* 8 (1982): 17-29.

—. "OT 'Woe' Oracles." In *The Anchor Bible Dictionary*. Edited by D.N. Freedman, 6:945-46. New York: Doubleday, 1992.

—. "Patterns in the Prophetic Canon." In *Canon and Authority*. Edited by G.W. Coats, and B.O. Long, 42-55. Philadelphia: Fortress, 1977.

—. *Prophecy and Covenant*. Studies in Biblical Theology 43. London: SCM Press, 1965.

—. "Wisdom and Old Testament theology." In *Wisdom in Ancient Israel: Essays in Honour of J.A. Emerton*. Edited by John Day, Robert P. Gordon, and H.G.M. Williamson, 269-86. Cambridge: Cambridge University Press, 1995.

Clendenen, E. Ray. "C.J.H. Wright's 'Ethical Triangle' and the Threefold Structure of Malachi." In *Annual Meeting of the Evangelical Theological Society 2003*, 1-16. Nashville: Broadman & Holman Publishers, 2003.

—. "The Structure of Malachi: A Textlinguistic Study." *Criswell Theological Review* (1987): 3-17.

Clifford, Richard J. "Rhetorical Criticism in the Exegesis of Hebrew Poetry." In *SBL 1980 Seminar* Papers, 17-28. SBL Seminar Papers Series 19. Chico: Scholars Press, 1980.

—. "The Use of *HÔY* in the Prophets." *Catholic Biblical Quarterly* 28 (1966): 464-85.

Clines, David. "The Arguments of Job's Three Friends." In *Art and Meaning: Rhetoric in Biblical Literature*. Edited by David Clines, David Gunn, and Alan Hauser, 199-214. Journal for the Study of the Old Testament Supplement 19. Sheffield: JSOT Press, 1982.

Clines, David J.A., and J. Cheryl Exum. "The New Criticism." In *The New Literary Criticism and the Hebrew Bible*. Edited by J. Cheryl Exum, and David J.A. Clines, 11-25. Sheffield: Sheffield Academic Press, 1993. Reprint, Valley Forge: Trinity Press, 1994.

Coats, George W. "The King's Loyal Opposition: Obedience and Authority in Exodus 32-34." In *Canon and Authority*. Edited by G.W. Coats, and B.O. Long, 91-109. Philadelphia: Fortress, 1977.

Coggins, Richard. "An Alternative Prophetic Traditions?" In *Israel's Prophetic Traditions: Essays in Honour of Peter R. Ackroyd*. Edited by Richard Coggins, Anthony Phillips, and Michael Knibb, 77-94. Cambridge: Cambridge University Press, 1982.

Coleman, Shalom. "The Dialogue of Habakkuk in Rabbinic Doctrine." *Abr-Nahrain* 5 (1964-65): 57-85.

Cooper, Alan. "In Praise of Divine Caprice: The Significance of the Book of Jonah." In *Among the Prophets: Language, Image and Structure in the Prophetic Writings*. Edited by Philip R. Davies, and David J.A. Clines, 144-63. Journal for the Study of The Old Testament Supplement Series 144. Sheffield: Sheffield Academic Press, 1993.

Copeland, P.E. "The Midst of the Year." In *Text as Pretext: Essays in Honour of Robert Davidson*. Edited by R.P. Carroll, 91-105. Journal for the Study of the Old Testament Supplement Series 138. Sheffield: JSOT Press, 1992.

Cornelius, Izak. *Iconography of the Canaanite Gods Reshef and Ba'al: Late Bronze and Iron Age I Periods*. Freiburg: Vandenhoeck & Ruprecht, 1994.

Coxon, Peter. "Nebuchadnezzar's Hermeneutical Dilemma." *Journal for the Study of the Old Testament* 66 (1995): 87-97.

Craigie, Peter C. *Psalms 1-50*, 2d ed. Word Biblical Commentary. Vol 19. Nashville: Nelson, 2004.

Craigie, Peter C., Page H. Kelley, and Joel F. Drinkard, Jr. *Jeremiah 1-25*. Word Biblical Commentary. Vol 26. Dallas: Word, 1991.

Crenshaw, James L. "The Concept of God in Old Testament Wisdom." In *In Search of Wisdom: Essays in Memory of John G. Gammie*. Edited by Leo G. Perdue, Bernard Brandon Scott, and William Johnston Wiseman, 1-18. Louisville: Westminster John Knox Press, 1993.

—. *Defending God: Biblical Responses to the Problem of Evil*. New York: Oxford University Press, 2005.

—. "In Search of Divine Presence: Some Remarks Preliminary to a Theology of Wisdom." *Review and Expositor* 74 (1977): 353-69.

—. "The Influence of the Wise upon Amos: The 'Doxologies of Amos' and Job 5 9-16 9 5-10." *Zeitschrift für die alttestamentliche Wissenschaft* 69 (1967): 42-51.

—. "A Living Tradition: The Book of Jeremiah in Current Research." *Interpretation* 37 (1983): 117-29.

—. "Method in Determining Wisdom Influence upon 'Historical' Literature." *Journal of Biblical Literature* 88 (1969): 129-42.

—. "Popular Questioning of the Justice of God in Ancient Israel." *Zeitschrift für die alttestamentliche Wissenschaft* 82 (1970): 380-95.

—. *Prophetic Conflict: Its Effect Upon Israelite Religion*. New York: Walter de Gruyter, 1971.

—. "The Shift from Theodicy to Anthropodicy." In *Theodicy in the Old Testament*. Edited by James L. Crenshaw, 1-16. Philadelphia: Fortress, 1983.

—. "Theodicy." In *Anchor Bible Dictionary*. Edited by D.N. Freedman, 6:444-47. New York: Doubleday, 1992.

—. "Theodicy and Prophetic Literature." In *Theodicy in the World of the Bible*. Edited by Antti Raato, and Johannes C. de Moor, 236-55. Leiden: Brill, 2003.

—. "Theodicy in the Book of the Twelve." In *Thematic Threads in the Book of the Twelve*. Edited by Paul L. Redditt, and Aaron Schart, 175-91. New York: Walter De Gruyter, 2003.

—. "*Wədōrēk 'al-bāmôtê 'āres*" *The Catholic Biblical Quarterly* 34 (1972): 39-53.

—. "Wisdom." In *Old Testament Form Criticism*. Edited by John Hayes. 225-64. San Antonio: Trinity University Press, 1977.

—. *A Whirlpool of Torment: Israelite Traditions of God as an Oppressive Presence*. Overtures to Biblical Theology. Philadelphia: Fortress, 1984.

Cross, Frank Moore. *Canaanite Myth and Hebrew Epic: Essays in the History of the Religion of Israel.* Cambridge, MA: Harvard University Press, 1973.

—. "Notes on a Canaanite Psalm in the Old Testament." *Bulletin of the American Schools of Oriental Research* 117 (1950): 19-21.

Cross, Frank Moore, and David Noel Freedman. *Studies in Ancient Yahwistic Poetry*, 2d ed. Grand Rapids: Eerdmans, 1997.

Curtis, John Briggs, "On Job's Response to Yahweh." *Journal of Biblical Literature* 98 (1979): 498-511.

Dangl, Oskar. "Habakkuk in Recent Research." *Currents in Research: Biblical Studies* 9 (2001): 131-68.

Daniels, D.R. "Is there a 'Prophetic Lawsuit' Genre?" *Zeitschrift für die alttestamentliche Wissenschaft* 99 (1987): 339-60.

Davidson, A.B. *Nahum, Habakkuk, and Zephaniah.* The Cambridge Bible for Schools and Colleges. Cambridge: Cambridge University Press, 1896.

Davidson, Robert. *The Courage to Doubt: Exploring an Old Testament Theme.* London: SCM Press, 1983.

Davies, G.I. "Were There Schools in Ancient Israel?" In *Wisdom in Ancient Israel: Essays In Honour of J.A. Emerton.* Edited by John Day, Robert P. Gordon, and H.G.M. Williamson, 199-211. Cambridge: Cambridge University Press, 1995.

Day, John. "Echoes of Baal's Seven Thunders and Lightnings in Psalm 29 and Habakkuk 3:9 and the Identity of the Seraphim in Isaiah 6." *Vetus Testamentum* 29 (1979): 143-51.

—. "New Light on the Mythological Background of the Allusion to Reshep in Habakkuk 3:5." *Vetus Testamentum* 29 (1979): 353-54.

De Boer, P.A.H. "The Meaning of Psalm LXXIII 9." *Vetus Testamentum* 18 (1968): 260-64.

De Bruyn, Frans. "Genre Criticism." In *Encyclopedia of Contemporary Literary Theory: Approaches, Scholars, Terms.* Edited by Irena R. Makaryk, 79-84. Toronto: University of Toronto Press, 1993. Reprint, 1995.

De Roche, Michael. "Yahweh's *Rîb* against Israel: A Reassessment of the So-called 'Prophetic Lawsuit' in the Preexilic Prophets." *Journal of Biblical Literature* 102 (1983): 563-74.

Dentan, Robert C. "The Literary Affinities of Exodus XXXIV 6f." *Vetus Testamentum* 13 (1963): 34-51.

Diamond, A.R. *The Confessions of Jeremiah in Context: Scenes of Prophetic Drama.* Journal for the Study of the Old Testament Supplement Series 45. Sheffield: JSOT Press, 1987.

—. "Jeremiah's Confession in the LXX and MT: A Witness to Developing Canonical Function?" *Vetus Testamentum* 40 (1990): 33-50.

Dick, Michael Brennan. "Legal Metaphor in Job 31." *Catholic Biblical Quarterly* 41 (1979): 37-50.

Dimant, Devorah. "Pesharim, Qumran." In *The Anchor Bible Dictionary.* Edited by D.N. Freedman, 5:244-51. New York: Doubleday, 1992.

Dozeman, Thomas B. "Inner-Biblical Interpretation of Yahweh's Gracious and Compassionate Character." *Journal of Biblical Literature* 108 (1989): 207-23.

—. "OT Rhetorical Criticism." In *The Anchor Bible Dictionary*. Edited by D.N. Freedman, 5:712-15. New York: Doubleday, 1992.

Driver, G.R. "Critical Note on Habakkuk 3 7." *Journal of Biblical Literature* 62 (1943):121.

Dykes, Donna S. *Diversity and Unity in Habakkuk*. Ann Arbor: University Microfilm International, 1976.

Eaton, J.H. "The Origin and Meaning of Habakkuk 3." *Zeitschrift für die alttestamentliche Wissenschaft* 76 (1964): 144-71.

Eichrodt, Walther. "Faith in Providence and Theodicy in the Old Testament." In *Theodicy in the Old Testament*. Edited by James L. Crenshaw, 17-41. Philadelphia: Fortress, 1983.

Emerton, J.A. "The Textual and Linguistic Problems of Habakkuk II. 4-5." *Journal of Theological Studies* 28 (1977): 1-18.

—. "The Text of Psalm LXXVII 11." *Vetus Testamentum* 44 (1994): 183-94.

Engnell, Ivan. *Critical Essays on the Old Testament*. Translated by John T. Willis. London: SPCK, 1970.

Eissfeldt, Otto. *The Old Testament: An Introduction, Including the Apocrypha and Pseudepigrapha, and also the Works of Similar Type from Qumran: The History of the Formation of the Old Testament*. Translated by Peter R. Ackroyd. New York: Harper and Row, 1965. Reprint, 1966.

Evans, J. Ellwood. "The Song of Habakkuk." *Bibliotheca Sacra* 112 (1955): 62-67, 164-69.

Everson, A. Joseph. "The Canonical Location of Habakkuk." In *Thematic Threads in the Book of the Twelve*. Edited by Paul L. Redditt, and Aaron Schart, 165-74. New York: Walter de Gruyter, 2003.

Eybers, I.H. "Diverse Application of the Oracle of Habakkuk." *Theologia Evangelistica* (1969): 50-59.

Fishbane, Michael. *Biblical Interpretation in Ancient Israel*. Oxford: Clarendon Press, 1985.

—. "Jeremiah IV 23-26 and Job III 3-13: A Recovered Use of the Creation Pattern." *Vetus Testamentum* 21 (1971): 151-67.

Fitzmyer, J.A. "Habakkuk 2:3-4 and the New Testament." In *To Advance the Gospel: New Testament Studies*. New York: Crossroad, 1981.

Floyd, Michael H. "The מַשָּׂא (*Maśśā'*) as a Type of Prophetic Book." *Journal of Biblical Literature* 121 (2002): 401-22.

—. *Minor Prophets: Part 2*. Edited by Rolf P. Knierim, Gene M Tucker, and Marvin A. Sweeney. The Forms of the Old Testament Literature Vol. 22. Grand Rapids: Eerdmans, 2000.

—. "Prophecy and Writing in Habakkuk 2,1-5." *Zeitschrift für die alttestamentliche Wissenschaft* 105 (1993): 462-81.

—. "Prophetic Complaints about the Fulfillment of Oracles in Habakkuk 1:2-17 and Jeremiah 15:10-18." *Journal of Biblical Literature* 110 (1991): 397-418.

Fløysvik, Ingvar. "When God Behaves Strangely: A Study in the Complaint Psalms." *Concordia Journal* 21 (1995): 298-304.

Fohrer, G. "Das 'Gebet des Propheten Habakuk' (Hab 3,1-16)." In *Mélanges bibliques et orientaux en l'honneur de M. Mathias Delcor*. Edited by A. Caquot, S. Légasse, and M. Tardieu, 159-67. Alter Orient und Altes Testament 215. Neukirchen: Neukirchener Verlag, 1985.

—. *Introduction to the Old Testament*. Translated by David Green. London: SPCK, 1970.

Fokkelman, J.P. *Reading Biblical Poetry: An Introductory Guide*. Translated by Ineke Smit. Louisville: Westminster John Knox, 2001.

Freedman, David Noel. "The Biblical Idea of History." *Interpretation* 21 (1967): 32-49.

—. "Pottery, Poetry, and Prophecy: An Essay on Biblical Poetry." *Journal of Biblical Literature* 96 (1977): 5-26.

—. *Pottery, Poetry, and Prophecy: Studies in Early Hebrew Poetry*. Winona Lake: Eisenbrauns, 1980.

Fretheim, Terrence E. "Jonah and Theodicy." *Zeitschrift für die alttestamentliche Wissenschaft* 90 (1978): 227-37.

—. *The Suffering of God: An Old Testament Perspective*. Philadelphia: Fortress, 1984.

Friebel, Kelvin G. "Biblical Interpretation in the *Pesharim* of the Qumran Community." *Hebrew Studies* 22 (1981): 13-24.

Frost, Stanley Brice. "Asseveration by Thanksgiving." *Vetus Testamentum* 8 (1958): 280-90.

—. "The Death of Josiah: A Conspiracy of Silence." *Journal of Biblical Literature* 87 (1968): 369-82.

Frye, Northrop. *Anatomy of Criticism: Form Essays*. Princeton: Princeton University Press, 1957.

—. *The Great Code: The Bible and Literature*. New York: Harcourt Brace Jovanovich, 1982.

Fuller, Russell. "The Form and Formation of the Book of the Twelve: The Evidence from the Judean Desert." In *Forming Prophetic Literature: Essays on Isaiah and the Twelve in Honor of John D.W. Watts*. Edited by James W. Watts, and Paul R. House, 86-101. Journal for the Study of the Old Testament Supplement Series 235. Sheffield: Sheffield Academic Press, 1996.

Fyall, Robert S. *Now My Eyes Have Seen You: Images of Creation and Evil in the Book of Job*. New Studies in Biblical Theology 12. Downers Grove: InterVarsity Press, 2002.

Gabel, John B., and Charles B. Wheeler. *The Bible as Literature: An Introduction*. New York: Oxford University Press, 1986.

Gammie, John G. "Behemoth and Leviathan: On the Didactic and Theological Significance of Job 40:15-41:26" In *Israelite Wisdom: Theological and Literary Essays in Honor of Samuel Terrien*. Edited by John G. Gammie, Walter A. Brueggemann, W. Lee Humphreys, James M. Ward, 217-31. New York: Union Theological Seminary, 1978.

Gemser, B. "The *RĨB* or Controversy-Pattern in Hebrew Mentality." In *Wisdom in Israel and in the Ancient Near East*. Edited by M. Noth, and D. Winton Thomas, 120-37. Leiden: Brill, 1960.

Gerstenberger, Erhard. "Jeremiah's Complaints." *Journal of Biblical Literature* 82 (1963): 393-408.

—. "The Woe-Oracles of the Prophets." *Journal of Biblical Literature* 81 (1962): 249-63.

Gibson, John C.L. "On Evil in the Book of Job." In *Ascribe to the Lord: Biblical and Other Studies in Memory of Peter C. Craigie*. Edited by Lyle Eslinger and Glen Taylor, 399-419. Journal for the Study of the Old Testament Supplement Series 67. Sheffield: JSOT Press, 1988.

Gillingham, S.E. *The Poems and Psalms of the Hebrew Bible*. Oxford: Oxford University Press, 1994.

Good, Edwin M. "The Barberini Greek Version of Habakkuk III." *Vetus Testamentum* 9 (1959): 11-30.

—. "The Problem of Evil in the Book of Job." In *The Voice from the Whirlwind: Interpreting the Book of Job*. Edited by Leo G. Perdue, and W. Clark Gilpin, 50-69. Nashville: Abingdon, 1992.

Gowan, Donald E. "God's Answer to Job: How Is It an Answer?" *Horizons in Biblical Theology* 8.2 (1986): 85-102.

—. "Habakkuk and Wisdom." *Perspective* 9 (1968): 157-66.

—. *Theology of the Prophetic Books: The Death and Resurrection of Israel*. Louisville: Westminster John Knox, 1998.

—. *The Triumph of Faith in Habakkuk*. Atlanta: John Knox Press, 1976.

Gray, G.B. *Forms of Hebrew Poetry*. New York: KTAV, 1970.

Greenstein, Edward L. *Essays in Biblical Method and Translation*. Brown Judaic Studies 92. Atlanta: Scholars Press, 1989.

Greenwood, D. "Rhetorical Criticism and *Formgeschichte*: Some Methodological Considerations." *Journal of Biblical Literature* 89 (1970): 418-26.

Groves, Joseph W. *Actualization and Interpretation in the Old Testament*. Atlanta: Scholars Press, 1987.

Guerin, Wilfred L., Earle Labor, Lee Morgan, Jeanne C. Reesman, and John R. Willingham. *A Handbook of Critical Approaches to Literature*. 4th ed. New York: Oxford University Press, 1999.

Gunkel, Hermann. "The Close of Micah: A Prophetic Liturgy—A Study in Literary History." In *What Remains of the Old Testament*. Translated by A.K. Dallas, 115-49. London: George Allen Unwin Ltd., 1928.

—. *Introduction to Psalms: The Genres of the Religious Lyric of Israel*. Translated by James D. Nogalski. Macon: Mercer University Press, 1988.

—. "The Israelite Prophecy from the Time of Amos." In *Twentieth Century Theology in the Making: Themes of Biblical Theology*. Edited by Jaroslav Pelikan, 48-75. London: Collins, 1969.

—. *The Psalms: A Form Critical Introduction*. Translated by Thomas M. Horner. Philadelphia: Fortress, 1967.

# Bibliography

Gunn, David M., and Danna Nolan Fewell. *Narrative in the Hebrew Bible*. The Oxford Bible Series. New York: Oxford University Press, 1993.

Gunneweg, A.H.J. "Habakuk und das Problem des leidenden *sdyq*." *Zeitschrift für die alttestamentliche Wissenschaft* 98 (1986): 400-15.

Haak, Robert D. *Habakkuk*. Supplements to Vetus Testamentum 44. Leiden: Brill, 1991.

—. " 'Poetry' in Habakkuk 1:1-2:4?" *Journal of the American Oriental Society* 108 (1988): 437-444.

Habel, Norman C. "In Defense of God the Sage." In *The Voice from the Whirlwind: Interpreting The Book of Job*. Edited by Leo G. Perdue, and W. Clark Gilpin, 21-38. Nashville: Abingdon, 1992.

Hadley, J.M. *The Cult of Asherah in Ancient Israel and Judah: Evidence for a Hebrew Goddess*. Cambridge: Cambridge University Press, 2000.

Harmon, William. *A Handbook to Literature: Based on Earlier Editions by William Flint Thrall, Addison Hibbard, and C. Hugh Holman*, 9th ed. Upper Saddle River, NJ: Prentice Hall, 2003.

Harris, J.G. "The Laments of Habakkuk's Prophecy." *Evangelical Quarterly* 45 (1973): 21-29.

—. *The Qumran Commentary on Habakkuk*. London: A.R. Mowbray, 1966.

Harris, Wendell V. *Dictionary of Concepts in Literary Criticism and Theory*. New York: Greenwood Press, 1992.

Harrison, R.K. *Introduction to the Old Testament: With a Comprehensive Review of Old Testament Studies and a Special Supplement on the Apocrypha*. Grand Rapids: Eerdmans, 1969.

Hartley, John E. *The Book of Job*. New International Commentary on the Old Testament. Grand Rapids: Eerdmans, 1988.

Heflin, J.N. Boo. *Nahum, Habakkuk, Zephaniah, and Haggai*. Bible Study Commentary. Grand Rapids: Zondervan, 1985.

Herrmann, W. "Das Unerledigte Problem Des Buches Habakkuk." *Vetus Testamentum* 51 (2001): 481-96.

Hiebert, Theodore. "The Book of Habakkuk: An Introduction, Commentary, and Reflections." In *The New Interpreter's Bible*, 7:623-55. Nashville: Abingdon, 1996.

—. *God of My Victory: The Ancient Hymn in Habakkuk 3*. Harvard Semitic Monograph 38. Atlanta: Scholars Press, 1986.

—. "The Use of Inclusion in Habakkuk 3." In *Directions in Biblical Hebrew Poetry*. Edited by Elaine R. Follis, 119-40. Journal for the Study of the Old Testament Supplement Series 40. Sheffield: JSOT Press, 1987.

—. "Theophany in the OT." In *Anchor Bible Dictionary*. Edited by D.N. Freedman, 6:505-11. New York: Doubleday, 1992.

Hillers, Delbert. "A Convention in Biblical Hebrew Literature: The Reaction to Bad News." *Zeitschrift für die alttestamentliche Wissenschaft* 77 (1965): 86-90.

—. "*Hôy* and *Hôy*-Oracles: A Neglected Syntactic Aspect." In *The Word of the Lord Shall Go Forth: Essays in Honor of David Noel Freedman in Celebration of His Sixtieth Birthday*. Edited by Carol L. Meyers, and M.

O'Connor, 185-88. Philadelphia: American Schools of Oriental Research, 1983.

Holladay, William L. "The Background of Jeremiah's Self Understanding: Moses, Samuel, and Psalm 22." *Journal of Biblical Literature* 83 (1964): 153-64.

—. "Jeremiah and Moses: Further Observations." *Journal of Biblical Literature* 85 (1966): 17-27.

—. "Plausible Circumstances for the Prophecy of Habakkuk." *Journal of Biblical Literature* 120 (2001): 123-30.

Holt, J.M. "So He May Run Who Reads It." *Journal of Biblical Literature* 83 (1964): 298-302.

Horgan, Maurya P. *Pesharim: Qumran Interpretations of Biblical Books.* Washington, D.C.: The Catholic Biblical Association of America, 1979.

House, Paul R., ed. *Beyond Form Criticism: Essays in Old Testament Literary Criticism.* Winona Lake: Eisenbrauns, 1992.

—. "The Character of God in the Book of the Twelve." In *Reading and Hearing the Book of the Twelve.* Edited by James D. Nogalski, and Marvin A. Sweeney, 125-45. Atlanta: Society of Biblical Literature, 2000.

—. "Dramatic Coherence in Nahum, Habakkuk, and Zephaniah." In *Forming Prophetic Literature: Essays on Isaiah and the Twelve in Honor of John D.W. Watts.* Edited by James W. Watts, and Paul R. House, 195-208. Journal for the Study of the Old Testament Supplement Series 235. Sheffield: Sheffield Academic Press, 1996.

—. *The Unity of the Twelve.* Journal for the Study of the Old Testament Supplement 97. Sheffield: Almond Press, 1990.

—. *Zephaniah: A Prophetic Drama.* Journal for the Study of the Old Testament Supplement 69. Sheffield: Almond Press, 1988.

Huey, F.B. Jr. *Jeremiah, Lamentations.* The New American Commentary. Vol 16. Nashville: Broadmen & Holman Publishers, 1993.

Huffmon, Herbert B. "The Covenant Lawsuit in the Prophets." *Journal of Biblical Literature* 78 (1959): 285-95.

Hugenberger, G.P. "The Name אֲדֹנָי" In *Basics of Biblical Hebrew Grammar.* G.D. Pratico, and M.V. Van Pelt.269-70. Grand Rapids: Zondervan, 2001.

Hunter, J.H. "The Literary Composition of Theophany Passages in the Hebrew Psalms." *Journal of Northwest Semitic Languages* 15 (1989): 97-107.

Illman, Karl-Johan. "Theodicy in Job." In *Theodicy in the World of the Bible.* Edited by Antti Raato and Johannes C. de Moor, 304-33. Leiden: Brill, 2003.

Irwin, William A. "The Mythological Background of Habakkuk, Chapter iii." *Journal of Near Eastern Studies* 15 (1956): 47-50.

—. "The Psalm of Habakkuk." *Journal of Near Eastern Studies* 1 (1942): 10-40.

Jamieson-Drake, David W. "Literary Structure, Genre and Interpretation in Job 38." In *The Listening Heart: Essays in Wisdom and the Psalms in Honor of Roland E. Murphy, O.Carm.* Edited by Kenneth G. Hoglund, Elizabeth F.

Bibliography

Huwiler, Jonathan T. Glass, and Roger W. Lee, 217-35. Journal for the Study of the Old Testament Supplement Series 58. Sheffield: JSOT Press, 1987.

Janzen, J. Gerald. "Eschatological Symbol and Existence in Habakkuk." *Catholic Biblical Quarterly* 44 (1982): 393-414.

—. "Habakkuk 2:2-4 in the Light of Recent Philological Advances." *Harvard Theological Review* 73 (1980): 53-78.

Janzen, Waldemar. *Mourning Cry and Woe Oracle*. Berlin: de Gruyter, 1972.

Jefferson, Helen G. "Psalm LXXVII." *Vetus Testamentum* 13 (1963): 87-91.

Jepsen, A. "אָמַן" In *Theological Dictionary of the Old Testament*. Edited by G.J. Botterweck, H. Ringgren, and H.J. Farbry. Translated by D.E. Green. 1:317. Grand Rapids, 2003.

Jeremias, Jörg. *Kultprophetie und Gerichtsverkundigung in der späten Königszeit Israels*. Neukirchen-Vluyn: Neukirchener Verlag, 1970.

—. *Theophanie. Geschichte einer alttestamentlichen Gattung*. Neukirchen-Vluyn: Neukirchener Verlag, 1965.

Jöcken, P. *Das Buch Habakuk*. Bonner Biblische Beiträge 48. Köhn-Bonn: Peter Hanstein, 1977.

—. "War Habakuk ein Kultprophet?" In *Bausteine Biblischer Theologie*. Edited by H.J. Fabry, 319-32. Bonn: Bonner Biblische Beiträge, 1977.

Johnson, Aubrey. R. *The Cultic Prophet and Israel's Psalmody*. Cardiff: University of Wales Press, 1979.

Johnson, B. "צדק" In *Theological Dictionary of the Old Testament*. Edited by G.J. Botterweck, H. Ringgren, and H.J. Farbry. Translated by D.E. Green. 12:243-46. Grand Rapids, 2003.

Johnson, Marshall D. "The Paralysis of Torah in Habakkuk I 4." *Vetus Testamentum* 35 (1985): 257-66.

Jones, Barry A. "The Book of the Twelve as a Witness to Ancient Biblical Interpretation." In *Reading and Hearing theBook of the Twelve*. Edited by James D. Nogalski, and Marvin A. Sweeney, 65-74. Atlanta: Society of Biblical Literature, 2000.

Jones, Douglas R. Review of *God of My Victory*, by Theodore Hiebert. *Journal of Theological Studies* 41 (1990): 144-47.

Kaiser, Otto. "*Deus Absconditus and Deus Revelatus*: Three Difficult Narratives in the Pentateuch." In *Shall Not the Judge of All the Earth Do What Is Right? Studies on the Nature of God in Tribute to James L. Crenshaw*. Edited by David Penchansky, and Paul L. Redditt, 73-88. Winona Lake: Eisenbrauns, 2000.

Kaufman, U. Milo. "Expostulation with the Divine: A Note on Contrasting Attitudes in Greek and Hebrew Piety." *Interpretation* 18 (1964): 171-82.

Keil, Carl Friedrich. *The Twelve Minor Prophets*. Vol. 2. Translated by James Martin. Grand Rapids: Eerdmans, 1949.

Keller, C.A. "Die Eigenart der Prophetie Habakuks." *Zeitschrift für die alttestamentliche Wissenschaft* 85 (1973): 156-67.

Kelly, Fred. "The Strophic Structure of Habakkuk." *American Journal of Semitic Languages and Literatures* 18 (1901/1902): 94-122.

Kennedy, George A. *New Testament Interpretation through Rhetorical Criticism.* Chapel Hill: The University of North Carolina Press, 1984.

Kessler, Martin. "A Methodological Setting for Rhetorical Criticism." In *Art and Meaning: Rhetoric in Biblical Literature.* Edited by David Clines, David Gunn, and Alan Hauser, 1-19. Journal for the Study of the Old Testament Supplement 19. Sheffield: University of Sheffield Press, 1982.

—. "Rhetorical Criticism of Genesis 7." In *Rhetorical Criticism: Essays in Honor of James Muilenburg.* Edited by J.J. Jackson and M. Kessler, 1-17. Pittsburg Theological Monograph Series 1. Pittsburgh: Pickwick Press, 1974.

Kikawada, I.M. "Some Proposals for the Definition of Rhetorical Criticism." *Semitics* 5 (1977): 67-91.

King, Philip J., and Lawrence E. Stager. *Life in Biblical Israel.* Louisville: Westminster John Knox, 2001.

Kinnier Wilson, J.V. "A Return to the Problems of Behemoth and Leviathan." *Vetus Testamentum* 25 (1975): 1-14.

Klein, Ralph W. *Textual Criticism of the Old Testament: From the Septuagint to Qumran.* Philadelphia: Fortress, 1974.

Knierem, R. "Old Testament Form Criticism Reconsidered." *Interpretation* 27 (1973): 435-68.

Koch, Klaus. *The Growth of the Biblical Tradition: The Form Critical Method.* Translated by C.M. Cupitt. London: Adam and Charles Black, 1969.

—. "Is There a Doctrine of Retribution in the Old Testament?" In *Theodicy in the Old Testament.* Edited by James L. Crenshaw, 57-87. Philadelphia: Fortress, 1983.

Kolesnikoff, Nina. "Formalism, Russian." In *Encyclopedia of Contemporary Literary Theory: Approaches, Scholars, Terms.* Edited by Irena R. Makaryk, 53-60. Toronto: University of Toronto Press, 1993. Reprint, 1995.

Kramer, Samuel Noah. " 'Man and His God': A Sumerian Variation on the 'Job' Motif." In *Wisdom in Israel and in the Ancient Near East.* Edited by M. Noth, and D. Winton Thomas, 170-82. Leiden: Brill, 1960.

Kselman, John S. "Design and Structure in Hebrew Poetry." In *SBL 1980 Seminar Papers.* Edited by Paul J. Achtemeier, 1-16. SBL Seminar Papers Series 19. Chico: Scholars Press, 1980.

Kugel, J. *The Idea of Biblical Poetry.* New Haven: Yale University Press, 1981.

Kuntz, J. Kenneth. "Biblical Hebrew Poetry in Recent Research, Part I." *Currents in Research* 6 (1998): 31-64.

—. "Biblical Hebrew Poetry in Recent Research, Part II." *Currents in Research* 7 (1999): 35-79.

—. "The Canonical Wisdom Psalms of Ancient Israel—Their Rhetorical, Thematic, and Dimensions." In *Rhetorical Criticism: Essays in Honor of James Muilenburg.* Edited by J.J. Jackson and M. Kessler, 186-222. Pittsburgh Theological Monograph Series 1. Pittsburgh: Pickwick Press, 1974.

Bibliography

—. "The Contribution of Rhetorical Criticism to Understanding Isaiah 51:1-16." In *Art and Meaning: Rhetoric in Biblical Literature*. Edited by David Clines, David Gunn, and Alan Hauser, 140-71. Journal for the Study of the Old Testament Supplement Series 19. Sheffield: University of Sheffield Press, 1982.

—. "Reclaiming Biblical Wisdom Psalms: A Response to Crenshaw." *Currents in Biblical Research* 1 (2003): 145-54.

Lallemon-de Winkel, Hetty. *Jeremiah in Prophetic Tradition: An Examination of the Book of Jeremiah in the Light of Israel's Prophetic Traditions*. Leuven: Peeters, 2000.

Laurin, Robert. "The Theological Structure of Job." *Zeitschrift für die alttestamentliche Wissenschaft* 84 (1972): 86-9.

Leigh, B.Y. "A Rhetorical and Structural Study of the Book of Habakkuk." Ph.D. diss., Golden Gate Baptist Theological Seminary, 1994.

Lescow, Theodor. "Die Komposition der Bücher Nahum and Habakuk." *Bibische Notizen* 77 (1995): 59-85.

Lete, G. Del Olmo. "Deber." In *Dictionary of Deities and Demons in the Bible*. Edited by K. Van der Toorn, B. Becking, P.W. Van der Horst. 231-2. New York: Brill, 1995.

Levenson, Jon Douglas. *Creation and the Persistence of Evil: The Jewish Drama of Divine Omnipotence*. San Francisco: Harper and Row, 1988.

—. *The Book of Job in Its Time and in the Twentieth Century*. Cambridge: Harvard University Press, 1972.

Levinson, B.M. *Deuteronomy and the Hermeneutics of Legal Innovation*. New York: Oxford University Press, 1997.

Lichtenstein, Murray. "The Poetry of Poetic Justice: A Comparative Study in Biblical Imagery." *Journal of the Ancient Near Eastern Society of Colombia University* 5 (1973): 255-65.

Lim, Timothy H. "Eschatological Orientation and the Alteration of Scripture in the Habakkuk Pesher." *Journal of Near Eastern Studies* 49 (1990): 185-94.

—. "The Wicked Priests of the Groningen Hypothesis." *Journal of Biblical Literature* 112 (1993): 415-25.

Limburg, James. "The Root ריב and the Prophetic Lawsuit Speeches." *Journal of Biblical Literature* 88 (1969): 291-304.

Lindbeck, George A. "Postcritical Canonical Interpretation: Three Modes of Retrieval." In *Theological Exegesis: Essays in Honor of Brevard S. Childs*. Edited by Christopher Seitz, and Kathryn Greene-McCreight, 26-51. Grand Rapids: Eerdmans, 1999.

Lindblom, Johannes. "Wisdom in the Old Testament Prophets." In *Wisdom in Israel and in the Ancient Near East*. Edited by M. Noth, and D. Winton Thomas, 192-204. Leiden: Brill, 1960.

Lindström, Fredrik. "Theodicy in the Psalms." In *Theodicy in the World of the Bible*. Edited by Antti Raato, and Johannes C. de Moor, 256-303. Leiden: Brill, 2003.

Lloyd-Jones, D. Martyn. *From Fear to Faith: Studies in the Book of Habakkuk*. London: The Inter-Varsity Fellowship, 1953.

Longman, Tremper III. "Biblical Narrative." In *A Complete Literary Guide to the Bible*. Edited by Leland Ryken, and Tremper Longman III, 69-79. Grand Rapids: Zondervan, 1993.

—. "Biblical Poetry." In *A Complete Literary Guide to the Bible*. Edited by Leland Ryken, and Tremper Longman III, 80-91. Grand Rapids: Zondervan, 1993.

—. "Form Criticism, Recent Developments in Genre Theory, and the Evangelical." *The Westminster Theological Journal* 47 (1985): 46-67.

—. *How to Read the Psalms*. Downers Grove: InterVarsity Press, 1988.

—. "The Literature of the Old Testament." In *A Complete Literary Guide to the Bible*. Edited by Leland Ryken, and Tremper Longman III, 95-107. Grand Rapids: Zondervan, 1993.

—. *Literary Approaches to Biblical Interpretation*. Foundations of Contemporary Interpretation Volume 3. Grand Rapids: Zondervan, 1987.

López, García. "תּוֹרָה" In *Theological Dictionary of the Old Testament*. Edited by G.J. Botterweck, H. Ringgren, and H.J. Farbry. Translated by D.E. Green. 15:609-44 Grand Rapids, 2003.

Lundbom, Jack R. "The Double Curse in Jeremiah 20:14-18." *Journal of Biblical Literature* 104 (1985): 589-600.

—. *Jeremiah: A Study in Ancient Hebrew Rhetoric*. SBL Dissertation Series 18. Missoula: Scholars Press, 1975.

Macintosh, A.A. "Hosea and the Wisdom Tradition: Dependence and Independence." In *Wisdom in Ancient Israel: Essays in Honour of J.A. Emerton*. Edited by John Day, Robert P. Gordon, and H.G.M. Williamson, 124-32. Cambridge: Cambridge University Press, 1995.

MacKenzie, R.A.F. "The Purpose of the Yahweh Speeches in the Book of Job." *Biblica* 40 (1959): 435-45.

Manson, Thomas W. "The Argument from Prophecy." *Journal of Theological Studies* 46 (1945): 129-36.

Margolis, Max. "The Character of the Anonymous Greek Version of Habakkuk, Chapter 3." *American Journal of Semitic Languages and Literatures* 25 (1907/1908): 76-85.

Margulis, Baruch. "The Day the Sun Did Not Stand Still: A New Look at Joshua X 8-15." *Vetus Testamentum* 42 (1992): 466-91.

—. "The Psalm of Habakkuk: A Reconstruction and Interpretation." *Zeitschrift für die alttestamentliche Wissenschaft* 82 (1970): 409-42.

Markl, Dominik. "Hab 3 in intertextueller und kontextueller Sicht." *Biblica* 85 (2004): 99-108.

Marks, Herbert. "The Twelve Prophets." In *The Literary Guide to the Bible*. Edited by Robert Alter, and Frank Kermode, 207-33. Cambridge: The Belknap Press of Harvard University Press, 1987.

Mason, Rex. *Zephaniah, Habakkuk, Joel*. Old Testament Guides. Sheffield: JSOT, 1994.

# Bibliography

Marti, K. *Das Dokekapropheten*. Tübingen: J.C.B. Mohr, 1903.

Matties, Gordon H. *Ezekiel 18 and the Rhetoric of Moral Discourse*. Atlanta: Scholars Press, 1990.

Mays, James Luther. "Justice: Perspectives from the Prophetic Tradition." *Interpretation* 37 (1983): 5-17.

McCann, J. Clinton, Jr. "Psalm 73: A Microcosm of Old Testament Theology." In *The Listening Heart: Essays in Wisdom and the Psalms in Honor of Roland E. Murphy, O. Carm*. Edited by Kenneth G. Hoglund, Elizabeth F. Huwiler, Jonathan T. Glass, and Roger W. Lee, 247-57. Journal for the Study of the Old Testament Supplement Series 58. Sheffield: JSOT Press, 1987.

McCarter, P. Kyle, Jr. *Textual Criticism: Recovering the Text of the Hebrew Bible*. Philadelphia: Fortress, 1986.

McCarthy, Carmel. "Emendations of the Scribes [תקוני סופרים *Tiqqune Sopherim*]." In Supplementary volume to *Interpreter's Dictionary of the Bible*. Nashville: Abingdon, 1976.

McGlasson, Paul C. "The Significance of Context in Theology: A Canonical Approach." In *Theological Exegesis: Essays in Honor of Brevard S. Childs*. Edited by Christopher Seitz, and Kathryn Greene-McCreight, 52-72. Grand Rapids: Eerdmans, 1999.

McKane, William. "Jeremiah and the Wise." In *Wisdom in Ancient Israel: Essays in Honour of J.A. Emerton*. Edited by John Day, Robert P. Gordon, and H.G.M. Williamson, 142-51. Cambridge: Cambridge University Press, 1995.

McKenzie, John L. "Reflections on Wisdom." *Journal of Biblical Literature* 86 (1967): 1-9.

McKim, Donald K., ed. *A Guide to Contemporary Hermeneutics: Major Trends in Biblical Interpretation*. Grand Rapids: Eerdmans, 1986.

Melugin, Roy F. "Muilenburg, Form Criticism, and Theological Exegesis." In *Encounter with The Text, Form and History in the Hebrew Bible*. Editied by M.J. Buss, 91-100. Philadelphia: Fortress, 1979.

—. "Propetic Books and the Problem of Historical Reconstruction." In *Prophets and Paradigms: Essays in Honor of Gene M. Tucker*. Edited by Stephen Breck Reid, 63-78. Journal for the Study of the Old Testament Supplement Series 229. Sheffield: Sheffield Academic Press, 1996.

—. "The Typical Versus the Unique Among the Hebrew Prophets." In *Society of Biblical Literature 1972 Proceedings*. Edited by Lane C. McGaughty, 2:331-34. Missoula: SBL, 1973.

Mendenhall, George E. "Ancient Oriental and Biblical Law." *Biblical Archaeologist* 17 (May 1954): 26-46.

Mettinger, Trygge N.D. "The God of Job: Avenger, Tyrant, or Victor?" In *The Voice from the Whirlwind: Interpreting The Book of Job*. Edited by Leo G. Perdue, and W. Clark Gilpin, 39-49. Nashville: Abingdon, 1992.

Miller, H.P. "מָשָׁא." In *Theological Dictionary of the Old Testament*. Edited by G.J. Botterweck, H. Ringgren, and H.J. Farbry. Translated by D.E. Green. 9:20-24 Grand Rapids, 2003.

Miller, Patrick D., Jr. *Sin and Judgment in the Prophets: A Stylistic and Theological Analysis*. Society of Biblical Literature Monograph Series 27. Chico: Scholars Press, 1982.

Mitchell, David C. "'God Will Redeem My Soul from Sheol': The Psalms of the Sons of Korah," *Journal for the Study of the Old Testament* 30 (2006): 365-84.

Möller, K. "Prophets and Prophecy." In *Dictionary of the Old Testament: Historical Books*. Edited by Bill T. Arnold and H.G.M. Williamson. 825-29. Downers Grove: InterVarsity Press, 2005.

Morgan, Donn F. *Wisdom in the Old Testament Traditions*. Atlanta: John Knox, 1981.

Mowinckel, Sigmund. "Psalms and Wisdom." In *Wisdom in Israel and in the Ancient Near East*. Edited by M. Noth, and D. Winton Thomas, 205-24. Leiden: Brill, 1960.

Muenchow, Charles. "Dust and Dirt in Job 42:6." *Journal Biblical Literature* 108 (1989): 597-611.

Muilenburg, James. "Baruch the Scribe." In *Proclamation and Presence: Old Testament Essays in Honour of Gwynne Henton Davies*. Edited by John I. Durham, and J.R. Porter, 215-38. London: SCM Press, 1970. New Corrected Edition, Macon: Mercer University Press, 1983.

—. "The Biblical Understanding of the Future." *Journal of Religious Thought* 19 (1962/1963): 99-108.

—. "Form Criticism and Beyond." *Journal of Biblical Literature* 88 (1969): 1-18.

—. "The Linguistic and Rhetorical Uses of the Particle *kî* in the Old Testament." *Hebrew Union College Annual* 32 (1961): 135-60.

—. "The Speech of Theophany." *Harvard Divinity Bulletin* 28 (1963/1964): 35-47.

Murphy, Roland E. "Assumptions and Problems in Old Testament Wisdom Research." *Catholic Biblical Quarterly* 29 (1967): 407-18.

—. "A Consideration of the Classification, 'Wisdom Psalms'." In *Congress Volume: Bonn, 1962*. Edited by Martin Noth, 156-67. Supplements to Vetus Testamentum 9. Leiden: Brill, 1963.

Nations, Archie L. "Historical Criticism and the Current Methodological Crisis." *Scottish Journal of Theology* 36 (1983): 59-71.

Neiman, David. *The Book of Job*. Jerusalem: Massada, 1972.

Nicholson, E.W. "The Limits of Theodicy as a Theme of the Book of Job." In *Wisdom in Ancient Israel: Essays in Honour of J.A. Emerton*. Edited by John Day, Robert P. Gordon, and H.G.M. Williamson, 71-82. Cambridge: Cambridge University Press, 1995.

Niehaus, Jeffrey J. *God at Sinai: Covenant and Theophany in the Bible and Ancient Near East*. Grand Rapids: Zondervan, 1995.

Nielsen, E. "The Righteous and the Wicked in Habaqquq." *Studia Theologica* 6 (1953): 54-78.

Nogalski, James D. "Intertextuality in the Twelve." In *Forming Prophetic Literature: Essays on Isaiah and the Twelve in Honor of John D.W. Watts*. Edited by James W. Watts, and Paul R. House, 102-24. Journal for the Study of the Old Testament Supplement Series 235. Sheffield: Sheffield Academic Press, 1996.

——. " 'Joel as 'Literary Anchor' for the Book of the Twelve." In *Reading and Hearing the Book of the Twelve*. Edited by James D. Nogalski and Marvin A. Sweeney, 91-109. Atlanta: Society of Biblical Literature, 2000.

——. *Literary Precursors to the Book of the Twelve*. Berlin: W. de Gruyter, 1993.

——. *Redactional Processes in the Book of the Twelve*. Beihefte zur *Zeitschrift für die alttestamentliche Wissenschaft* 218. Berlin/New York: W. de Gruyter, 1993.

——. "The Redactional Shaping of Nahum 1 for the Book of the Twelve." In *Among the Prophets: Language, Image and Structure in the Prophetic Writings*. Edited by Philip R. Davies, and David J.A. Clines, 193-202. Journal for the Study of the Old Testament Supplement Series 144. Sheffield: Sheffield Academic Press, 1993.

——. "Recurring Themes in the Book of the Twelve: Creating Points of Contact for a Theological Reading." *Interpretation* 61 (2007): 125-36.

Nordin, John P. " 'There is Nothing on Earth that I Desire': A Commentary on Psalm 73." *Currents in Theology and Missions* 29 (Aug 2002): 258-64.

O'Brien, Julia M. *Nahum, Habakkuk, Zephaniah, Haggai, Zechariah, Malachi*. Abingdon Old Testament Commentaries. Nashville: Abingdon, 2004.

——. "Nahum-Habakkuk-Zephaniah: Reading the 'Former Prophets' in the Persian Period." *Interpretation* 61 (2007): 168-83.

O'Connell, Kevin G. "Habakkuk—Spokesman to God." *Currents in Theology and Mission* 6 (1979): 227-31.

O'Connor, Kathleen M. *The Confessions of Jeremiah: Their Interpretation and Role in Chapters 1-25*. SBL Dissertation Series 94. Atlanta: Scholars Press, 1988.

——. "Wild, Raging Creativity: The Scene in the Whirlwind (Job 38-41)." In *A God So Near: Essays on Old Testament Theology in Honor of Patrick D. Miller*. Edited by Brent A. Strawn and Nancy R. Bowen, 171-9. Winona Lake: Eisenbrauns, 2003.

O'Connor, M. *Hebrew Verse Structure*. Winona Lake: Eisenbrauns, 1980.

O'Neal, G. Michael. *Interpreting Habakkuk as Scripture: An Application of the Canonical Approach of Brevard S. Childs*. New York: Peter Lang, 2007.

O'Rourke Boyle, Marjorie. "The Covenant Lawsuit of the Prophet Amos: III 1-IV 13." *Vetus Testamentum* 21 (1971): 338-62.

Oswalt, John N. *The Book of Isaiah Chapters 1-39*. New International Commentary on the Old Testament. Grand Rapids: Eerdmans, 1986.

Otto, Eckart. "Die Stellung der Wehe-Worte in der Verkundigung des Propheten Habakuk." *Zeitschrift für die alttestamentliche Wissenschaft* 89 (1977): 73-107.

—. " Die Theologie des Buches Habakuk." *Vetus Testamentum* 35 (1985): 274-95.

Otto, Rudolf. *The Idea of the Holy: An Inquiry into the Non-Rational Factor in the Idea of the Divine and Its Relation to the Rational.* Translated by John W. Harvey. London: Oxford University Press, 1925.

Pardee, Dennis. "*YPH* ! 'Witness' in Hebrew and Ugaritic," *Vetus Testamentum* 28 (1978): 204-13.

Patrick, Dale, and Allen Scult. *Rhetoric and Biblical Interpretation.* Journal for the Study Of the Old Testament Supplement Series 82. Sheffield: Almond Press, 1990.

Patrick, Dale. "The Translation of Job XLII 6." *Vetus Testamentum* 26 (1976): 369-71.

Patterson, Richard D. "A Literary Look at Nahum, Habakkuk, and Zephaniah." *Grace Theological Journal* 11 (1991): 17-27.

—. *Nahum, Habakkuk, Zephaniah.* The Wycliffe Exegetical Commentary. Chicago: Moody Press, 1991.

—. "Old Testament Prophecy." In *A Complete Literary Guide to the Bible.* Edited by Leland Ryken, and Tremper Longman III, 296-309. Grand Rapids: Zondervan, 1993.

—. "The Psalm of Habakkuk." *Grace Theological Journal* 8 (1987): 163-94.

Peake, A.S. "Job: The Problem of the Book." In *Theodicy in the Old Testament.* Edited by James L. Crenshaw, 100-8. Philadelphia: Fortress, 1983.

—. *The Problem of Suffering in the Old Testament.* London: Kelly, 1904.

Peckham, Brian. *History and Prophecy: The Development of Late Judean Literary Traditions.* New York: Doubleday, 1993.

—. "Tense and Mood in Biblical Hebrew." *Zeitschrift für Althebräistik* 10 (1997): 139-68.

—. "The Vision of Habakkuk." *Catholic Biblical Quarterly* 48 (1986): 617-36.

—. Review of *God of My Victory*, by Theodore Hiebert. *Hebrew Studies* 30 (1989): 143-45.

—. "Writing and Editing." In *Fortunate the Eyes that See: Essays in Honor of David Noel Freedman in Celebration of His Seventieth Birthday.* Edited by Astrid B. Beck, Andrew H. Bartelt, Paul R. Raabe, and Chris A. Franke, 364-83. Grand Rapids: Eerdmans, 1995.

Penchansky, David, and Paul L Redditt, eds. *Shall Not the Judge of All the Earth Do What is Right? Studies on the Nature of God in Tribute to James L. Crenshaw.* Winona Lake: Eisenbrauns, 2000.

Petersen, David L. "A Book of the Twelve?" In *Reading and Hearing the Book of the Twelve.* Edited by James D. Nogalski and Marvin A. Sweeney, 3-10. Atlanta: Society of Biblical Literature, 2000.

Petersen, David L., and Kent Harold Richards. *Interpreting Hebrew Poetry.* Old Testament Series. Minneapolis: Fortress Press, 1992.

Pfeiffer, R.H. *Introduction to the Old Testament.* London: Black, 1952.

Pinker, Aron. "Better Bitter River." *Zeitschrift für die alttestamentliche Wissenschaft* 114 (2002): 112-5.

—. " 'Captors' for 'Years' in Habakkuk 3:2." *Revue Biblique* 112 (Jan 2005): 20-6.

—. "Casternets." *Zeitschrift für die alttestamentliche Wissenschaft* 114 (2002): 618-21.

—. "God's C3 in Habakkuk 3." *Zeitschrift für die alttestamentliche Wissenschaft* 115 (2003): 261-65.

—. "On the Meaning of מטיו in Habakkuk 3,14a." *Biblica* 86 (2005): 376-86.

—. "The Lord's Bow in Habakkuk 3,9a." *Biblica* 84 (2003): 417-20.

—. "The Targum on Hab 2:2." *Revue Biblique* 111 (2004): 28-30.

—. "Was Habakkuk Presumptuous?" *Jewish Bible Quarterly* 32 (Jan-Mar 2004): 27-34.

Pope, Marvin H. *Job: A New Translation with Introduction and Commentary.* The Anchor Bible 15. New York: Doubleday, 1973.

Priest, John F. "Where is Wisdom to be Placed?" *Journal of Bible and Religion* 31 (1963): 275-82.

Prinslo, G.T.M. "Habakkuk 1 – a Dialogue? Ancient Unit Delimiters in Dialogue with Modern Critical Interpretation." *Old Testament Essays* 17 (2004): 621-45.

—. "Life for the Righteous, Doom for the Wicked: Reading Habakkuk from a Wisdom Perspective." *Skrif en Kerk* 21 (2000): 621-40.

—. "Reading Habakkuk as a Literary Unit: Exploring the Possibilities." *Old Testament Essays* 12 (1999): 515-35.

—. "Reading Habakkuk 3 in its Literary Context: A Worthwhile Exercise or Futile Attempt?" *Journal for Semitics* 11 (2002): 83-111.

—. "Yahweh the Warrior: An Intertextual Reading of Habakkuk 3." *Old Testament Essays* 14 (2001): 475-93.

Rabinowitz, Isaac. " '*Pēsher/Pittāron*' Its Biblical Meaning and Its Significance in the Qumran Literature." *Revue de Qumran* 8 (1972-75): 219-32.

Rad, Gerhard von. "The Confessions of Jeremiah." In *Theodicy in the Old Testament.* Edited by James L Crenshaw, 88-99. Philadelphia: Fortress, 1983.

Rainey, Anson F., and R. Steven Notley. *The Sacred Bridge: Carta's Atlas of the Biblical World.* Jerusalem: Carta, 2006.

Ramsey, George W. "Speech-Forms in Hebrew Law and Prophetic Oracles." *Journal of Biblical Literature* 96 (1977): 45-58.

Rast, Walter E. "Habakkuk and Justification by Faith." *Currents in Theology and Mission* 10 (1983): 169-75.

Rendtorff, Rolf. "How to Read the Book of the Twelve as a Theological Unity." In *Reading and Hearing the Book of the Twelve.* Edited by James D. Nogalski & Marvin A. Sweeney, 75-87. Atlanta: Society of Biblical Literature, 2000.

Roberts, J.J.M. *Nahum, Habakkuk, and Zephaniah: A Commentary.* Old Testament Library. Louisville: Westminster John Knox, 1991.

Robertson, David A. *Linguistic Evidence in Dating Early Hebrew Poetry.*
Missoula: SBL, 1972.

—. *The Old Testament and the Literary Critic.* Old Testament Series.
Philadelphia: Fortress Press, 1977.

Robertson, O.P. *The Books of Nahum, Habakkuk, and Zephaniah.* The New
International Commentary on the Old Testament. Grand Rapids: Eerdmans,
1990.

—. " 'The Justified (by Faith) Shall Live by His Steadfast Trust'—Habakkuk
2:4." *Presbyterion* 9 (1983): 52-71.

Rogerson, J.W. "The Enemy in the Old Testament." In *Understanding Poets
and Prophets: Essays in Honour of George Wishart Anderson.* Edited by A.
Graeme Auld, 284-93. Journal for the Study of the Old Testament
Supplement Series 152. Sheffield: JSOT Press, 1993.

Rooker, M.E. "Theophany." In *Dictionary of the Old Testament: Pentateuch.*
Edited by T. Desmond Alexander, and David W. Baker. 859-64. Downers
Grove: InterVarsity Press, 2003.

Rudolph, W. *Micha-Nahum-Habakuk-Zephania.* Kommentar zum alten
Testament 13:3 Guttersloh: Mohn, 1975.

Ryken, Leland. "The Bible as Literature: A Brief History." In *A Complete
Literary Guide to the Bible.* Edited by Leland Ryken, and Tremper Longman
III, 49-68. Grand Rapids: Zondervan, 1993.

—. *How to Read the Bible as Literature.* Grand Rapids: Zondervan, 1984.

—. "Literary Criticism of the Bible: Some Fallacies." In *Literary Interpretation
of Biblical Narratives.* Edited by Kenneth Gros Louis, et al., 24-40.
Nashville: Abingdon, 1974.

—. *Words of Delight: A Literary Introduction to the Bible.* Grand Rapids:
Baker, 1987.

Sack, Ronald H. "Nebuchadnezzar." In *Anchor Bible Dictionary.* Edited by
D.N. Freedman, 4:1058-9. New York: Doubleday, 1992.

Sakenfeld, Katherine Doob. "Ezekiel 18:25-32." *Interpretation* 32 (1978): 295-
300.

Sanders, J.A. "Habakkuk in Qumran, Paul, and the Old Testament." *The
Journal of Religion* 39 (1959): 232-44.

—. "Text and Canon: Concept and Method." *Journal of Biblical Literature* 98
(1979): 5-29.

Savage, Mary. "Literary Criticism and Biblical Studies: A Rhetorical Analysis
of the Joseph Narrative." In *Scripture in Context: Essays on the
Comparative Method.* Edited by Carl D. Evans, William W. Hallo, and John
B. White, 79-100. Pittsburgh Theological Monograph Series 34. Pittsburgh:
Pickwick Press, 1980.

Schaper, Joachim. "Exilic and Post-Exilic Prophecy and the Orality/Literacy
Problem." *Vetus Testamentum* 55 (2005): 324-42.

Schart, Aaron. "Reconstructing the Redaction History of the Twelve Prophets:
Problems and Models." In *Reading and Hearing the Book of the Twelve.*
Edited by James D. Nogalski and Marvin A. Sweeney, 34-48. Atlanta:
Society of Biblical Literature, 2000.

Schiffman, Lawrence H., and James C. VanderKam, eds. *Encyclopedia of the Dead Sea Scrolls*. Vol. 1. New York: Oxford University Press, 2000.

Schmidt, N.F., and P.J. Nel. "Theophany as Type-scene in the Hebrew Bible." *Journal for Semitics* 11 (2002): 256-81.

Scholnick, Sylvia Huberman. "The Meaning of *Mišpat* in the Book of Job." *Journal of Biblical Literature* 104 (1982): 521-29.

—. "Poetry in the Courtroom: Job 38-41." In *Directions in Biblical Hebrew Poetry*. Edited by Elaine R. Follis, 185-204. Journal for the Study of the Old Testament Supplement 40. Sheffield: Sheffield Academic Press, 1987.

Scott, James M. "A New Approach to Habakkuk II 4-5A." *Vetus Testamentum* 35 (1985): 330-40.

Scott, R.B.Y. "Priesthood, Prophecy, Wisdom, and the Knowledge of God." *Journal of Biblical Literature* 80 (1961): 1-15.

—. "The Study of the Wisdom Literature." *Interpretation* 24 (1970): 20-45.

Seitz, Christopher R. *Prophecy and Hermeneutics: Toward a New Introduction to the Prophets.* Grand Rapids: Baker, 2007.

Seybold, Klaus. *Nahum, Habakuk, Zephanja*. Zürcher Bibelkommentare 24. Zürich: Theologischer Verlag, 1991.

Shupak, Nili. "The God from Teman and the Egyptian Sun God: A Reconsideration of Habakkuk 3:3-7." *Journal of the Ancient Near Eastern Society* 28 (2001): 97-116.

Silberman, Lou H. " 'You Cannot See My Face': Seeking to Understand Divine Justice." In *Shall Not the Judge of All the Earth Do What Is Right? Studies on the Nature of God in Tribute to James L. Crenshaw*. Edited by David Penchansky, and Paul L. Redditt, 89-95. Winona Lake: Eisenbrauns, 2000.

Skinner, John. *Prophecy and Religion: Studies in the Life of Jerusalem*. Cambridge: Cambridge University Press, 1922. Reprint, 1955.

Slomovic, Elieser. "Towand an Understanding of the Exegesis in the Dead Sea Scrolls." *Revue de Qumran* 7 (1969-71): 3-15.

Smith, Gary V. *The Prophets as Preachers: An Introduction to the Hebrew Prophets*. Nashville: Broadman & Holman, 1994.

Smith, R.L. *Micah-Malachi*. Word Biblical Commentary 32. Waco: Word, 1984.

Snaith, Norman. *Hymns of the Temple*. London: SCM, 1951.

Snyman, S.D. "Non-Violent Prophet and Violent God in the Book of Habakkuk." *Old Testament Essays* 16 (2003): 422-34.

Soggin, J.A. "Amos and Wisdom." In *Wisdom in Ancient Israel: Essays in Honour of J.A. Emerton*. Edited by John Day, Robert P. Gordon, and H.G.M. Williamson, 119-23. Cambridge: Cambridge University Press, 1995.

Soulen, Richard N, and R. Kendall Soulen. *Handbook of Biblical Criticism*, 3d ed. Louisville: Westminster John Knox, 2001.

Stenzel, Meinrad. "Habakkuk 2,1-4.5a." *Biblica* 33 (1952): 506-10.

—. "Habakkuk II, 15-16." *Vestus Testamentum* 3 (1953): 97-99.

Stephens, Farris. "The Babylonian Dragon Myth in Habakkuk 3." *Journal of Biblical Literature* 43 (1924): 290-93.

Sternberg, Meir. "The Bible's Art of Persuasion: Ideology, Rhetoric, and Poetics in Saul's Fall." In *Beyond Form Criticism: Essays in Old Testament Literary Criticism*. Edited by Paul R. House, 234-71. Winona Lake: Eisenbrauns, 1992.

—. *The Poetics of Biblical Narrative: Ideological Literature and the Drama of Reading*. Bloomington: Indiana University Press, 1987.

Sturch, R.L. "Theodicy." In *New Dictionary of Christian Ethics and Pastoral Theology*. Downers Grove: InterVarsity Press, 1995.

Sweeney, Marvin A. "Habakkuk, Book of." In *The Anchor Bible Dictionary*. Edited by D.N. Freedman, 3:1-6. New York: Doubleday, 1992.

—. "Habakkuk." In *Berit Olam: Studies in Hebrew Narrative and Poetry, The Twelve Prophets*. Vol. 2, *Micah, Nahum, Habakkuk, Zephaniah, Haggai, Zechariah, Malachi*. Edited by David W. Cotter, 453-88. Collegeville: The Liturgical Press, 2000.

—. "Habakkuk." In *The Harper Collins Bible Commentary*, rev. ed. Edited by James L. Mays, 668-70. San Francisco: Harper, 2000.

—. "Sequence and Interpretation in the Book of the Twelve." In *Reading and Hearing the Book of the Twelve*. Edited by James D. Nogalski and Marvin A. Sweeney, 49-64. Atlanta: Society of Biblical Literature, 2000.

—. "Structure, Genre, and Intent in the Book of Habakkuk." *Vetus Testamentum* 41 (1991): 63-83.

Széles, Maria Eszenyei. *Wrath and Mercy: A Commentary on the Books of Habakkuk & Zephaniah*. Translated by George A.F. Knight. International Theological Commentary. Grand Rapids: Eerdmans, 1987.

Tate, Marvin E. *Psalms 51-100*. Word Biblical Commentary. Dallas: Word Books, 1990.

Tate, W. Randolph. *Interpreting the Bible: A Handbook of Terms and Methods*. Peabody: Hendrickson, 2006.

Taylor, J. Glen. *Yahweh and the Sun: Biblical and Archaeological Evidence for Sun Worship in Ancient Israel*. Journal for the Study of the Old Testament Supplement 111. Sheffield: JSOT Press, 1993.

Terrien, Samuel. "Amos and Wisdom." In *Israel's Prophetic Heritage*. Edited by Bernhard W. Anderson, and Walter Harrelson, 108-15. New York: Harper and Brothers, 1962.

—. *The Psalms: Strophic Structure and Theological Commentary*. Grand Rapids: Eerdmans, 2003.

Thompson, J.A. *The Book of Jeremiah*. The New International Commentary on the Old Testament. Grand Rapids: Eerdmans, 1980.

Thompson, Michael E.W. "Prayer, Oracle and Theophany: The Book of Habakkuk." *Tyndale Bulletin* 44 (1993): 33-53.

Tov, Emanuel. "Exegetical Notes on the Hebrew Vorlage of the LXX of Jeremiah 27 (34)." *Zeitschrift für die alttestamentliche Wissenschaft* 91 (1979): 73-93.

—. *Textual Criticism of the Hebrew Bible*, 2d rev. ed. Minneapolis: Fortress, 2001.

Trible, Phyllis. *Rhetorical Criticism: Context, Method, and the Book of Jonah*. Old Testament Series. Philadelphia: Fortress, 1994.

Tsevat, Matitiahu. *The Meaning of the Book of Job and Other Biblical Studies: Essays on the Literature and Religion of the Hebrew Bible*. New York: Ktav, 1980.

Tsumura, David Toshio. "Habakkuk 2 2 in the Light of Akkadian Legal Practice." *Zeitschrift für die alttestamentliche Wissenschaft* 94 (1982): 294-95.

—. "Janus Parallelism in Hab. III 4." *Vetus Testamentum* 54 (2004): 124-26.

—. "Literary Insertion (AXB Pattern) in Biblical Hebrew." *Vetus Testamentum* 33 (1983): 468-82.

—. "Niphal with Internal Object in Habakkuk 3:9a" *Journal of Semitic Studies* 31 (1986): 11-16.

—. "Ugaritic Poetry and Habakkuk 3." *Tyndale Bulletin* 40 (1989): 24-48.

—. "The 'Word Pair' *qšt* and *mṯ* in Habakkuk 3:9 in the Light of Ugaritic and Akkadian." In *Go to the Land I Will Show You: Studies in Honor of Dwight W. Young*. Edited by Joseph Coleson and Victor Matthews, 353-61. Winona Lake: Eisenbrauns, 1996.

Tucker, Gene M. *Form Criticism of the Old Testament*. Old Testament Series. Philadelphia: Fortress, 1971.

—. "Prophetic Speech." In *Interpreting the Prophets*. Edited by James Luther Mays, and Paul J. Achtemeier, 27-40. Philadelphia: Fortress, 1987.

—. "Prophetic Superscriptions and the Growth of a Canon." In *Canon and Authority*. Edited by G.W. Coats, and B.O. Long, 56-70. Philadelphia: Fortress, 1977.

Tuttle, Gary A. "Wisdom and Habakkuk." *Studia Biblica et Theologica* 3 (1973): 3-14.

Ungerer, W. J. *Habakkuk: The Man with the Honest Questions*. Grand Rapids: Baker, 1976.

Van der Toorn, K. "Yahweh יהוה" In *Dictionary of Deities and Demons in the Bible*. Edited by K. Van der Toorn, B. Becking, P.W. Van der Horst, 910-19. New York: Brill, 1995.

Van der Wal, A.J.O. "*Lō' Nāmūt* in Habakkuk I 12: A Suggestion." *Vetus Testamentum* 38 (1988): 480-82.

Van Leeuwen, Raymond C. "Scribal Wisdom and Theodicy in the Book of the Twelve." In *In Search of Wisdom: Essays in Memory of John G. Gammie*. Edited by Leo G. Perdue, Bernard Brandon Scott, and William Johnston Wiseman, 31-49. Louisville: Westminster John Knox Press, 1993.

Vanderhooft, David Stephen. *The Neo-Babylonian Empire and Babylon in the Latter Prophets*. Harvard Semitic Monographs 59. Atlanta: Scholars Press, 1999.

VanGemeren, Willem A. "Psalms." In *The Expositor's Bible Commentary*. Edited by Frank E. Gaebelein, 5:475-504. Grand Rapids: Zondervan, 1991.

Vaux, Roland de. *Ancient Israel: Its Life and Institutions*. Translated by J. McHugh. Grand Rapids: Eerdmans, 1977.

Walker, H.H., and N.W. Lund. "The Literary Structure of the Book of Habakkuk." *Journal of Biblical Literature* 53 (1935): 355-70.

Waltke, Bruce K., and M. O'Connor. *An Introduction to Biblical Hebrew Syntax*. Winona Lake: Eisenbrauns, 1990.

Walton, John H., Victor H. Matthews, and Mark W. Chavalas. *The IVP Bible Background Commentary: Old Testament*. Downers Grove: InterVarsity Press, 2000.

Watson, Wilfred G.E. *Classical Hebrew Poetry: A Guide to its Techniques*. Journal for the Study of the Old Testament Supplement Series 26. Sheffield: JSOT Press, 1984.

Watts, John D.W. *The Books of Joel, Obadiah, Jonah, Nahum, Habakkuk and Zephaniah*. Cambridge: Cambridge University Press, 1975.

—. "A Frame for the Book of the Twelve: Hosea 1-3 and Malachi." In *Reading and Hearing theBook of the Twelve*. Edited by James D. Nogalski, and Marvin A. Sweeney, 209-17. Atlanta: Society of Biblical Literature, 2000.

—. "Superscriptions and Incipits in the Book of the Twelve." In *Reading and Hearing the Book of the Twelve*. Edited by James D. Nogalski, and Marvin A. Sweeney, 110-24. Atlanta: Society of Biblical Literature, 2000.

Watts, James W. "Psalmody in Prophecy: Habakkuk 3 in Context." In *Forming Prophetic Literature: Essays on Isaiah and the Twelve in Honor of John D.W. Watts*. Edited by James W. Watts, and Paul R. House, 209-23. Journal for the Study of the Old Testament Supplement Series 235. Sheffield: Sheffield Academic Press, 1996.

Weis, Richard D. "A Definition of the Genre *Maśśā'* in the Hebrew Bible." Ph.D. diss., Claremont Graduate School, 1986.

—. "Oracle." In *The Anchor Bible Dictionary*. Edited by D.N. Freedman, 5:28-29. New York: Doubleday, 1992.

Weiss, M. *The Bible from Within: The Method of Total Interpretation*. Jerusalem: Magnes Press, 1984.

Wendland, Ernst. " 'The Righteous Live by Their Faith' in a Holy God: Complementary Compositional Forces and Habakkuk's Dialogue with the Lord." *Journal of the Evangelical Theological Society* 42 (1999): 591-628.

Wenham, Gordon J. *Story as Torah: Reading Old Testament Narrative Ethically*. Grand Rapids: Baker, 2000.

Westermann, Claus. *Basic Forms of Prophetic Speech*. Translated by Hugh Clayton White. Philadelphia: Westminster, 1967.

—. *Praise and Lament in the Psalms*. Translated by Keith R. Crim and Richard N. Soulen. Atlanta: John Knox, 1981.

—. *The Psalms: Structure, Content, and Message*. Translated by Ralph D. Gehrke. Minneapolis: Augsburg, 1980.

—. "The Role of the Lament in the Theology of the Old Testament." *Interpretation* 28 (1974): 20-38.

Whedbee, J. William. *Isaiah and Wisdom*. Nashville: Abingdon, 1971.

Whitley, C.F. "A Note on Habakkuk 2:15." *Jewish Quarterly Review* 66 (1975/1976): 143-47.

Whybray, R. N. " 'Shall Not the Judge of All the Earth Do What Is Just?' God's Oppression of the Innocent in the Old Testament." In *Shall Not the Judge of All the Earth Do What Is Right? Studies on the Nature of God in Tribute to James L. Crenshaw*. Edited by David Penchansky, and Paul L. Redditt, 1-19. Winona Lake: Eisenbrauns, 2000.

—. "The Wisdom Psalms." In *Wisdom in Ancient Israel: Essays in Honour of J.A. Emerton*. Edited by John Day, Robert P. Gordon, and H.G.M. Williamson, 152-60. Cambridge: Cambridge University Press, 1995.

Wilcox, John T. *The Bitterness of Job: A Philosophical Reading*. Ann Arbor: The University of Michigan Press, 1989.

Williams, James G. "Deciphering the Unspoken: The Theophany of Job." *Hebrew Union College Annual* 49 (1978): 59-72.

—. "Irony and Lament: Clues to Prophetic Consciousness." *Semeia* 8 (1977): 51-71.

—. "You Have Not Spoken Truth of Me": Mystery and Irony in Job. *Zeitschrift für die alttestamentliche Wissenschaft* 83 (1971): 231-55.

Williams, Ronald J. "Theodicy in the Ancient Near East." In *Theodicy in the Old Testament*. Edited by James L. Crenshaw, 42-56. Philadelphia: Fortress, 1983.

—. *Hebrew Syntax: An Outline*, 2d ed. Toronto: University of Toronto Press, 1976.

Williamson, H.G.M. "Isaiah and the Wise." In *Wisdom in Ancient Israel: Essays in Honour of J.A. Emerton*. Edited by John Day, Robert P. Gordon, and H.G.M. Williamson, 133-41. Cambridge: Cambridge University Press, 1995.

Willis, John T. "Alternating (ABA'B') Parallelism in the Old Testament Psalms and Prophetic Literature." In *Directions in Biblical Hebrew Poetry*. Edited by Elaine R. Follis, 49-76. Journal for the Study of the Old Testament Supplement Series 40. Sheffield: JSOT Press, 1987.

—. "Redaction Criticism and Historical Reconstruction." In *Encounter with the Text: Form and History in the Hebrew Bible*. Edited by M.J. Buss, 83-89. Philadelphia: Fortress, 1979.

Wilson, Robert R. *Prophecy and Society in Ancient Israel*. Philadelphia: Fortress, 1980.

Wolfe, Rolland Emerson. "The Editing of the Book of the Twelve." *Zeitschrift für die alttestamentliche Wissenschaft* 53 (1935): 90-129.

Wolff, Hans Walter. "Prophecy from the Eighth through the Fifth Century." *Interpretation* 32 (1978): 17-30.

Wuellner, Wilhelm. "Where is Rhetorical Criticism Taking Us?" *Catholic Biblical Quarterly* 49 (1987): 448-63.

Würthwein, Ernst. *The Text of the Old Testament: An Introduction to the Biblia Hebraica*. Translated by Erroll F. Rhodes. Grand Rapids: Eerdmans, 1979.

Xella, P. "Resheph." In *Dictionary of Deities and Demons in the Bible*. Edited by K. Van der Toorn, B. Becking, P.W. Van der Horst. 700-703. New York: Brill, 1995.

Zemek, George J. "Interpretive Challenges Relating to Habakkuk 2:4b." *Grace Theological Journal* 1 (1980): 43-69.

Zuck, Roy B. *Job*. Chicago: Moody Press, 1978.

Zuckerman, Bruce. *Job the Silent: A Study in Historical Counterpoint*. New York: Oxford University Press, 1991.

ND - #0097 - 090625 - C0 - 229/152/12 - PB - 9781842278505 - Gloss Lamination